Working Effectively with Faculty

Guidebook
for Higher Education
Staff and Managers

Working Effectively with Faculty

Guidebook for Higher Education Staff and Managers

Susan Christy, Ph.D.

UNIVERSITY
RESOURCES
PRESS

BERKELEY, CALIFORNIA

Working Effectively with Faculty
Guidebook for Higher Education Staff and Managers
by Susan Christy, Ph.D.

Copyright © 2010 by Susan Christy

ISBN: 978-0-9827476-0-5

E-Book ISBN: 978-0-9827476-1-2

LCCN: 2010933448

Published by:
University Resources Press
Berkeley, California

Editing: Jude Berman
Cover design: Steve Oerding
Typography and design: Desta Garrett

This book is designed to provide accurate information in regard to the subject matter covered. It is sold with the understanding that neither the author nor the publisher is engaged in rendering legal or other professional services. If legal advice or other expert assistance is required, the services of a competent professional should be sought.

See Contact Information for consulting services, speaking engagements, and book purchasing on pages 261–262. Volume discounts on bulk quantities of books are available to professional associations, colleges and universities, educators, trainers, and others. A special edition with your institution's logo and/or a letter from your president or dean can be arranged.

University Resources Press
P.O. Box 237, 1748 Shattuck Avenue
Berkeley, CA 94709
Phone 510 222-2992 • Toll free 888 408-9059
www.UniversityResourcesPress.com

Susan Christy, Ph.D. is passionate about helping college and university managers, staff, and faculty create the best in education, research, and organizational effectiveness. She has provided consulting, training, and presentations to help thousands of people in higher education understand academic culture and enhance their people skills as well as management and leadership abilities. Susan gained an appreciation for the complexity of staff-faculty relationships through her experience as a tenured psychology professor at Asnuntuck Community College in Enfield, CT; as a member of the board of trustees at The California Institute of Integral Studies in San Francisco, CA; as president of Christy Consulting, Inc.; and as vice president of HighGain, Inc. in San Francisco.

Christy Consulting, Inc. was listed as one of the top fifteen management consulting firms by the *East Bay Business Times*. Many clients appreciate the combination of her doctorate in psychology and her credential as a certified management consultant by the Institute of Management Consultants.

To my parents

for their generosity, love of life,

and life-long learning

Acknowledgments

I'd like to thank Kathleen Sexton at Stanford University's Training and Organizational Development Department for embracing my idea for a staff training on this topic. Special thanks to the many participants and audience members from several colleges and universities who have offered their wisdom, resources, and suggestions during my trainings and presentations. I am so sorry I have no way to track and credit each and every individual contribution.

I'd like to thank Sara Buono, my trustworthy assistant, who has shared this five-year journey from training manual to book publication. I send deep gratitude to Jude Berman, my editor, for her wordsmithing and superb collaboration. Steve Oerding, artist extraordinaire, has provided feedback on early drafts, creative artwork, and general hand-holding during the last year.

And deep appreciation to my husband, Marlin Boisen, who has loved and supported me on this journey in a thousand ways. Words cannot express the depth of my affection. He knows.

Here is a list of colleagues, clients, friends, and experts who have generously shared their feedback and ideas along the way. Thank you for your collaboration. I could not have done it without you.

Eve Abbott
Annmarie Belda
Debbie Bell
Paul Brentson
Michele Castillo
Imber Coppinger
Cate Corcoran
Janice Corner
Keith Crestman
Rebecca Davis
Barbara De Luca
Jan Dickens
Nancy Dill
Allen Doyle
Moira Fitzgerald
Thomas Fulton
Ramana Linnea Gasch
Christine Gibo
Coquelicot Gilland
Walter Gmelch
Maye Lynn Gon-Soneda
Lynn Gore
Toni Grimes
Lorna Groundwater
Esti Hall
Bettyann Hinchman
Ian Jacobsen
Kaila Jimenez
Jamelyn Johnson
Ysabel Johnston
Randall Jones
Judith Kirmmse
Eunice LeMay

Selma Lewis
Dagmar Logie
Jonathan London
Randy Lopez
Mary Beth Mears
Elizabeth Meyer
Cheryl Miller
Carina Celesia Moore
Rebecca Morgan
Judith Moss
Sally Neal
Donna Olssen
Frances O'Neil
Suzanne Orcutt
Barry Oshry
Alan Plum
Michael Ray
Linda Rose
Leslie Sandberg
Josh Schimel
Heidi Schmidt
Bev Scott
David Sibbet
Kristian Simsarian
Ed Streeter
Else Tamayo
Mary Taylor-Huber
Barbara Twale
Jacqueline Ward
Barbara Waugh
Marcia Wienert
Finis (Pete) Wilson
Nancy Wilson

Contents

SECTION I—Working with Faculty in Academia 1

Introduction. 3

    My Background and Perspective 5

    About This Book. 6

1   I Hear You 9

    The Eight Challenges 12

    Putting On Your Shoes 18

    Where Do You Stand? 19

    Summary—I Hear You. 20

2   Faculty and Staff: Getting Acquainted 21

    The Species Test 22

    Early One Monday Morning. 23

    Faculty and Staff Characteristics. 25

    A Faculty Portrait. 27

    Your Work with Faculty 32

    Where Do You Stand? 34

    Summary—Faculty and Staff: Getting Acquainted 36

SECTION II—Ways to Think about Staff-Faculty
               Interactions 37

3   A Systems Perspective 39

    A Personal Problem 40

    A Broader View. 43

    Understanding Systems and Systems Thinking 45

    Looking through the Systems Lens. 52

    We Have a Choice. 54

    Where Do You Stand? 55

    Summary—A Systems Perspective 56

4   Staff-Faculty Partnerships 57

    Systems Thinking and Power 58

    Difficult-to-Talk-About Relationships. 60

    Do I Work *For* Faculty or *With* Faculty? 62

    Different Views of the Organization. 63

    Where Do You Stand? 67

    Summary—Staff-Faculty Partnerships. 68

5   **Adopt a Growth Mindset** 69

The Power of Mindset 70

What Is Your Mindset? 71

Value Strong Relationships with Faculty 72

View Faculty as Colleagues. 74

Hold the Big Picture. 76

Balance Commitment with Healthy
    Detachment. 77

Focus on What Is Working. 79

Adopt an Experimenter's Mindset. 81

How to Develop a Growth Mindset 82

Faculty Mindset 85

Summary—Adopt a Growth Mindset. 87

**SECTION III—Working with Faculty: Practices
    and Suggestions** 89

6   **Communicating with Faculty: Basic Skills** 91

Active Listening 92

Questioning. 97

I-Messages 100

Directing Others. 102

Giving Feedback 104

Summary—Communicating with Faculty:
    Basic Skills. 110

7   **How To Establish a Partnership with Faculty**. 111

How do I convince faculty I can be of help? 113

How do I get (and hold) faculty's attention? 114

How do I address faculty? 118

How can I get faculty to respond? 120

Summary—How To Establish a Partnership
    with Faculty. 124

8   **How To Say No and Deliver Bad News** 125

Establishing Healthy Boundaries. 126

Delivering Bad News 129

Summary—How to Say No and
    Deliver Bad News 136

9 Continuing the Partnership with Faculty 137

How can I orient faculty to university policies
and procedures? 137

How can I identify and work with a faculty
member's resistance? 141

How can I have more productive one-on-one
meetings with faculty? 142

Is there anything I shouldn't say? 145

How can I engender respect? 150

What should I do next? How do I follow up? 153

Summary—Continuing the Partnership
with Faculty. 155

10 Become Organizationally Savvy and Build Your Resources. . 157

Inform Yourself. 158

Identify Stakeholders 160

Assemble or Create Resources 161

Get Organized with Your Computer 168

Develop a Network of People 169

Do as Much Behind-the-Scenes Work as Possible 172

Conclusion 175

Summary—Become Organizationally Savvy
and Build Your Resources. 176

**Section IV—Dealing with Individual Faculty Members
and Their Stresses** 177

11 Faculty Stress Reactions and What You can Do. 179

The Toughest Part of the Job 180

The Faculty Stress Cycle 181

Faculty Stressors. 182

Faculty Perceptions 185

Faculty Stress Reactions 186

Consequences 188

An Ah-Ha! Moment. 188

What You Can Do 189

Conclusion 194

Summary—Faculty Stress Reactions and
What You Can Do 195

12 Strategies for Working Skillfully with Difficult Faculty......197

Who Is Difficult for You?................................. 198

Characteristics of Faculty Who Are Difficult............. 199

Faculty Who Are Self-Centered.......................... 202

Faculty Who Are Aggressive 205

Faculty Who Are Manipulative........................ 208

Faculty Who Are Unresponsive.........................210

Conclusion 215

Summary—Strategies for Working Skillfully
    with Difficult Faculty 216

SECTION V—Take Care of Yourself and Your Career........... 217

13 Be Resilient and Recover from Being Criticized,
Beaten Up, or Worn Down 219

How Resilient Are You?................................. 221

Warning Signs... 223

Know Your Stress Cycle................................ 224

Stand Up for Yourself................................. 229

Know Your Rights..................................... 232

How to Recover from Being Criticized,
    Beaten Up, or Worn Down.......................... 233

Become More Resilient 234

Conclusion 237

Summary—Be Resilient and Recover from Being
    Criticized, Beaten Up, or Worn Down................. 239

14 A Career That Works for You 241

The Ingredients of Satisfaction......................... 241

Job or Career 245

Adopt a Career Mindset 246

Define a Career Path 246

How You Can Further Your Career...................... 251

Amplify What Brings Heart and Meaning to
    Your Work 253

Conclusion 255

Summary—A Career That Works for You................. 256

References 257

Contact Information.. 261

SECTION I

Working with Faculty
in Academia

Introduction   3

1. I Hear You   9

2. Faculty and Staff: Getting Acquainted   21

www.WorkingWithFaculty.com

1

Introduction

- **My Background and Perspective**
- **About This Book**

This book is about a relationship dear to my heart—the one between staff and faculty. Over the years I've experienced both sides. As a tenured professor of psychology, I saw many of the issues you likely encounter daily in your work as staff. More recently, as an organizational consultant and staff/management development trainer for many colleges and universities, I've worked closely with staff and faculty at all levels.

By staff I mean all employees who are not faculty; that is, all the people who contribute to the economic enterprise, manage the people and facilities, and provide equipment and support to the faculty. Staff are classified in a hierarchy comprising employees, managers, and directors, which exists side by side with the faculty hierarchy of instructors and adjunct professors, and assistant, associate, and full professors. This complex structure of academic institutions can be cumbersome and confusing for staff and faculty alike. Staff-faculty working relationships are likely to be challenging, too.

In my seminars, staff members talk about their love for their jobs and appreciation for the faculty members with whom they work. They also speak openly about their frustrations: how difficult it can be to get things done in academia, how working with faculty has challenges that are different from those in other organizations, how painful the staff-faculty relationship can be at times. The increasing pressures associated with funding for academia; administrative cost-cutting measures; and the pressures of smart, highly specialized faculty members competing for grants, promotions, or lab space only magnify the challenges. As a consultant and trainer, it's been my job to listen to all points of view, to understand people, academic culture, organizational systems, business principles, and best practices. The focus of my work is on empowering others, mediating conflicts, building bridges, and helping both staff and faculty cope with the inevitable tensions in academia.

This guidebook is based on a training for staff called "How to Work Effectively with Faculty" that I've offered at Stanford University, UC Davis, University of San Francisco, St. Mary's College, and other institutions. This training evolved from consulting and staff development workshops and presentations I gave during the previous twenty years at many universities and colleges—research and teaching oriented, public and private, large and small.

To give you the flavor, here are samples of the feedback I received from participants in my trainings:

- "Personal experience shared was great. Thank you, Dr. Christy, for keeping it real."

- "You nailed faculty behavior patterns very well. Now I realize that a different approach is needed."

- "Your research and preparation made for a good presentation."

- "Lots of good useable information. The 'Communicate with Faculty' section was great."

- "Thank you for the opportunity to learn how important my role is to my department."

- "This helped me understand my husband better. He is a scientist."

- "I was here five years before I understood the dynamics. I wish someone could have described what you are teaching when I first got this job."

- "Should be a required training for all new staff."

4

Many staff participants suggested I write this book. They wanted something in writing, something they could walk away with and use when they felt the need, as situations arose on the job. Also, they pointed out that staff who might not have the opportunity to attend a workshop would benefit from a guidebook.

In preparation for writing this guidebook, I researched the relevant literature, interviewed hundreds of university staff and faculty, and discussed the issues with professionals in many fields. I was surprised to find relatively little written about staff-faculty relationships, although there are thousands of useful books and resources about leadership, management, communication, and organizational effectiveness. The advances in systems thinking and communication have been impressive in the last few decades. I am especially grateful for all the generous ideas and practices, wisdom and know-how offered by thousands of participants in my workshops over the years. I wish I could give each of you individual credit.

My Background and Perspective

My career has taken fascinating twists and turns. At age 25, I taught my first psychology courses at Lowell State College in Massachusetts and subsequently took a full-time position at Asnuntuck Community College in Connecticut, where I became a tenured associate professor. At the time, humanistic psychology, systems thinking, and experiential learning were quite new. The field of psychology was growing in important ways. I was thrilled to create new courses or modules: Psychology of the Family, Psychology of Women and Men, and Group Dynamics, to name a few.

In 1984, I had the opportunity to take a sabbatical and study in San Francisco. Although that hadn't originally been my plan, I decided to leave my academic position and join a small communications training firm that served large corporations. Our work focused on training corporate managers and employees in communication skills, and it was rewarding to move into the field of applied psychology.

After five years of working in business and organizational development, I started my own consulting and training business. In 1989, I presented a brown-bag lunch talk on "How to Work with Difficult People" to staff in UCSF's Human Resources Department. It was a joy for me to be back on a campus. Based on that talk, I was hired by UCSF to give ongoing staff development trainings and consultation to staff and faculty. Nowadays, about half of my work is on university and college campuses.

Perhaps I should add that my history in learning to communicate with faculty actually goes way back. My father, Hiram H. Hardesty, M.D., was an ophthalmology professor at Western Reserve Medical School. As a young girl, I felt challenged to communicate with my brilliant father, who often seemed preoccupied with his research, journal articles, and clinical practice. As a teenager, I helped him edit journal articles and worked in his office. While I worked on this book, the lessons I learned from my father frequently came to mind.

About This Book

I call this a *guidebook* because it is intended to offer you guidance. You can read it cover to cover, or you may prefer to read only those chapters or portions of chapters that are of particular interest to you. I suggest you read Chapter 3, in which I present the model for improving staff-faculty relationships that informs the rest of the chapters. At any rate, please make the book *yours*. And do visit my Website at www.WorkingWithFaculty.com, which serves as an interactive companion and resource for this book. There you'll find more information and updates, as well as the opportunity to ask questions and share your ideas.

Throughout the book, I present stories of staff and faculty. Their names and other identifying information have been altered to protect anonymity. I struggled with the best way to easily distinguish staff from faculty. In the end, I decided to call staff by their first names and faculty by their titles. I'm aware this is not the conventional form of address on many campuses today; I hope you will forgive me for sacrificing a modicum of political correctness for the sake of clarity.

Many of my examples come from universities, but I think you will find most apply equally to colleges, community colleges, professional schools, stand-alone graduate schools, and the hospitals and research centers affiliated with universities. To work effectively with faculty, it helps to understand college and university structures as well as faculty behavior, to be able to navigate a complex organization, know what to expect at work, and apply the approaches and techniques others have found successful. Of course, no technique or approach works all the time with everyone. Generalizations are helpful but don't always apply. Universities and colleges differ greatly from one another; departments differ too, and individuals even more so. It takes extraordinary sensitivity and humility to work with human beings—in any organization. We handle each interaction the best we can and proceed to the next moment, creative and willing to move forward. Each step of the way, we want to build constructive relationships as we accomplish important tasks together.

I know people can be maddening—unresponsive, rude, manipulative, unfair, abusive, emotional, and irrational. And, the fact is, some people will never change. Difficult people can make others' jobs impossible. I have had more than a few desperate calls from university staff members who are burning out, burdened by unrealistic demands, starved for appreciation, or trying to please someone who will never be satisfied. They often are too exhausted and beaten down to initiate change for themselves.

At the same time, I am impressed with the business and people skills I've observed in the staff and faculty with whom I work. Many people do change. They do the hard inner work and take responsibility for their impact on others. In fact, some people who've taken my workshops tell me they see few difficult people around anymore. I suspect these individuals have learned to head off trouble from the get-go. And you can do the same. Although expecting faculty to change in fundamental ways may be unrealistic, you may be able to influence how they treat you. It's my strong conviction that savvy staff have a knack for bringing out the best in everyone and can influence faculty in creative ways.

May this guidebook serve you well!

1

I Hear You

- The Eight Challenges
- Putting On Your Shoes
- Where Do You Stand?
- Summary

When I lead workshops for college and university staff, I often start by asking participants whether they experience working with faculty as a challenging part of their jobs. When the chorus of "Sure do!" "Yes!" and "Need you ask?" dies down, I ask if they'd be willing to share some instances of interactions with faculty that didn't go smoothly. And I ask them to let me and the rest of the group know how these interactions left them feeling. Sometimes it's as though I've opened the valve on a fire hose of pent-up exasperation.

Let's listen to some typical stories.

- "A faculty member wanted to hire someone she'd already picked out to be the new language lab manager. I had to try to convince her that, for legal reasons, fairness, and compliance with university rules, we had to go through a hiring process that included interviewing other people and hiring the best qualified. She actually said to me, 'Do what you need to do, just get me the person

I want.' I felt so disrespected. And I felt caught between the rules I'm paid to follow and this professor who couldn't have cared less about the rules."

- "I work in the medical school, which can be very vibrant and exciting. But it wasn't so exciting when one faculty member invited a group of European professors to watch his new surgery techniques when they came to the U.S. The faculty member didn't work with me or anyone on staff to arrange the visit. When the professors arrived, they discovered that no permissions had been obtained from patients to allow observation of the surgery. This would take days to arrange, and the professors wouldn't be in town that long. I felt so frustrated because I knew I could have arranged it all if I'd been given the chance. And the snafu made our department look disorganized, which in turn made me and my colleagues look bad to our superiors. And, to tell the truth, I felt sad the visiting professors missed the opportunity to learn about the new surgery, which could have helped patients in their countries."

- "I work in the registrar's office, and while most of the faculty at this community college are great, a few never seem to get their grades in on time. Yesterday I ended up leaving work late because I had to go over to a professor's office and stand next to her while she emailed me the document that was due last week. It was the only way to get her to do it. I kid you not! And the whole time, she was complaining about how much bother I was causing her. It was all I could do to bite my tongue and get out of there as quick as possible. Really, I'm tired of chasing these laggards down. Someone should do something to make them appreciate how much extra work they're creating for staff."

- "I work as a program coordinator in the Philosophy Department. I support ten full-time faculty and thirteen adjuncts. It's a big job and I find it really stimulating. Recently, I was talking and laughing with three faculty members before a meeting, when two faculty from another department came up and joined in. We'd all been talking together for a while, when I realized they thought I was another faculty member. When they learned I was an assistant, they stopped making eye contact and talking directly to me. The next day, one of them passed me in the hallway and didn't say hello. Obviously, I'm not part of the *in* crowd! I felt hurt and treated like a second-class citizen. Ouch."

• "I am a research assistant working full-time for a geology professor. Most of my job is administering his big grant. Just yesterday, an adjunct professor who was in the building to teach an afternoon class came up to my desk and asked me to duplicate handouts for his upcoming class. Even though this was totally outside my job description, and I had plenty to do otherwise, I did it. But later in the day I found myself fuming. Does this adjunct think that because I'm staff, I'm at her beck and call?"

And the stories keep coming.

So, can we conclude that these staff members hate their jobs? Are they poring over job listings looking for a way out? Hardly. Most of them tell me they love their jobs. They find working within academia fulfilling and meaningful, and they're quick to point out what they see as its many benefits. The environment feels alive with learning. It's stimulating to get to know some of the professors, and perhaps to get involved with a research project or take an interesting class. Staff enjoy a multitude of opportunities—both within academic departments and in such areas as human resources, accounting, business services, student services, research administration, facilities, and the police department, to name a few.

Yet, when I make it clear to staff that I want to hear the full story, when I invite them to open that fire hose valve, they often are more vocal about their challenges than they are about their opportunities. Even if they've had just a few painful experiences along the way, these can loom large. If only some faculty, they say, would make a greater effort to meet their deadlines, learn university procedures, respect the importance of staff contributions, understand what it takes to accomplish requests, and appreciate staff's hard work. Basically, they want to see faculty change. And they look to me to help them find a way to make this happen.

Of course, this desire to change the faculty is a valid perspective, at least in the sense that it is based on staff's legitimate experience. The desire to change how other people operate is a feeling that tends to arise when people feel frustrated. Perhaps you, as staff, can relate to this feeling. But there's an important catch. Quite simply, if you haven't noticed...over the long haul, it doesn't work!

We are going to examine closely in the chapters that follow why this is the case. But for now, let me say that this approach doesn't work for several important reasons. To begin with, trying to change others is a questionable strategy under any circumstances. Moreover, when staff pursue this strategy, it actually keeps them from getting their jobs done as well as they otherwise could. Then, too, staff morale is likely to suffer. Staff who try to change faculty's behavior or attitudes often find their relationships with those faculty members becoming increasingly uncomfortable.

The Eight Challenges

Before we try to change anything, it is usually a good idea to be clear about what we want to change and what we want to accomplish. Simply put, we need to define the problem.

Over the years of consulting and leading workshops for staff members, I've collected participants' descriptions of their challenges working with faculty. Of course, their experiences vary by institution, by department, by individual faculty member, by encounters on a daily or even moment-to-moment basis. The truth is, staff-faculty relationships are quite complex. However, by listening closely to the nuances staff members have expressed to me, I came up with eight challenges commonly faced by staff.

To be clear from the start, these are not categorical statements about faculty. I don't want you to take them as demands, or even requests, for faculty to change their habits. As I said, that strategy wouldn't be effective. Rather, these challenges represent the perspective of staff. I've really been listening to what staff have been telling me over the years.

1. **Faculty often seem disorganized.** Because they put their energy into other priorities, some faculty can seem preoccupied and unsystematic when it comes to responding to what staff need. As a result, they are dependent on help from staff members. This in and of itself is not a problem. After all, as staff, you are there to provide support. The challenge arises when staff feel that faculty fail to value the help on which they depend. For example, the checklist you created for getting their class materials produced on time may seem like a petty detail to them, and as a result they may not get the material to you on time. Some faculty may require hand holding beyond what staff job descriptions indicate. Other faculty may impose last-minute demands on staff

because of their own lack of organization.

What staff have said....

- "We are affected by their disorganization. I'm always waiting for them to find a paper that is lost in those piles on the desk, chairs, and floor."
- "Faculty change their minds after production."
- "I feel like the designated nanny. Getting the urology faculty off to a conference is like getting the boys off to camp."
- "Faculty change their schedules at the last minute and don't see the ripple effect. We're the ones who face the wrath of students who get notified at the last minute."
- "I try to help the professor use her time wisely. She's so disorganized. I feel like I have to tidy up a scatterbrained Ph.D."
- "I have to remind faculty to sign the academic forms, show up at meetings on time, follow the grant proposal time lines. Sometimes they get irked about it."

2. Faculty often are unavailable. The term *academic freedom* refers to the freedom of intellectual pursuit, but faculty also enjoy considerable freedom and flexibility in their daily routine. One of the benefits of a faculty position is that it is not a nine-to-five job. Faculty can and often must work evenings and weekends, and can work out of a home office if they choose. So, even though faculty may be working a sixty-hour work week, staff may find them unavailable when needed for time-sensitive issues and decisions.

What staff have said....

- "Faculty often aren't on campus. It's hard to locate them."
- "Sometimes I forge the mandatory faculty signatures so we can meet the deadlines."
- "It's nerve racking when I have to draft important letters without faculty input."
- "We have to be prepared to make so-called executive decisions, and then to stand by them."
- "It's hard to keep in touch with eighteen adjunct professors. Some of them teach at satellite campuses, and I never see them."

13

3. Faculty may not understand the volume and complexity of staff jobs. Staff often say they do not feel understood by faculty. Some faculty, staff say, are not well oriented to staff responsibilities and how things get done on campus. They may not realize what it takes for staff to deal with personnel issues, union contracts, patents, or complex procurement procedures. They may not know how long it takes to do the many routine things staff accomplish, such as getting signatures for promotion applications, hiring assistants, or getting them a visa to China.

What staff have said....

- "We doubled our enrollment, but the number of program assistants stayed the same."
- "Faculty do not know what it takes to meet their requests. They don't know how long it takes us to do some things. They think it's a one-minute job."
- "I'm overworked and overcommitted. All twelve faculty members in the English Department expect me to be their personal assistant."
- "Faculty say, 'I'll sign off on it, but I won't do the work.' This increases my work load."
- "Sometimes faculty are not responsive to our initiatives. I put in a proposal for a mentoring program for program assistants, and never heard back."

4. Faculty members often do not follow procedures. University procedures and policies are often complex and not always widely known. Many faculty prefer to have someone else "just handle the logistics." In this case, the department manager or program coordinator can search the university intranet for policies or consult with human resource specialists or research administrators to clarify what to do.

Faculty sometimes interpret academic freedom and tenure as license to do what they please. On occasion, universities actually reward faculty for not following procedures. This may make the faculty happy, but it can be challenging for staff. For example, staff in one Physics Department told me the chairperson and faculty got more than their share of university resources because they demanded loudly, manipulated the system skillfully, and had a dean who advocated for them. Staff in other departments had to get by with less.

What staff have said....

- "Faculty don't bother to find out the policies and procedure, like they're not allowed to do a human study without human-study protocols."

- "Faculty asks us to set a new policy. We do, and then they don't follow it. They even created a portfolio process themselves, and then did not follow it."

- "Some faculty are like an old boys' club. They do what they please, protect one another, and get away with murder."

- "They won't listen to you if you say, 'It can't be done.' They just turn around and go over your head, directly to the registrar or dean, to get what they want."

5. Faculty may have unrealistic expectations. Because of their lack of understanding about the scope of staff job responsibilities and their inattention to university procedures, faculty may have unrealistic or unclear expectations. According to staff, some faculty seem to think the best university staff members are invisible. Faculty may assume you can do something with a snap of your fingers, and fail to take into account the various and time-consuming steps you need to follow. Faculty may assume staff have the same privileges they have as faculty members. For example, when one faculty member sent a staff assistant to the library to make photocopies from a book, the assistant discovered that book was not part of the general collection and required faculty permission to access it. The faculty member was upset because he didn't have the material when he needed it.

What staff have said....

- "I always hear, 'The old program coordinators used to do XYZ. Why don't you...?' Hey, it's not in my job description."

- "It's hard to draw the line when they ask you to do personal tasks." (Specific examples staff have mentioned include going to Fed Ex on Saturday, and taking signed papers to a roofing contractor.)

- "I do it once and it becomes my job forever."

- "We have to respond if they think it's important, even if it's not a priority for us. One faculty member asked, 'Find out why they're digging a hole outside my window.'"

- "They think we have a magic wand in our desks and can just make things magically happen." (In one large university I visited, a staff member in the Mechanical Engineering Department has a toy magic wand in her drawer, which she occasionally uses to emphasize what she has to say to a faculty member or co-worker!)

6. Faculty may not communicate well. Staff report that communication skills do not feature prominently in the repertoire of some faculty. This may be especially true of faculty in the hard sciences or other technical, non-people-oriented fields. Faculty are not likely to be trained as communicators or managers. Even if you, as a staff member, have good interpersonal skills, it may be challenging to engage with faculty. In general, faculty do not look to organizational leaders or managers to define, direct, or evaluate their work. Yet there you are, in your staff job, doing things in ways that run counter to their preferences. As a result, what you communicate may be perceived by faculty as an interruption, pain-in-the-neck policies, or "administrivia."

What staff have said....

- "Sometimes I can't figure out what they are saying, what they really want. We're expected to be mind readers."
- "I've noticed the loudest and most manipulative or abusive faculty and departments are the most likely to get what they want."
- "I struggle to find the best way to contact faculty. I mean, who likes email and who wants a phone call?"
- "It's hard to say no or deliver bad news. The other day, I had to say, 'Sorry, but you can't write off a $500 suitcase for your conference in Spain.'"

7. Faculty may come across as critical, disrespectful, or cynical. Faculty's annoyance with administration may be expressed through a lack of civility toward administrators and staff members across campus. Twale and De Luca (2008) have written about what they call "faculty incivility" and the "bully culture" in academia, and provide a wealth of examples. Some faculty members can be critical, demanding, demeaning, or unresponsive. When this happens, there is little protection for staff members because the university needs these faculty as its academic stars.

A staff member told me the following anecdote. She said, "One admin position is always being filled. We've had seven different administrative assistants in three years. This admin reports to an amazing scientist who does cutting-edge work, brings in a lot of money, works with the army and venture capitalists. All the brightest students want to work with him. But he can be a real jerk, very pushy. If he doesn't get what he wants, he goes to someone who will get it. He won't take no for an answer, even if it's against the law. He says things that belittle people, like asking how far they've gone in school.... When the admins can't stand it anymore, they quit. They usually find other jobs on campus. New admins will continue through the revolving door that leads to unrealistic demands, degrading criticism, and lack of appreciation. From one point of view, admins are expendable; this faculty member is not. You just have to understand, they [the university] want him here."

What staff have said....

- "Faculty tend to treat staff as impersonal parts of a machine, and not relate to us as whole people."

- "Faculty are cynical. They think the administration is out to get them."

- "When we have to shut down the facility or the network to do maintenance, the faculty have a fit."

- "They don't think much of us—they are surprised to learn I am on a board or am an elected official. If it doesn't pertain to them, they think it's competing with my fulfilling their demands."

- "Faculty can be aggressive, selfish, or micromanage at times when they need what they need. They seem disrespectful."

8. The institution may not provide sufficient staff orientation or training. Although this challenge is not about faculty per se, it contributes to the struggles staff experience in their work with faculty. While a few academic institutions provide excellent orientation for staff members, it is haphazard in most college and university settings. Staff may not understand the academic structure, culture, policies, or procedures, and faculty may be unaware of staff needs for training. Faculty may expect staff to do things they have not been oriented to do.

What staff have said....

- "It takes a long time to learn the job. We don't get an orientation when we first get hired."

- "There's no organization chart, no structure, or only an amorphous structure. Reporting relationships are not clear."
- "There are so many different policies to be aware of, such as copyright laws. How can I be expected to know all that stuff?"
- "We need more training on PowerPoint, BlackBoard, and other software, and how to post assignments online, to be able to help faculty."
- "Faculty provide us with a very brief description of what they want. Then we must draw our own conclusions and get it right."

Putting On Your Shoes

These are the challenges I have heard most commonly from staff. Participants in my workshops say these problems often feel overwhelming and quite mysterious. On their bad days, they come to some pretty dark conclusions about why working with faculty can be as hard as it sometimes is. Maybe the whole university environment is somehow "broken" or "screwed up." Maybe faculty are (choose your pejorative): inconsiderate, clueless, arrogant, self-centered, unappreciative as people. Staff know this doesn't define the complete picture, but they are just trying to make sense of the bad days.

So then, how to mitigate the pain?

What comes to mind is a Buddhist saying I like a lot: if you want your journey to be less painful, it's easier to put on shoes than to cover the earth with leather. Isn't that a great image? And so true. We don't need to try to change everything and everyone in the world out there. We only need a deeper understanding of what is going on and what we can realistically influence.

You could think of this book as shoes for your journey toward a better working relationship with faculty. As I do with staff who attend my workshops, I am going to guide you to develop new ways of understanding and perceiving, communicating and partnering with, and appreciating faculty. What I offer will help you not only to survive, but also to thrive as you work with faculty.

We're going to embark on this journey in the next chapter by looking first at the different characteristics and roles of staff and faculty that contribute to what we could consider the interpersonal culture of academia. This culture is the fertile ground in which many of the challenges we have just discussed take root and grow. So, whether you've worked as staff for a week or your whole career, your ability to work well with faculty depends on understanding these important aspects of your workplace.

Where Do You Stand?

I've tried to represent the range of feelings and reactions expressed by staff who attend my workshops. Some challenges may have resonated more with you than did others. Ultimately, what matters is your ability to minimize challenges so you can take full advantage of the many opportunities that come with your job. So, before we continue, I suggest you take a quick inventory of what we have discussed so far.

- What do you see as the three most important opportunities for you in your work with faculty?

- What do you see as the three most important challenges for you in your work with faculty?

- Think of three strong emotions you feel or have felt in your working relationships with faculty. Are these feelings you wish to experience more often or less often?

- How do you deal with emotions and challenges that arise at work? Do you have a colleague or friend with whom can you speak openly and honestly about them?

[See Summary—I Hear You on the following page.]

Summary

I Hear You

- As staff, you may find your job fulfilling and meaningful. Nevertheless, at times you may find working with faculty can be confusing, frustrating, and challenging.

- I list eight challenges that staff often report, including faculty who seem disorganized, are unavailable, do not follow procedures, have unrealistic expectations, and are disrespectful to staff.

- Trying to change faculty members (or anyone else) can be frustrating and futile. In this book, I guide you to develop new ways of understanding and perceiving, as well as communicating and partnering with faculty.

2

Faculty and Staff: Getting Acquainted

- The Species Test
- Early One Monday Morning
- Faculty and Staff Characteristics
- A Faculty Portrait
- Your Work with Faculty
- Where Do You Stand?
- Summary

"Faculty are a different species, immersed in a different culture."
When a manager made this provocative comment during a training I was leading at a university, the other staff members all nodded in agreement. I have since picked up on his metaphor and used it in other workshops. I find staff often resonate with this image. To me, it suggests a world populated with a variety of colorful species who operate in importantly different ways that can, at times, put them at odds with one another.

Through the eyes of staff, faculty can indeed seem different in many ways. As the manager said in my workshop, not only do faculty seem like a different species, but their overall culture is confounding to many staff. This can be especially disconcerting if you work closely with faculty.

The Species Test

So, how are faculty and staff different? Please note, when I say *different*, I don't mean better than or worse than—just different.

Here is a questionnaire intended to help you find out whether you think, act, or characterize yourself more like a typical staff or a typical faculty member. Take just a minute and have some fun with this. Read each of the statements in **The Species Test**, and without giving it too much thought, circle the number on the 1–5 scale that you feel best describes you *while on the job* in your current staff position. (Note that the high rating is always on the right side, even though the order of the numbers varies.)

Table 2.1 The Species Test

Describes me in my work environment:	Not at all	Some-what	Very much		
1. I am an abstract thinker.	5	4	3	2	1
2. I'm a people person.	1	2	3	4	5
3. I take a very concrete and practical approach.	1	2	3	4	5
4. I am a visionary.	5	4	3	2	1
5. I stay in touch with colleagues at other institutions.	5	4	3	2	1
6. I leave work at the same time every day.	1	2	3	4	5
7. I can be absent-minded when it comes to details.	5	4	3	2	1
8. I carefully follow university procedures.	1	2	3	4	5
9. I work most weekends.	5	4	3	2	1
10. I support other people's goals and ambitions.	1	2	3	4	5
Calculate the sum of all circled numbers.	Total ____				

© 2010 Susan Christy, Ph.D.

If the total of your answers (you may want to pull out a calculator) is greater than 32, there's a good chance you may be more like a typical member of the staff species than a typical member of the faculty species. Of course, you realize this isn't a formally validated instrument. So I can't guarantee the accuracy of its results, and I certainly don't plan to publish them! But you can keep them in mind in a general way as we compare and contrast these two "species."

Early One Monday Morning

Okay, play with me on this for a moment. I'd like you to imagine it is Monday morning on a large university campus, and we're looking in on two individuals: Kyle Stickman, professor of economics, and Gwen Brooks, the project manager for one of his research grants. Dr. Stickman's office at the end of the hall in the Department of Economics has windows overlooking the sculpture garden. It's 8:45 a.m. He's just walked in and sets his briefcase beside the desk, which is piled too high with papers to hold another item. (By the way, I'm calling Gwen by her first name and Dr. Stickman by his title because that is how they often refer to themselves; for more about the appropriate ways to address faculty, see Chapter 7.) Before Dr. Stickman can pick up the ringing phone, there's a tap at the door. Gwen pokes her head in. He motions her to sit while he takes the call. It's his wife, with some things she didn't get a chance to tell him before he left the house. Gwen looks over some notes while she waits. For the past hour, she's been busy in her office, which she shares down the hall with two other staff members.

When Dr. Stickman gets off the phone, he has only five minutes to talk before he needs to rush to his first lecture. Gwen has a list of items to discuss, which she quickly reassesses and skips straight to the highest priority: the PowerPoint he needs for his presentation at a conference the next day. Dr. Stickman listens attentively, then rises from his chair and says with a warm and genuine smile, "You're always on top of everything!" Gwen thanks him for his confidence in her, promises to make sure the appropriate slides get into PowerPoint, and asks if they can meet later in the day so he can look them over.

By now, Dr. Stickman is halfway out the door. He says he has a faculty lunch, then a search committee meeting and two student conferences in the afternoon. His most open time is around 5 p.m., if Gwen can stay that late. She says she'll take a long lunch and adjust her schedule. "Good," he says, "because, you see, I had a breakthrough this weekend. I thought of a whole new way to present my data." He catches her before she can object. "Don't worry," he says. "It'll only mean creating a couple of new slides." He then spends five minutes describing the slides to her, only stopping when she asks, "Aren't you going to be late for class?"

Before we go any further, I want to be absolutely clear: I'm not trying to create or advocate or reinforce stereotypes about either staff or faculty. Geri-Ann Galanti (1991) made an important distinction that applies here. She defined a *stereotype* as an "ending point" that is applied to individuals without checking the truth of the statement. A *generalization,* on the other hand, is a "beginning point" and is used to identify trends, rather than to tag individuals. So the latter is what we are interested in here.

If we take Dr. Stickman and Gwen's interaction as a beginning point, what do we see?

As a faculty member, Dr. Stickman is focused on big picture ideas. Everyone says he's brilliant. He gets excited about new theories and intellectual challenges, so much so he's happy to spend evenings and weekends working on them. This, after all, is his life's work. The reason his wife didn't get to talk to him was because he was up at 5 a.m. for a phone conference with colleagues in Sweden. Their goal is to get more funding next year and to collaborate on an international study. Dr. Stickman is passionate about his research because he believes it will influence major economic policy decisions. His success already has given a big boost to his publications and even landed him on a presidential committee. He is highly ambitious and idealistic.

Dr. Stickman also is dedicated to teaching and gets satisfaction from seeing his students learn. However, lately he's been a bit disgruntled because the department increased his undergrad course load and required him to advise more grad students, all of which takes time away from his research. He is used to juggling many things, but sometimes he wonders how it all gets done. The details drive him nuts. He simply doesn't want to be bothered with university policies and procedures or too many day-to-day tasks. He's notorious for forgetting when reports are due to his research funding agencies and for the Dean's Office. His eyes glaze over when staff start talking about time lines and action steps, or suggest that he clean up his desk. When someone jokes that Dr. Stickman is early to a meeting because he's only fifteen minutes late, he reminds that person how fortunate he feels to be surrounded by such qualified and competent staff. Although he truly values them, staff don't always get that feeling. Talking among themselves, they sometimes say he treats them as underlings.

Gwen began working as an administrative assistant in Dr. Stickman's department before he had tenure, more than a decade ago. She likes the academic environment and never felt a need to look elsewhere.

Initially, she supported several of the younger faculty, but now she is central to the successful running of the entire department office. Many of the professors come to her first when they need something done because they know they can count on her. In addition, she has supervisory responsibilities for the four office staff members.

Gwen has a logical mind and is very organized. But she also is what you might call a people person. She has a strong network around campus, and often calls on one or another person to help with department needs. On this particular day, she contacts a graphic artist in another department to help her adjust one of Dr. Stickman's slides. She never forgets a person's name, even if they've met only once. Her coworkers used to teasingly call her a "walking Rolodex." Gwen has good working relationships with others in her department, although on occasion she's been criticized for being too rigid when it comes to all the university procedures she so meticulously follows and all the paperwork she asks faculty to complete. Usually she listens to their concerns, and still gets them to comply. On most days, she is able to leave the office by 5 p.m., feeling satisfied with herself and her accomplishments.

Faculty and Staff Characteristics

Table 2.2 summarizes some generalizations we might make about faculty and staff, based on Dr. Stickman's and Gwen's examples, as well as on my observations at many institutions over many years. Keep in mind that although staff and faculty may come across as two species with different priorities, like two species in an ecosystem, both are essential to a university's operation and success. Every role is important. Faculty and staff are interdependent, even if different priorities sometimes put them at cross-purposes. However, what may be essential for your job may seem trivial for theirs. And vice versa. [See Table 2.2 on the following page.]

Gwen, by the way, scored as we might expect a typical staff member to do when she took The Species Test. This is a reflection both of her practically oriented organizational abilities and her orientation toward serving people. What if you, despite your staff job, took the test and scored more like faculty? It can happen and does on occasion.

So, if you did not score as staff on the Species Test, the caveat is this. There are a wide range of staff work styles, roles, and positions. Staff differ from one another in terms of their educational backgrounds,

Table 2.2 Faculty and Staff Characteristics

	Faculty	Staff
Strength	Intellectual athletes	Organizational wizards
Thinking Style	Abstract, analytical, creative	Concrete, practical
Background (training)	Specialized graduate education; usually not trained in leadership, administration, or communication	Educated in a variety of fields; on-the-job training; some specialized training (e.g., management, accounting, information technology)
Seek to understand	Theories, skills, and knowledge of an academic field; cutting edge concepts and possibilities	How to get things done, given the procedures and people involved; who is who; what's going on
Work style	Primarily independent, solitary; works from home some of the time	Team player
Work schedule	Work many hours, not necessarily scheduled	Scheduled work day; frequent interruptions
Orientation to work	Academic work is a central focus of life's meaning and activity	Work usually is a valued occupation; much of life's meaning is derived from outside of work
What they manage	Their own research, publishing, teaching, and career	Implementation processes, people, projects, budgets, departmental/interdepartmental relationships, and own career
Approach to implementation	May see implementation as the "easy part" after their intellectual efforts; may need to learn about procedures and how to mobilize resources	Know how to mobilize resources and follow university procedures; creatively "work" their network of relationships to create results
Network	Academics worldwide in their field, students at the university	Faculty, students, and other staff within the department and university
Negative stereotypes (to avoid)	Absent-minded, disorganized, last-minute, prima donna, alpha dog, spread too thin	Bureaucratic (create red tape, make others jump though hoops), nitpicker, rigid and uptight

© 2010 Susan Christy, Ph.D.

job responsibilities, relationships with faculty, pay stubs, and many other ways. Here, we are focusing on the commonalities of the staff experience, as it relates to working with faculty. But we always want to remember and honor our diversity.

A Faculty Portrait

The value of any generalization is apparent in its application. That's what makes it a true "beginning point," in Geri-Ann Galanti's words. One of the main purposes of this book is to consider what the contrasting styles, perspectives, and goals we discuss in this chapter—our beginning point—suggest in terms of their application for your work with faculty. In Sections II and III, I offer many suggestions about how you can approach faculty and communicate to meet your needs—and theirs. For starters, it helps to appreciate that faculty can be viewed as a different species, immersed in a different culture. I suggest you have fun, play with this image. If you were going to pick a species to describe yourself as a staff member, what might it be?

Also for starters, I think it is helpful to get to know faculty better. Let's take a closer look at some of their typical characteristics, as suggested in Table 2.2.

Faculty as intellectual athletes. The work faculty do is intellectual in nature, and so they tend to live largely in the realm of the intellect. They enjoy exploring and critiquing abstract theories and constructs. They may even enjoy ideas for the sake of ideas, much as one relishes the mental stimulation from doing a crossword or jigsaw puzzle.

Like star athletes, faculty usually are hard working, dedicated, self-motivated, disciplined, persistent, and competitive. Keeping fit for them may mean keeping up with advances in their field, considering new approaches that will reach beyond the known, and working harder than other faculty members.

Daniel Salter (2006), who studied the personality types of faculty as measured by the Myers-Briggs Type Indicator (MBTI), confirms that most faculty, especially those at large universities, are introverted "thinking" types. In contrast, Barbara Barron-Tieger and Paul Tieger (1995) found that 75% of people in the general population are extraverts. I think it's fair to say staff are representative of the general population, and thus are likely to be extraverted and "feeling" types. Of course, the science of personality preferences is much more complex than I can

27

discuss here. But the point here is that the natural personality styles and work styles of faculty and staff often are different, and this can complicate working relationships.

Faculty's high level of intellectual interest may be accompanied by a lower level of interest and skill when it comes to administrative tasks and work relationships. They may expect staff to step in and handle logistics and practical details. Policies and procedures may be low on their list of priorities. At times, you as staff may feel the contrast between their passion for what they do and their lack of passion for what you do.

Faculty as stars. Even without specific research to back it up, I think it's safe to say most professors were star students during their early education. They learned to study, organize themselves, and compete for good grades and for recognition from teachers and parents. As undergraduate and graduate students, they probably were singled out by their professors and mentored to become professors and researchers. Thus, they began their academic careers as stars, and now as faculty they must compete with other star scholars to distinguish themselves as excellent educators and innovative thinkers and researchers. They frequently see themselves on a personal mission to make a difference in the world.

In *The College Administrator's Survival Guide*, C. K. Gunsalus (2006) counsels deans and department chairs to be aware that faculty members may expect special treatment and recognition based on their status and expertise. She cautions that "the star system, academic freedom, the general reluctance of those in academia to be managed, and disdain for those in management positions" (p. 45) are all aspects of the faculty culture that can lead to tension in the workplace. Similarly, as staff, you may experience challenges working in an environment in which faculty are viewed as stars. In Section II, we will explore ways to think through your interactions with faculty, and in Section III, I offer specific strategies.

Faculty prefer an independent work style. Faculty tend to be independent and self-motivated. Most of their scholarly work is done in relative isolation from others. Even the planning and teaching of classes is accomplished by the professor as an individual. Many faculty prefer to spend as little time in meetings as possible.

Many faculty find it challenging to make enough time to follow their own creative and independent process while working within an academic institution. They appreciate the academic freedom that is pivotal to higher education. At the same time, you might say faculty's dynamic combination of inspiration and perspiration doesn't like to be managed or confined by university procedures or time lines. Rather than accepting direction from others, faculty put more emphasis on the independent pursuit of what interests them most. They are intrigued by the content and methodology of their subject and excited about how they can contribute to their field and to students' education.

Because faculty are so focused on intellectual activities, they may become preoccupied and pay little attention to interpersonal relationships, such as their working relationships with staff. They may be unaware of the impact their actions or tone of voice or hectic schedules have on staff. They may overlook the feelings of others or even their own feelings. Faculty may keep their ideas or strategies to themselves for too long, believing others see things the same way. At times they may appear distant, unfeeling, arrogant, or otherwise disinterested in others.

Academic work as a central life-focus for faculty. Faculty tend to be passionate about what they do. They are noted for being identified with and dedicated to their academic discipline. I think it's fair to say their livelihood is a way of life. What they do at the university and how they live in general tend to be highly integrated. When I was a professor, I didn't stop paying attention to the psychological dimension of my world when I left the campus at the end of each day. Many of my friends shared the same interests, and we went to workshops together. Even today, years after I stopped being a professor, these interests continue to be closely integrated into all aspects of my life.

Faculty see themselves as experts in their field, not merely as service providers for students. Richard Ruch (2001) speaks about a management consultant who was called in to assist faculty and staff at a private university. The question this consultant posed at a meeting of faculty and administrators was "Who is your customer?" No one could agree. Some thought faculty were the main customers; others thought students were the main customers; yet others rejected the whole notion of customers as an imposition from the world of business onto academia. Ultimately they fired the consultant because he didn't understand academic culture well enough to help with their issues. I mention this incident because it illustrates how faculty's orientation to work can inject confusion into staff-faculty relationships.

Faculty under stress. Many faculty are extremely busy, and feel pulled in many directions simultaneously. They may find their multiple priorities overwhelming. Faculty receive many requests to participate in meetings, committees, conferences, and speaking engagements. Often they are hounded by students seeking attention and advice. And on top of all this, they have to respond to requests from you as staff. Faced with these competing pressures, faculty often become protective of their time and solitude. They know their success depends on their ability to carve out time for thinking and writing and other projects. As a result, they may avoid interactions with others, including staff, and may work from a home office part of the time, which makes it even more difficult to contact them.

Researchers David Buckholdt and Gale Miller (2009) report that, despite widespread assumptions to the contrary, faculty members experience higher levels of stress than do people in many other professions. Moreover, stress appears to be on the increase among faculty as a result of recent financial, technological, and other developments in the higher education setting. *The Chronicle of Higher Education* (2009) predicted that the faculty of the future will be "leaner, meaner, more innovative, and less secure" as a result.

As I just mentioned, faculty tend to be self-motivated, which can put them at odds with the demands in their environment. Motivation can be internal (or intrinsic) or external (extrinsic). Examples of internal drivers include love of learning and desire to make a difference in the world. Examples of external drivers include criteria defined by the academic institution, such as job requirements, performance review standards, the dean's expectations, and academic rewards. Table 2.3 lists some common internal drivers and external drivers for faculty. [See Table 2.3 on the following page.]

Sometimes internal and external drivers can work harmoniously together. Faculty want to do what they are required to do to get ahead in academia. However, when their internal and external drivers are in conflict, the result can be considerable stress. Many faculty in research universities would prefer to focus on teaching and community service, but these activities are not as likely to lead to promotion as is publication. Many faculty in teaching institutions find repeatedly teaching introductory courses gets monotonous.

Table 2.3 Internal and External Drivers

Internal drivers (what motivates faculty)	External drivers (what universities expect of / offer to faculty)
• Genuine interest in an academic field • Love of learning, research, exploration, discovery, and new insights • Desire to share what they know with students and others • Desire to contribute new ideas, research findings, practical applications to their field and (often) to the world • Opportunity to work in a respected academic institution • Financial security (e.g., through tenure and consulting) • Academic freedom • Need for success as defined by their own values and criteria	• Need to play the game being played, not the game they might prefer • Pressure to get hired, get promoted, get tenure • Pressure to publish, do research on important topics, teach a popular course • Expectation to deliver papers at professional meetings • Need to get grants and other funds to support their work and the institution • Requirement to teach a set number of courses • Expectation to contribute to the reputation of the university or college • Responsibility for administration, committees, meetings, paperwork • Need to adhere to policies, procedures, time lines, deadlines, budgets • Requirement to advise students, sit on dissertation committees

Faculty must learn to play the game being played, not necessarily the game they'd prefer to play. For example, Dr. Weinstein enjoys and values helping people improve their grammar and writing skills (internal driver). The fact that the English Department requires (external driver) her to teach three courses on this subject is satisfying to her. However, Dr. Weinstein resists the department chair's expectation that she write a book on literary criticism in her field. She'd rather spend her extra time writing short fiction. This is causing conflict between Dr. Weinstein and her department chair, and she fears that as a result she may not receive a promotion. Of course, Dr. Weinstein can choose the heights to which she aspires, but if promotion is her priority, she may want to put her energy into the book on literary criticism. In Section IV, we will look more closely at how faculty stress develops, and how you as staff can work effectively with faculty who are stressed.

Your Work with Faculty

Perhaps you've heard the expression "Working with faculty is like herding cats." We all know that herding cats is a waste of time, not to mention that it annoys the cats. Similarly, faculty members don't like to be herded. As we've just discussed, much like cats, faculty prefer to maintain their independence. Typically, they work on their own, in their own way, with as little management as possible. Now, you or I might find a creative way to influence cats, perhaps with an open can of tuna fish. Of course, you and I can't make the faculty want to partner with us in more constructive ways, take an interest in the logistics of our work, or prioritize how to help us succeed. But if we think about it and use our imagination, we can probably discover the academic equivalent of an open can of tuna.

We can choose options that naturally encourage improved staff-faculty relationships. There is no value in feeling frustrated, beleaguered, bewildered, or waking up in the middle of the night wishing some professor were different. There *is* value in increasing our perspectives, business and political know-how, communication skills, and campus resources to make our work as easy and effective as possible.

Our goal is to move beyond the tendency to automatically and unconsciously react to faculty behavior or engage in us-them thinking. We can approach faculty as individuals, while recognizing their mindsets and the pressures impinging upon them. We can appreciate faculty for who they are, without taking their behavior as a personal affront.

We will spend much of the rest of the book examining how to work effectively with faculty; for now, I'd like you to consider these general principles.

Forge harmonious and responsible relationships. Influencing faculty is a fine art. It is a balancing act. You want to support faculty's goals, and at the same time you want to stay true to and carry out the university's goals and policies. You don't want to herd faculty or bother them, but rather you want to work within the procedures and time lines of a complex institution.

As staff, it is your job to forge harmonious and responsible relationships with faculty. This includes understanding the structures and policies involved and having empathy for all the players. You can respect where faculty are coming from and recognize that they are doing what makes sense to them, given their perspective. If you find yourself in a bind between what a faculty member wants and the institution's rules, be sure to tune in to your own integrity.

Partnership is essential, if not equal. As staff, you may find yourself working in a system that seems tipped to the advantage of faculty. You may feel you have information and skills, but not overt power. This can be disconcerting, especially if you are new to academia. Your partnerships with faculty may not be equal in nature, but they are essential nonetheless. It is likely to be up to you as staff to find creative and skillful ways to partner with faculty. This is the case even if faculty may not seem receptive. This guidebook will help you do so.

Understand the university system and policies. As staff who work with faculty, your job is likely to include interpreting and implementing institutional policies and procedures for and with faculty. You can't easily and effectively do this unless you clearly understand how the institution functions. If you haven't already, I suggest you familiarize yourself with the many positions required to manage the complex academic enterprise in which you work. In addition to all the managers and staff within academic departments, there is a multitude of people who manage the economic enterprise of education—the business offices, the facilities, and community services that provide for students, faculty, and others on and off campus. Building a network with these staff members will ensure you have the resources you need in your work with faculty.

Service is a choice. Your job as staff is to support the academic enterprise, and often to support and serve individual faculty. When you decide to take a staff position, it can be helpful to understand the service aspect of your job. In a service-oriented position, your work may be largely behind the scenes. Good staff work is often invisible. Many staff tell me they derive satisfaction from knowing they are there to serve something greater than themselves. They enjoy serving the university, and recognize that one way to do so is through helping faculty be successful. Staff who regard service as something imposed upon them, rather than a choice they have made, are more likely to feel resentful and dissatisfied in their work with faculty.

Appreciate the other species. Staff often do not understand the pressures and politics faculty routinely experience. At the same time, faculty may not appreciate a staff member's business perspective, specialized responsibilities, or time lines. They speak in the technical jargon of their academic field and may resist business concepts used by staff, such as customer service, cost containment, and budgeting constraints. I have seen staff furious at how long it takes to get faculty to sign a document or make a simple decision necessary for the staff to proceed with their work. As staff, you can break this cycle by cultivating appreciation and empathy for the other species. Instead of creating an "us and them," make an effort in each situation to delve more deeply into what's going on for both faculty and staff:

- Goals and purposes
- Current circumstances
- Background pressures, concerns
- Perceived vulnerabilities, personal risks
- Assumptions and perceptions

You are valuable. Staff often report they are not seen as valuable individuals, or are not treated respectfully. In fact, faculty may perceive you and other staff as lower-echelon people who are there just to serve them. Faculty may seem entitled, impersonal, insensitive, or unappreciative. As you read this book, I am hopeful that you will see that this is something that, should it happen to you, you need not take personally.

Where Do You Stand?

Throughout much of this chapter, we've been talking about faculty in generalities. As I mentioned, we aren't interested in creating stereotypes, yet sometimes generalizations can be of value. That value is meaningful, however, only if we can apply it to our own unique situation. Take a minute now and bring to mind one faculty member with whom you interact on a regular basis. This experiment will work best if you interact with one or more faculty members on a daily basis. If you don't, just adapt the steps to fit your own experience of faculty.

- For one day, observe this faculty person. Do so with fresh eyes, even if you have worked together for a long while. Walk in his or her shoes; observe through his or her point of view. What do you think are this faculty member's priorities at work? Career goals? Stressors? What can you observe about his or her work style?

- How do you think this person experiences you and your working relationship with him or her?

- List three things you admire about this faculty member.

- Now list three things you imagine you would do differently if you were in this person's position, and were the one wearing the faculty hat.

- Finally, if you have the time and interest, you can expand this exercise by applying it to two or three faculty members. See how different they are from each other.

[See Summary—Faculty and Staff: Getting Acquainted on the following page.]

Summary

Faculty and Staff: Getting Acquainted

- To staff, faculty can seem like a different species, immersed in a different culture. Staff and faculty have different characteristics, roles, work styles, and priorities.

- Faculty can be described as intellectual athletes and academic stars who prefer an independent work style and see their work as a central life focus.

- Faculty experience higher levels of stress than do people in many other professions. Although they are self-motivated (e.g., by their love of learning and desire to make a difference in the world), their goals and priorities can put them at odds with institutional policies and staff priorities.

- To work more effectively with faculty, you can appreciate the service aspect of your staff job, partner with faculty, help them interpret procedures, and understand the pressures impinging upon them.

SECTION II

Ways to Think about
Staff-Faculty Interactions

3. A Systems Perspective   39

4. Staff-Faculty Partnerships   57

5. Adopt a Growth Mindset   69

www.WorkingWithFaculty.com

3

a Systems Perspective

- A Personal Problem
- A Broader View
- Understanding Systems and Systems Thinking
- Looking through the Systems Lens
- We Have a Choice
- Where Do You Stand?
- Summary

Rosa Ruiz, the student services manager in the Material Sciences and Engineering Department at a large university, is in charge of planning the orientation meeting for freshmen. For the last seven years, Dr. Joseph Fall, a world-renowned engineer, has welcomed the new students. Every year, Rosa presents department logistics and discusses student resources; then Dr. Fall gives a brief speech about current trends in his specialized field of engineering. Over the years, many freshmen have experienced this orientation as a rite of passage, an initiation into becoming a full-fledged university student. This event has become part of Rosa and Dr. Fall's annual routine.

At the beginning of this academic year, as always, the new students were excited to attend their first Engineering Department function and to see Professor Fall in person. In fact, many of the students had come to this university specifically to study with him. However, three days before the event, which was scheduled for Thursday, Dr. Fall realized he had a conflicting personal obligation. He asked Rosa to find another faculty member to take his place. Although it was short notice, she assumed she could find someone else. First she called four senior engineering professors, all of whom were unavailable. Then she stopped by the offices of two younger faculty members and appealed to them to welcome the freshmen. No luck.

Rosa realized she didn't have any options left. The meeting had to go on as planned; it was on all the freshmen's schedules. So she decided to facilitate it herself, without a faculty presentation. She stayed up late that evening to rehearse in front of the bathroom mirror.

The next day, Rosa successfully welcomed the new class. She apologized for Dr. Fall not being available due to another unavoidable commitment. The meeting ended earlier than usual, although of course the students didn't have a basis for comparison. Some students came up to Rosa afterward, shook her hand, and thanked her for the meeting and the great refreshments. Only one student expressed disappointment that he didn't have a chance to meet Dr. Fall.

A few days later, Rosa was sitting at her desk when she overheard Dr. Fall chatting with a colleague. He mentioned that he had been at home last Thursday, when his new hot tub was installed, so he could surprise his wife. When she heard "Thursday," a light bulb went on in Rosa's head. So that was his important personal obligation!

A Personal Problem

For a minute, put yourself into Rosa's shoes. Perhaps you've been there already. You are a staff member in charge of an event or project or activity involving many other people, such as the students in this example. You have a lot of responsibility for how the event turns out, whether it ultimately succeeds or fails. And also you are highly capable, the best person for the job, right?

But wait. Even though you feel large and in charge, you don't actually have the final say-so. When it comes right down to it, someone else in the university has greater authority over this particular event or project. He or she can do or say something—or in this case, not be there and not say anything—that will have a determining impact on the outcome. In fact, as you see it, the problem may be more than just that person's greater power. His or her personality also has an impact. And if those two forces—power plus personality—wield their influence in tandem...whew!

So, you have a problem on your hands. How do you handle it?

Again, imagine you are Rosa as she drives home after the freshman orientation she facilitated. Consider each of the following questions. How would you expect Rosa to respond? How would *you* respond?

- Suppose you're speaking to a friend after work. How do you describe what happened?

- How do you feel about Dr. Fall right now?

- What would you really like to say, but won't ever say, to Dr. Fall?

- How will this incident affect how you do your job in the following days and weeks?

In our example, it's easy to imagine how Rosa's angst might have sounded as she drove home: "What's wrong with the faculty? They've got to step it up. Freshmen pay $40,000 a year to come here! Besides, why can't the engineers enjoy this? I mean, if I were a faculty member, I'd love to be the first to welcome students, just to see their fresh, eager faces. Dr. Fall really let those students down. And me, as well. We need to see a little more cooperation around here!" Along with these thoughts, we might expect some frustration, anger, resentment, and annoyance.

Barry Oshry (2007) discusses some of the personal feelings and reactions that are likely to arise in work relationships. He cites six common feelings/reactions: burdened, oppressed, unsupported or isolated, can't please anyone, unreasonably judged, and feeling done-to (p. 126). Using Oshry's terms and Rosa's experience as a jumping-off point, let's look more closely at each feeling that can be experienced by staff, specifically Rosa, in the university setting.

We can feel *burdened* when a work situation presents multiple and possibly conflicting demands on us, or our workload seems unmanageable. Rosa might have felt burdened when she had to scurry around to find a last-minute substitute for Dr. Fall. Leading the presentation herself might have felt burdensome because it was a new role for her. We could call this a clash between our expectations and the demands placed on us by a situation.

Feeling *oppressed* refers to the emotions directed toward other individuals that can arise when we feel at the mercy of their demands at work. Staff can feel angry at faculty, resentful toward them, or disappointed in their behaviors. Rosa might have felt oppressed when she found out that Dr. Fall was at home installing a hot tub while she had to deal with the orientation crisis. She might have felt angry or resentful because he made a personal choice without taking into account its impact on her. We could call this a clash between how people treat us and how we expect them to treat us.

It is easy to feel *unsupported* or *isolated* when we are out on a limb, working hard but without what we perceive as needed responses or support from faculty. These feelings tend to be less intense than the feeling of being oppressed. Rosa might have felt unsupported when she knocked on faculty's doors and no one agreed to substitute for Dr. Fall. In this case, we have a clash between the support we expect and the support we actually receive.

The feeling that we *can't please anyone* can arise when we find ourselves in a no-win situation. This can happen at work when we are responsible for resolving issues we didn't create. It can happen when we are torn between serving the needs of different faculty simultaneously, or when we want faculty to appreciate us but they don't show it. When a student complained to Rosa about not meeting Dr. Fall, she might have felt frustrated knowing that, no matter how good her presentation was, it wasn't as good as meeting the professor himself. We all know the letdown that comes from wanting approval or appreciation and not receiving it.

We can feel *unreasonably judged* when we think we are being responsible and are doing a reasonably good job, but others are critical of us through their words or actions. This feeling can be accentuated if the supposed judgment comes from a faculty member. For example, faculty may judge us if they have unrealistic expectations about our job performance or about how the system should work. Rosa might have felt unreasonably judged by the student who wanted to hear from Dr. Fall at the orientation. This is a clash between how we want others to see us and how they seem to see us.

Feeling done-to refers to situations in which we feel powerless, taken advantage of, even possibly victimized. Instead of feeling we are the ones in control of our own work performance, we see others as making decisions that determine what happens to us. We may be filled with righteous indignation: "How could he or she have done this to me?"

Rosa might have felt done-to when she realized she had to give the presentation without a faculty member there. She knew she would be evaluated on the success of the event because she was the coordinator, so she had no other options. The student who expected to see Dr. Fall might have felt done-to, as well. This is a clash between wanting to feel in control and feeling imposed on by others.

These are some of the feelings common to work situations, especially when a crisis occurs. At the height of the crisis, we can get caught up in our reaction and not try to analyze the situation. But sooner or later, most of us find a way to explain what has happened. We typically do this in one of several ways:

- We focus on the personal characteristics of the people involved. We say, "He is aggressive." "She is selfish." "She is a blamer." "He is insecure." "She doesn't have a clue."

- We speculate about what the other person is thinking or feeling. For example, we say, "He doesn't respect me." "She doesn't understand what it takes to...." "He is pre-occupied with...." "She is stressed out."

- We second guess the other person's motivations. For example, "He will do anything to get what he wants." "She is acting arrogant because she feels so powerless here." "He cares about students, but not about staff."

Our friend Rosa Ruiz could easily have explained her situation by saying, "Dr. Fall is insensitive. He doesn't care about students. He has no people skills. He thinks I'll turn my life upside down for this job. All that matters to him is publishing that book he's writing and then retiring in a few more years." She may even have speculated about why he made surprising his wife with a new hot tub a higher priority than participating in the student orientation.

A Broader View

I have just described many of the things Rosa *might* have felt or thought or said. Notice that I was careful to keep my description in the realm of conjecture. The truth is, I've been holding out on you! The real individual on whom Rosa's story was based responded in a very different manner. Here is how she actually explained her feelings about the situation.

The real Rosa did not suffer angst. She may have felt burdened, oppressed, or unsupported for a few moments, but she is an experienced, university-savvy staff member and so quickly moved beyond her initial reaction. Rosa appreciates the dynamics of university systems, particularly the Engineering Department in this prestigious university. She also understands the student experience, the faculty experience, and the staff experience. When she was planning the orientation, she knew the students would be thrilled to catch a glimpse of Dr. Fall. She also appreciated that Dr. Fall had come to the orientation every year out of his loyalty to the department and the kindness of his heart. When he told her he wasn't available this year, she did not take it personally. She did not feel a need to impugn his motives or belittle his decision. She assumed he did not intend to create difficulty for her. In fact, it occurred to her that, from Dr. Fall's point of view, prioritizing the hot tub to surprise his wife may have been the right choice for him.

Just as Rosa understood Dr. Fall's choice not to present to the freshmen, she also was not surprised the other faculty turned her down. Her people skills are excellent, and she used her best influencing skills to frame her request in terms of each professor's interests and values. At the same time, she is aware most engineering faculty prefer not to take on speaking engagements that cannot further their professional career goals. She accepts it as a fact of her job that she does not have position power, and she knows that much staff work involves influence without authority.

Rosa was willing to step up and give the presentation herself. Her role in the department is one of facilitator, both for faculty and students. In this capacity, she was comfortable filling in as the speaker. Also, she was used to presenting the logistics, so she used that as a starting point. She did feel nervous about how the additional part of the presentation would go, but when it was all over she appreciated the opportunity to practice some new skills.

How do we account for these two vastly different approaches (i.e., how I initially described her response, and how she really responded) to the same situation?

In the first case, Rosa viewed everything that happened in purely personal terms. That is, she considered only her own experience, needs, and point of view. In the second case, Rosa saw everything from a broader perspective. Instead of just herself, she considered Dr. Fall and the other professors, the situation, and the university culture. This broader view reflects an approach known as *systems thinking*.

I first learned about systems thinking, as it applies to interpersonal relationships, from Virginia Satir in the 1970s, when she and others were developing family systems theory. I introduce it here because I think it will help you better understand your work with faculty.

Understanding Systems and Systems Thinking

A system is defined as a unit whose parts are integrated and work together. A system can be as small as the digestive system of a flea (or smaller, for that matter) or as vast as the solar system. Each of its parts serves a different function or plays a different role, while simultaneously working together with the other parts for the survival of the whole. Because these parts continuously affect one another, a change occurring in one can result in a change for the whole.

Systems thinking focuses on understanding how the parts of a system work together. It helps us to understand the interrelationships among the parts, recognizing patterns, and identifying alternative ways to work within the system. It is a way of thinking and solving problems that does not view people or parts of an organization as isolated entities.

Systems in Academia

Systems thinking can easily be applied to the academic setting. A college or university can be thought of as a system whose parts work together. A department can be thought of as a subsystem of the university system. Alternatively, a department can be seen as its own system and culture. Faculty as a group also can be seen as a system within the institution. Each individual faculty member can be seen as a system, with his or her own patterns and ways of doing things.

Here are a few of the subsystems that represent many levels within a college or university system:

- Formal policies and procedures (e.g., the tenure process, research guidelines)
- The curriculum
- Faculty and staff as groups
- Faculty and staff as individuals
- Office groups (e.g., student services, security)

- Channels of communication
- Football team
- Informal culture, attitudes, perceptions

Notice that some of these subsystems are more tangible and easily identifiable than are others. The attitudes of faculty and staff, for instance, may be harder to pin down than the pay scale for teaching assistants or the established procedures for grant applications; however, each is part of the university system and affects the other parts.

Systems Thinking for Interpersonal Relationships

Systems thinking can help us understand ourselves (our motivations, emotions, actions) and enhance our understanding of another person. It helps us recognize the impact we have on a faculty member and the impact he or she has on us. Virginia Satir (1988) described the process of interpersonal communication as the interaction of three related parts: self, other, and context. All three affect one another in a dynamic way. Any communication can be understood in terms of yourself, the other person(s), and the context (the situation as it is unfolding) (Figure 3.1).

Figure 3.1
Self-Other-Context
Diagram

(The situation and the
university environment)

If we think once again about Rosa, and apply this model, we see that she considered herself, Dr. Fall, and the circumstances before reacting (Table 3.1). She was able to see both herself and Dr. Fall as individuals with different roles and different points of view within the context of the freshman orientation in the Engineering Department. Systems thinking enabled her to understand the interdependencies of each part and the effect her possible actions might have on the other people and the situation. She was able to accept Dr. Fall's unavailability and make other appropriate choices as the situation evolved. She recognized the shifting context and adapted accordingly.

Table 3.1 Rosa's System Thinking

Self (Rosa)	Other (Dr. Fall)	Context
Her experience	His experience	Scheduled freshman orientation program, precedent of prior years
Her role, thoughts priorities, and point of view	His role, thoughts, priorities, and point of view	Dr. Fall's unavailability, Rosa's responsibility for the Freshman orientation
Her needs	His needs	Faculty priorities
Her behaviors	His behaviors	Student expectations

Virginia Satir elaborated on the self-other-context model by describing five seemingly universal stances people take in interpersonal communication. Each stance includes an attitude as well as a pattern of communication. The first stance (congruent) enables us to see interactions between self, other, and context in ways that facilitate our understanding, communication, and problem solving. The other four stances (placating, blaming, super-reasonable, and irrelevant) are known as survival stances. We enter one of the survival stances when we are feeling stressed or threatened, or don't want to reveal our weakness (Table 3.2).

Table 3.2 Healthy and Survival Stances

1. In congruent, we are aware and accepting of self, other, and context.	Healthy stance
2. In placating, we discount or ignore our own needs, feelings, and perceptions. 3. In blaming, we discount or ignore the other person's needs, feelings, and perceptions. 4. In super-reasonable, we discount or ignore the needs and feeling of both ourselves and the other person. We focus only on the task or needs of the situation. 5. In irrelevant, we discount or ignore ourselves, the other person, and the context. We focus on something that has nothing to do with the situation or the immediate needs of the people involved.	Survival stances

Paying attention to ourselves, the other person, and the context allows us to understand interpersonal dynamics from a systems perspective and to plan our communications more effectively. Although we often can see all five stances in ourselves and the individual faculty members with whom we work, most of us tend to use a few of the stances more often than we do the others. The following descriptions can help you recognize the five stances and communication patterns in yourself and others.

Congruent. According to Virginia Satir, to be congruent, we communicate from a position of caring for ourselves and for other people, with an awareness of the present circumstances or context (Figure 3.2). We are aware of our feelings and can acknowledge and accept them. We manage our feelings and take responsibility for our impact on others and the situation. Congruence includes keeping our self-esteem intact, even when we feel threatened. It does not mean being happy and without problems, or being polite regardless of the situation.

Figure 3.2
Congruent Diagram

When we communicate congruently, our words, tone of voice, and gestures are all consistent with our message. For example, if a professor has just dropped off a pile of papers with a Post-it note attached, you might say, "I want to be clear about what you want. Do you have two minutes right now or can we meet very briefly sometime later today?"

When we as staff communicate congruently with faculty, we use our inner and outer resources to work toward mutual goals. We acknowledge our own and the faculty member's points of view, strengths, and vulnerabilities. We approach other people and situations with curiosity and openness. We are willing to take risks and be flexible. From this congruent stance, we may be able to observe with empathy others' communication patterns, such as placating, blaming, super-reasonable, and irrelevant. Congruence is a growth stance, rather than a survival stance.

Placating. We placate when we disregard our own feeling of worth, hand over our power to someone else, and go along with whatever the other person wants (Figure 3.3). Placating messages include "Whatever you want is okay" and "I'm just here to make you happy." In an attempt to please others, we may talk in ingratiating ways, either by apologizing or by agreeing even if we do not mean it. We discount our point of view, needs, or feelings so we can survive without disappointing or angering someone else. We do not voice our own opinions, set limits with others, or assert ourselves to find solutions that will be good for everyone involved. People who are codependent frequently also engage in placating.

Figure 3.3
Placating Diagram

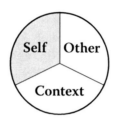

Staff who placate faculty may take on too much work, try to respond to unrealistic demands, wear themselves out, or become resentful. They may forsake their own needs and personal boundaries and agree with or go along with a faculty member when it would be better to set appropriate limits. When talking with faculty, staff who placate appear to lack confidence. Their behavior may even invite faculty to discount them and their talents.

Blaming. Whereas placating discounts our own self, blaming makes others wrong. We sometimes blame so others will regard us as strong, not weak or vulnerable. Blaming messages include "You never do anything right," "What's the matter with you?" "If it weren't for you, we wouldn't be in this mess," and "You're stupid." If we blame, we may act superior, find fault, accuse, harass, dictate, explode, or want to change the other person. We may talk critically about people behind their backs. Blaming does not allow for empathic connection with the other person (Figure 3.4).

Figure 3.4
Blaming Diagram

Staff who blame faculty often are ineffective because their simplistic thinking prevents them from figuring out what faculty need or from helping faculty think through problems.

Super-reasonable. People who are super-reasonable are so focused on the work or task at hand (context) that they ignore the feelings and needs of both themselves and others (Figure 3.5). When we are super-reasonable, work is so all important that we don't allow ourselves or others to focus on feelings or personal needs.

Figure 3.5 Super-reasonable Diagram

Faculty or staff who are super-reasonable may come across as heady or "academic," or even appear robotic. They may be all nose-to-the-grindstone, lack empathy, and communicate using overly technical jargon or unnecessary details. For example, stating to a faculty member who has been working long hours on a report, "Your request for expedited copies is unacceptable. The copy center's required turnaround times are printed on page 2 of this brochure," would be a super-reasonable message.

People who are super-reasonable may create or go along with an out-of-balance task orientation that hurts the relationships among the people involved. Super-reasonable staff often are seen as bureaucrats who thoughtlessly create or enforce rules. Super-reasonable faculty may cause staff great suffering with their unaware behavior or casual lack of respect.

Irrelevant. People who are irrelevant change the subject, talk about unrelated topics (often about themselves), or shift the focus away from what needs to be done. In this way, they avoid whatever may be threatening in a situation. They discount self, other, and context (Figure 3.6). Irrelevant messages include "Oh, what you just said reminds me of something I saw on television last night" and "This wastebasket is too full. The janitor is going through a divorce, you know, and just can't get his act together."

Figure 3.6 Irrelevant Diagram

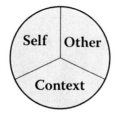

Staff who bring up seemingly irrelevant policies or cumbersome procedures may come across as irrelevant to a faculty member who is focused on his or her next steps. Also, staff may be seen as irrelevant when they try to be entertaining or overly friendly when a faculty member wants to move forward with work.

Not So Personal

When we apply systems thinking to the work environment, often it is apparent that what seemed personal is not necessarily so personal. Systems thinking can help us avoid a knee-jerk emotional reaction and can create more emotional distance for ourselves. Stepping back helps us recognize hurt feelings as expected outcomes in certain situations. Of course, these emotions are personal in the moment we feel them. Nevertheless, we can understand that the situation probably is not about us personally. With this perspective, stress and pain can be more endurable.

You might ask, "Isn't what's happening sometimes personal?"

That's a legitimate question. And it certainly can feel personal and could be a personal attack, especially when feelings are high. However, I would suggest that in most, if not all, cases we also can find a systems explanation for what has happened. Remember, systems thinking doesn't negate our emotions or personal experiences; rather, it places them in a context. It offers us the opportunity to become more aware, to be open to a broader range of possibilities, and to make better choices about what to say or how to respond. We can avoid the unconscious patterns Barry Oshry (1995) calls the "Dance of Blind Reflex." In this dance, we perceive our work through the lens of the personal, and then react blindly and habitually. Oshry (2007, p. xvi) says,

> "When we don't see systems—
>
> we fall out of the possibility of partnership with one
>   another;
>
> we misunderstand one another;

we make up stories about one another;

we have our myths and prejudices about one another;

we hurt and destroy one another;

we become antagonists when we could be collaborators;

we separate when we could remain together happily;

we become strangers when we could become friends;

we oppress one another when we could live in peace;

and our systems—organizations, families, task forces, faith groups—squander much of their potential.

All of this happens without awareness or choice."

When we don't see systems, we are at their mercy. When we recognize the "Dance of Blind Reflex," we can recognize our feelings in a systems context. We often can understand faculty members in new ways that engender empathy and guide us to be more proactive. When we honor our own and faculty members' strengths and limitations, all of us can make our best contributions. Identifying the components of a system and how they interact often gives us the capacity to make things work better at the individual, departmental, and institutional levels. We can influence the flow of information, pull together available resources, communicate congruently, and prevent problems from brewing.

Looking through the Systems Lens

I've introduced systems thinking and Satir's model of self-other-context in this chapter. However, if we look back at the previous chapters, we see all the elements were there. Now we can begin to consider what the world of staff looks like through the systems lens.

How can you think and act in ways that support the well-being and growth of yourself, other staff, the faculty, the department, and the college or university? Often it is a fine balancing act. It takes more than simple formulas, jumping to conclusions, stereotyping, or giving in. There are guidelines but no hard rules. It takes our utmost sensitivity; keen awareness; and good choices about how to think, communicate, and behave. It enhances our dignity. Here are some of the advantages systems thinking offers when we stop doing the "Dance of Blind Reflex," or at least initially begin to slow it down.

Common patterns become apparent. It becomes easier to identify common patterns in the way the department or institution works. Indeed, staff members probably are having similar experiences in universities and colleges around the world, but may be doing so in relative isolation. We can begin to communicate about our commonalities and learn from one another. We can pay attention to how these patterns affect us and faculty.

Roles are better defined. We find it easier to see past the personalities and recognize the roles we play as staff and faculty. Often our roles can become obscured by the personalities involved. Being conscious of roles helps us understand why individuals say what they say and do what they do. When we think in terms of roles rather than the personalities who play those roles, it is easier to see that we are not wrong or bad, and neither are the other people involved.

Relationships with faculty improve. Staff can operate from higher ground when we become more aware of what is going on in our relationships with faculty. We can honor our own and faculty members' pressures and patterns, limitations and strengths in ways that enable all of us to make our best contributions. Have you noticed, staff often seem to understand faculty members better than the faculty members understand themselves? In a system context, this knowledge can be useful for staff in helping faculty follow procedures and succeed in their endeavors.

Compassion increases, tensions decrease. Rather than merely being responsive to others' needs, agendas, and priorities, we can maintain independence of thought and action. When we are less reactive, we become more compassionate with ourselves and others. We are less likely to focus on "us" and "them." By applying systems thinking, faculty and staff at all levels come to appreciate how their partnerships can best serve themselves, one another, and the institution.

New options emerge. Focusing on the systemic rather than the personal opens up avenues for more effective partnerships with faculty. Often people think the easiest intervention is at the level of rules, structures, processes, information flow, reward systems, and control mechanisms. Peter Senge (1990) notes the tendency in organizations to resolve problems with quick fixes of this nature. However, these can create unintended consequences that only make the situation worse. Suppose a few professors get their grades in late. So the Registrar's

Office sets an earlier deadline and creates new forms that all professors must use to report grades. Over time, this decision engenders resentment about all the paperwork and unrealistic deadlines. Even more professors get their grades in late. The quick fix backfired! By using systems thinking, staff might get input from a few professors who often are late and identify what prevents them from getting their grades in on time. Instead of a poorly thought-out switch of rules, staff in the Registrar's Office may be able to find a more effective solution.

We Have a Choice

I offer systems thinking and Satir's self-other-context model as an invitation for you to look at your own perspective and decision-making process. As Peter Senge points out, given the interdependencies within a system, we have a wide range of available options in most situations. Each alternative has the potential for desired results as well as unintended consequences elsewhere in the system. The art of systems thinking involves learning to anticipate the implications and tradeoffs of the actions we choose. It is up to us to examine the advantages and disadvantages of each alternative before taking action. At times, this may entail accepting uncertainty and ambiguity and holding several options, without jumping to conclusions too soon.

Systems thinking helps us make solid choices and work toward long-range solutions and productive partnerships with faculty. Rather than blaming any one person, we can explore what each person brings to the situation and how it is evolving. Rather than placating faculty or taking their criticism personally, we can maintain our self-esteem and choose to communicate congruently. Of course, it can be a challenge to communicate skillfully with a faculty member who is blaming us or has taken on one of the other survival stances. However, the self-other-context model can help us recognize their communication pattern as a survival stance. It can reveal the tension or threat they may be feeling. With this new understanding, we are more likely to maintain our composure, communicate congruently, and calm the upset faculty member. We come across as thoughtful and mature.

Because faculty may not be attuned to organizational nuances, it's often up to staff to craft productive partnerships with faculty. Faculty are unlikely to be offered training about how to work effectively with staff. If a program were offered, most probably would not sign up for it.

Their priorities and attention are elsewhere. In general, faculty:

- Are more focused on their academic fields than on the running of the university
- See themselves as individual contributors with goals related to their academic work
- Are less likely than many staff members to be tuned into the interpersonal dimension of the workplace
- Are less likely than staff members to build collaborative relationships across campus to address their professional needs

In the chapters that follow, I suggest how you can draw upon systems thinking to communicate with and support faculty in ways that serve both of you and your common goals. I'll offer some practical tips you can use while working with faculty. As we discuss them, we'll explore how systemic factors, such as academic traditions, culture, and assumptions about faculty and staff, can influence how you interact with faculty. For example, we will look at how faculty reward systems affect faculty's priorities and at ways in which faculty are dependent on staff for their success. Systems thinking points out these kinds of interdependencies. At the same time, it suggests we examine each situation or relationship from many different perspectives.

Where Do You Stand?

Systems thinking can be applied to a million and one incidents in the workplace. Think about an incident involving a staff-faculty relationship that has left a bad taste in your mouth, one for which you would like to see a better resolution.

- Explaining what happened from a purely personal perspective, what can you say about yourself? About other staff, if any, who were involved? About the faculty involved?
- Applying systems thinking, how do you explain this incident?
- What differences do you see between the personal and systems perspectives in this case?
- Does your analysis suggest a different resolution for this incident?

[See Summary—A Systems Perspective on the following page.]

Summary

A Systems Perspective

- Feelings that commonly arise in work relationships include the following: burdened, oppressed, unsupported or isolated, can't please anyone, unreasonably judged, and feeling done-to. These often arise from taking others' actions personally.

- Systems thinking focuses on understanding how the parts of a system work together, rather than as isolated entities. Parts of a system (i.e., people or departments in an organization) are viewed as constantly changing and as interacting in a dynamic way.

- Virginia Satir, a systems thinker, explained interpersonal communication as the interaction of three related parts: self (you), other (faculty), and context (the situation or academic culture).

- Congruent communication takes into account self, other, and context, and leads to healthy, productive relationships. Four unhealthy communication patterns (i.e., placating, blaming, super-reasonable, and irrelevant) are based on fear and lead to dysfunctional and unhealthy relationships.

- When you, as staff, choose to view your work relationships through a systems lens, roles become better defined, relationships with faculty improve, tensions decrease, and more alternative actions become apparent.

4

Staff-Faculty Partnerships

- Systems Thinking and Power
- Difficult-To-Talk-About Relationships
- Do I Work *For* Faculty or *With* Faculty?
- Different Views of the Organization
- Where Do You Stand?
- Summary

In the last chapter, we tried out the lens of systems thinking and looked at how this perspective helps us recognize the impact we have on the faculty members with whom we work, as well as the impact they have on us. I see this as a powerful lens. On the one hand, it offers a very wide-angle view. The basic principles of systems thinking have been applied to fields as diverse as interpersonal relationships, organizational development, information technology, environmental science, and manufacturing. This wide angle allows us to look broadly at the complex systems within which we work. On the other hand, systems thinking can operate like a pair of sharply focused binoculars. In this sense, it can allow us to zoom in and see with greater clarity and more intimate detail the dynamics of staff-faculty partnerships.

In this chapter I have drawn from various experts in the field of systems thinking and applied their wisdom to our work with faculty.

Systems Thinking and Power

One of the advantages of systems thinking is that it can shed light on the balance of power in relationships.

Where the power lies. Although staff and faculty fall into separate hierarchies within the university system, overt power and prestige within the institution rest primarily with the faculty. In general, faculty, students, and staff all tend to see faculty members as being more important than other people in the institution. This attribution of power can complicate effective communication.

When Sandy, a project manager for Dr. Kogan in the Education Department, was in charge of planning a conference for visiting professors from around the country, the professor told her he "trusted her to handle all the details." She felt empowered, and was proud of how effectively she organized everything. But the day before the conference, after all the participants had received their packets, Dr. Kogan passed by her desk and glanced at the schedule. With a frown, he said he had never been to the restaurant where the final dinner was being held. Sandy ended up spending hours changing the reservation and revising the schedule. Because the restaurant the professor said he wanted instead was unavailable at the original time, other events had to be switched around. By the time Sandy had reworked everything, not only was she exhausted, but she was worried about future communications with Dr. Kogan. What could she do to prevent him from undercutting her next time?

Knowing that someone has power over our work, our paycheck, the rules governing our activities, or is in a position to evaluate us can have an intimidating effect on even simple interactions. However, we don't have to view this as a personal issue; it is more accurately a reflection of the larger system in which we coexist.

Moreover, people who have or are perceived to have power over others often are not as sensitive as they might otherwise be to their impact on others. In our example, Dr. Kogan was unaware of how his request affected Sandy. In his mind, he was simply assuring that the group went to a restaurant he knew he liked. Although this may have appeared as personal insensitivity to Sandy, it reflects a level of deference many faculty expect. I often hear from staff that they feel obliged to defer to faculty, even for inconsequential matters. As Robert Sutton, a Stanford professor (2009), points out,

> Leaders in most organizations not only get paid more than others; they also enjoy constant deference and false flattery. A huge body of research—hundreds of studies—shows that when people are put in positions of power, they start talking more, taking what they want for themselves, ignoring what other people say or want, ignoring how less powerful people react to their behavior, acting more rudely, and generally treating any situation or person as a means for satisfying their own needs—and that being put in positions of power blinds them to the fact that they are acting like jerks. (pp. 71–72)

Sutton's insights about powerful people in organizations can add another dimension to staff seeking to understand their work with faculty. Many of the challenges described by staff in Chapter 1 are similar to the experience of less powerful people in organizations in general, and are not specific to academia or staff-faculty relationships.

Of course, I'm not suggesting it is helpful to label others as "jerks." A systems perspective discourages that kind of thinking. But we can use the sharply focused binoculars of systems thinking to look for more meaningful explanations. A professor in a school of business told me that based on what junior professors had confided in him about their worries and lack of confidence, he concluded that faculty insecurity often masquerades as arrogance. Similarly, Gunsalus points out in her book for academic deans and department chairs (who are themselves faculty) that people who are perceived as powerful don't necessarily feel they have power. She goes so far as to state that none of the groups in the university hierarchy feels empowered:

> It's a truism that everyone in universities feels powerless; undergraduates are at the mercy of everyone, the teaching assistants (who rarely recognize their power over their students and thus can be ripe for abusing it) feel they are at the bottom of the power curve, assistant professors feel disenfranchised and powerless, associate professors worry about who can vote for their promotion, full professors must jockey for position and perks, and department heads know they have little power. (p. 30)

Throughout her book, Gunsalus describes faculty who have excelled as students finding themselves up against great odds to excel in academia. She frequently refers to faculty as "insecure overachievers." Many staff members in my workshops had never considered that faculty may feel insecure or inadequate in their roles and aspirations. Gunsalus's viewpoint can help staff have greater compassion for some faculty behavior and concerns as well as greater willingness to partner with them.

Bending the power structure. In decades past, many staff members were called secretaries, and this is still the case in some institutions today. Professors sometimes have adopted the off-putting stereotypes of a boss-secretary relationship, further accentuating the imbalance of power. Now, large academic departments more typically have individual staff members dedicated to student services, finance, research administration, information technology, human resources, and other functions. To some extent, this wide array of positions emphasizes staff skills and expertise. However, faculty may fail to differentiate among specific staff roles. They think in terms of boss and subordinates, and may think any staff person should "just take care of" whatever they need to have done, thereby perpetuating old power relationships.

Here is an example. A group of professors had pizzas, salad, and dessert during a committee meeting. When they were finished, they hurried off, leaving leftover food and dirty paper plates on the table. Although a big wastebasket was positioned right next to the professors' table, they expected staff to come in and clean up after them. An administrative assistant who participated in a discussion about this incident during one of my trainings interpreted it as a symbol of being treated like second-class citizens. "Why couldn't they throw away their own trash?" he asked.

A manager from the department next door, who had encountered the same situation, offered a practical solution. She recommended having the faculty committee pay for a custodian to clean up. This is an approach that may or may not work in your circumstances. In later chapters, I offer more techniques and creative approaches to handle situations such as these, in ways that work for both you and faculty.

Difficult-to-Talk-About Relationships

I have found that talking about power relationships between any two groups of people can be difficult. For example, describing power dynamics between men and women, blacks and whites, liberals and conservatives, or teenagers and their parents can call forth defensiveness. The same holds true when describing relationships between staff and faculty. We run the risk of upsetting staff or faculty or both, for example, when we say:

- In academia, faculty are more powerful and important than staff.
- Staff are challenged to partner with faculty who may not seek to partner with them.
- Faculty tend to be thinking types and less focused on the interpersonal dimension.
- Staff who are following procedures can be roadblocks to faculty members' missions.

Yes, these generalizations are not true for many individuals. However, examining their ramifications can be useful if our goal is greater understanding, respect, and comfort in staff-faculty work relationships.

One way power relationships play out within the academic environment is along gender and racial/ethnic lines. You only need to walk from a faculty meeting to a staff meeting and look at the faces in the room to observe that a gender and cultural gap exists between the two groups. I have noticed that more women than men attend my workshops for university staff, a reflection of the predominance of women in staff positions.

Consider the statistics. Despite many years of affirmative action policies, the majority of university faculty continue to be white males. Martha West and John Curtis reported in 2006 that women only held 24 percent of full-professor positions in the U.S., and concluded that "women face more obstacles as faculty in higher education than women do as managers and directors in corporate America" (p. 4). This is not due to lack of education; the majority (53%) of Ph.D. recipients in recent years have been women. Similarly, women are overrepresented among non-tenured and part-time faculty, where they account for the majority, as well as in less prestigious institutions. Although some progress has been made in overcoming the gender gap in academia, West and Curtis cite research indicating that according to the most optimistic projections, it will take more than half a century to erase the gap completely.

The numbers are even more disproportionate for minorities. According to the American Council on Education (Jan, 2010), African

Americans and Hispanics constitute only 8.8 percent of tenure-line faculty nationwide. At some prestigious institutions, this figure is as low as 3 to 4 percent. This contrasts with approximately 46 percent of the total population who are African American or Hispanic.

What do these dramatic demographic differences mean for staff working with faculty, and why do I bring them up here? I believe simple awareness is a good place to begin. It is valuable to be aware that power relationships defined on the basis of gender or ethnicity can lead to stereotyping and can be especially difficult to talk about. In your work with faculty, it is helpful to acknowledge when these issues might be having an impact. When a relationship is run on assumptions that have not been clearly articulated, these assumptions can easily spiral into self-fulfilling prophesies and misunderstandings. In the following sections of this book, we will explore ways you can avoid these pitfalls.

Do I Work *For* Faculty or *With* Faculty?

This is a pivotal question for staff. And it comes up often, especially when staff become more attuned to the power dynamics of staff-faculty relationships and to the nuances of systems thinking. It is a natural question to pose to obtain clarity about the basic ground rules of the relationship.

When I interviewed staff members, I found answers to this question varied from one institution, department, or individual to another. Many staff members spoke about ambiguous reporting relationships and inconsistencies that reflect the complexity of academia. They often tried to reconcile the "for" and "with" aspects of the staff-faculty relationship. One senior human resources manager, for instance, told me, "Both. You work for the faculty member because it's his or her purposes you're supporting. But to be successful, you work with him or her in a partnership—not necessarily an equal partnership, but a partnership nevertheless."

A manager in a veterinary hospital clinic said, "We have faculty members who see their staff as collaborators toward common goals, and others who see themselves as boss over staff. When we collaborate to support one another in each other's work, we create better results. The approach 'I am your boss' can become dysfunctional." She continued by explaining the complex staff-reporting relationships in her state university: "University staff technically report to other staff in a separate hierarchy that is parallel to the faculty hierarchy. Staff report to their employer—the institution—through a staff manager, at least on paper. The union doesn't allow staff to report to faculty. The staff manager gets input from the faculty member before doing a performance review. However, staff often functionally report to faculty members."

I guess it's not a secret where I personally fall on this continuum. You only need to look as far as the title of this book! So, yes, I believe it is to staff's advantage to consider how they can work effectively *with* faculty. At the same time, I think it is important to be aware that this is not the only view held in academia.

Different Views of the Organization

I have learned over the years that faculty and staff are likely to understand the structure of the academic organization in different ways. They have varying views of the staff-faculty relationship and the system in which they both participate. Faculty, particularly those who have not worked outside of academia, tend to see the organization as similar to a professional office. For example, in a doctor's or lawyer's office, the professional hires the staff and sets the rules. Staff work for the professional to help him or her be successful. They manage the office however the professional desires, and often become good at influencing without having real authority.

Academic staff, particularly those who have worked in corporations or nonprofit organizations, tend to take into consideration the different roles and responsibilities faculty and staff have within the academic institution. They may assume that both faculty and staff work for the college or university and are all subject to the same policies and procedures.

In his classic book *Gods of Management*, published in the 1970s and updated in 1995, Charles Handy defines four cultures of organizational management: club culture (an informal network, centered around a product or service); role culture (based on roles and function); task culture (based on problem solving); and existential culture (centered around the individual). In the first three cultures, the participants are there to further the organization, but in the fourth culture, the organization exists to support the individual in accomplishing his or her purpose.

I think this model can be applied to staff and faculty in academic institutions. Faculty generally fall into the existential culture. Staff generally operate according to the role culture. Of course, both groups are subject to the same sets of rules and procedures, but they may respond to them differently, based on their viewpoints. In Table 4.1, I have taken these cultures, as Handy has described them, and illustrated how they apply to faculty and staff in the academic setting.

Table 4.1 Faculty and staff views of organizational management

In the eyes of faculty	In the eyes of staff
The organization is subordinate to the individual. The organization exists to help the individual achieve his or her purpose.	The individual is subordinate to the organization. Individuals are there to help the organization achieve its purpose.
Accomplishments and skills of individual faculty are the crucial asset of the organization.	Faculty and staff work together to provide education, research, and community service.
Professors and researchers preserve their individual identity and freedom. Management in the organization is done like housekeeping.	Faculty and staff have roles defined by the organization. Management occurs through flow charts, job descriptions, rules and procedures, manuals, budgets, and information systems.
Faculty seek success in their own terms and prefer not to be limited by organizational policies or procedures. They expect staff to understand their mindset and work style and to support them accordingly.	Staff look to the administration (president, deans, department chairs) to define rules and procedures. Staff are responsible for communicating about and implementing policies in their work with faculty.

These two views can lead to miscommunication and tension between staff and faculty. Even when they set out to work together, faculty and staff can find themselves becoming accidental adversaries. First coined by Jennifer Kemeny in 1994, the term *accidental adversaries* is a systems archetype commonly referenced by systems thinkers. It refers to groups of people who in all likelihood should be in partnership, but who wind up on opposing sides. They stand to gain from working closely together, but instead repeatedly put their own needs first, thus inadvertently obstructing the other's success. Table 4.2 illustrates some of what I have observed to be common misunderstandings by staff and faculty that can turn them into unintended adversaries I've included this list as a starting point for

Table 4.2 Common misunderstandings

Faculty assume that...	Staff assume that...
Staff understand how busy faculty are, how difficult what they do is	Faculty know how busy staff are
Staff must have all the facts and information on hand	Faculty know staff don't have all the facts and information at their fingertips
What staff do is easy	Faculty know how complex what staff do is, how long things take, and all the policies and people involved
Staff are not doing everything possible, otherwise there wouldn't be a problem	Faculty know staff are doing their best to resolve the problem
Staff are there to solve problems faculty encounter and can move mountains	Faculty understand staff may require more input or authority to correct a situation
Staff work evenings and weekends because faculty do	Faculty know staff don't usually work on weekends
Staff should never get angry, frustrated, or tired	Faculty know staff are only human
Faculty speak clearly and never make unreasonable requests.	Staff speak clearly and never make unreasonable requests

you to bridge some of the staff-faculty differences you may encounter.

While I was writing this chapter, an interesting thing happened. I emailed a professor whom I didn't know—I'll refer to him as Dr. Schmile—but whom a mutual acquaintance suggested I interview. I called him, described my book briefly, and asked if he would be willing to share some of his perspectives and experiences. We made an appointment for two weeks in the future. I was surprised to get an email from him the next day. It began as follows:

We are professors, and we know many things, some of which are even true:

1. We carry the mission of the university—we teach, do research, and perform service. The university is about us, and staff exist to allow us to carry out that mission.

Mostly true. We are the center of the university universe and staff exist to serve us. But what we don't recognize is that, while this is true at an organizational level, it is not true at a personal level. Staff exist to support us, not to serve us personally.

2. We are busy and our time is too important to be wasted by administrivia.
   Sort of true.

3. If the staff do what we want, when we want it, the system is working; if they don't, it is not.
   Not so true.

4. We are better than or above staff.
   Not true at all, at least not in any kind of human, rather than rank, way.

5. If a system or policy is inconvenient, it can and should simply be changed. We shouldn't be constrained or limited by administrative systems.
   Conceptually true perhaps, but often not practically true.

I was amazed when I read this list in Dr. Schmile's email. Without seeing any part of my manuscript, he had enumerated five assumptions faculty make about staff-faculty relationships that echo what I have presented in this chapter, as well as in Section I. Talk about confirmation! I also was impressed with the honest manner in which he stated the assumptions, owned them, and then repudiated most of them. Of course, I am aware other faculty members may not share his perspective.

Dr. Schmile elaborated on his view of how staff and faculty interact within the university system. I'd like to leave you with a quote from the rest of his email:

Both faculty and staff often forget we share a single mission and are on a single team. We each carry a different part of that mission, but without all of us, the mission can't be achieved. I may be the guy on the front lines, teaching the classes and doing the research, but without effective staff, my proposals won't get submitted, my money won't get managed, my classrooms won't be scheduled, and my equipment won't work. Of course, some university staff forget their mission, to the appropriate annoyance of faculty. I know of offices that forget their job is to support teaching and research, and think instead they are the center of the universe. Business services and the legal offices often seem to believe that covering the university's ass is more important than actually running classes and research.

Where Do You Stand?

When I was conducting interviews for this book, another person with whom I spoke was a staff member named Patricia, who is the Director of Employee and Labor Relations at a large university. She has been at the institution for thirty-five years, having moved up through the ranks by excelling at each position, helping her boss be successful, and designing better ways to support faculty and staff productivity. She was chosen to head her department, a position usually held by a senior lawyer, because of her vast experience and people skills. She developed a program in which consultants from her department meet with managers from other departments to help them deal with conflicts and performance issues as problems arise, rather than waiting for them to escalate.

I thought Patricia was in a good position to offer valuable insights for staff, so I asked her what she might advise. She offered the following three caveats for staff:

Maintain a healthy relationship with your work. Understand and be willing to accept your role. Many who fail as staff can't accept their role. They overstep their boundaries with faculty, get too emotionally involved advocating for students, or become too entwined in faculty's lives.

Don't allow yourself to be victimized, or isolated without resources.

Ask where you can add value in your work with faculty. When you add value, you are likely to be given greater responsibility and independence.

These golden nuggets from Patricia are a perfect lead-in to our next chapter, about adopting a growth mindset. Before we turn to that topic, however, her advice suggests some ways for you to apply the principles of systems thinking to your work with faculty. Take a few minutes to do an inventory of the following:

- To what extent do you understand and accept your role as staff, say, on a scale of 1 to 10?

- What aspects of your staff role are challenging for you to accept?

- How do you communicate your role and responsibilities to the faculty with whom you work?

- How, specifically, can you add value to your work with faculty?

[See Summary—Staff-Faculty Partnerships on the following page.]

Summary

Staff-Faculty Partnerships

- Faculty, students, and staff all tend to see faculty as more important than others in the institution. People in powerful positions in any organization often take advantage of less powerful people.

- In academia, the reporting relationships between staff and faculty are often confusing. This can lead to miscommunication and to staff feeling diminished.

- Faculty and staff often have different perspectives. Many faculty assume the institution exists to help them achieve their goals. Many staff assume both staff and faculty are there to help the institution achieve its goals, and that faculty and staff should all adhere to defined roles and procedures. These different views can put you and faculty at odds with one another.

- I encourage you to understand and accept your role as staff, not allow yourself to be isolated or victimized at work, and find creative ways to add value to your work with faculty.

5

Adopt a Growth Mindset

- The Power of Mindset
- What Is Your Mindset?
- Value Strong Relationships with Faculty
- View Faculty as Colleagues
- Hold the Big Picture
- Balance Commitment with Healthy Detachment
- Focus on What Is Working
- Adopt an Experimenter's Mindset
- How to Develop a Growth Mindset
- Faculty Mindset
- Summary

As I've worked in academia, I have observed that some staff and administrators are more successful and satisfied in their jobs than others are. I've seen some staff practically hanging on by their fingernails, while others thrive in the same environment. Of course, the contrast isn't always so dramatic.

But having seen enough staff differences on every campus, in managers and administrative assistants alike, I began to ask myself what could account for this phenomenon. With careful observation,

I realized one of the primary differences lies with *mindset*. Staff who are successful share a common personal stance toward their jobs and themselves. This stance is more than a particular attitude or concept. It is a deep understanding about the importance and role staff fulfill in their departments.

A successful stance can manifest outwardly in a variety of ways. Successful staff tend to come across to others as competent and mature. They appear to be self-aware, able to deal with their inevitable frustrations and willing to take responsibility for their behavior and their impact on others. They show little righteous indignation, and are more likely to respond to situations with equanimity and curiosity.

Successful staff stand tall in knowing their place in the scheme of things. As one research administrator who deals with many professors told me, "I know my place. I like my place." There is no resentment, blaming, or victimization in this kind of stance. Successful staff are not threatened by the eccentricities and foibles of faculty with whom they interact. They realize their job knowledge and people skills are crucial to the professors' success—and to their own success.

In workshops, I find it interesting to see successful staff alongside less successful colleagues who have the same job description but feel resentful, overwhelmed, or demeaned. They tend to blame or placate. These disgruntled staff spend their energy complaining and wishing faculty were different, or fighting something about the institution that is unlikely to change. I have seen workshop conversations between dissatisfied staff and more successful staff lead to powerful learning and to the adoption of a growth mindset. For the first time, dissatisfied staff hear other staff explain how they view their jobs: "I treasure the faculty." "I feel included and appreciated." Often the dissatisfied staff respond, "Wow, I didn't realize there was another way to look at this!"

If you are feeling frustrated or overwhelmed in your work with faculty members, you may be thinking about the situation in ways that aren't helpful to you or your success. In this chapter, let's look at the power of mindset as it relates to systems thinking. I'll share some ways you can reexamine your own mindset in light of what I've found to work for successful staff.

The Power of Mindset

When you hear about someone having a particular mindset, you might picture a person whose mind is set, rigid, not open to new ideas or to other people's perspectives. We speak about having our "mind set on" something when we aren't predisposed to changing our opinion or our goal. But psychologists make an important distinction between fixed mindsets and growth mindsets. A growth mindset is all about flexibility and willingness to learn. Virginia Satir's five stances, described in the last chapter, can be considered mindsets. In this case, congruence would be a growth mindset and the four survival stances—placating, blaming, super-reasonable, and irrelevant—would be fixed mindsets.

Carol Dweck of Stanford University, author of *Mindset: The New Psychology of Success* (2006), is a research pioneer in this area. She studied achievement and success, and made the rather startling discovery that people who have the mindset that they are talented or smart don't necessarily go on to develop their full potential. This is because their mindset is fixed on themselves as smart people. They can be too busy reinforcing their belief in their own smartness to tune into others or develop new skills. Others, however, might not consider themselves particularly talented but have the mindset that their commitment and hard work will lead to success. Often individuals outshine their supposedly more talented peers when it comes to actual accomplishments. The difference comes from having a growth mindset that allows them to be more fluid, to change and adapt and learn. Even if they start out less talented, they grow in the ways necessary to achieve success.

These ideas have been tested in corporations and other settings. Laura Kray and Michael Haselhuhn (2008) report, for example, that negotiators with a growth mindset are better able than negotiators with a fixed mindset to reach agreements that benefit both parties. You may be familiar with the idea of a winning mindset in sports. The field of sports psychology is based on the premise that attitude and mindset are as important as physical ability for successful athletes.

What Is Your Mindset?

Take a minute now and assess your own mindset. See to what extent yours could be considered a growth mindset. As you did in The Species Test, read each statement, and without giving it too much thought, circle the number on the 1–5 scale that you feel best describes you *while on the job* in your current staff position.

[See Table 5.1 The Staff Mindset Assessment on the following page.]

Table 5.1 The Staff Mindset Assessment

As a staff member:	Not at all	Some- what	Very much		
1. I tend to hold grudges against faculty.	5	4	3	2	1
2. I look at the big picture.	1	2	3	4	5
3. I remain professionally detached when conflicts occur.	1	2	3	4	5
4. I find many faculty intimidating or unreasonable.	5	4	3	2	1
5. I see a lot of personality conflicts at work.	5	4	3	2	1
6. I keep my sense of humor.	1	2	3	4	5
7. I avoid faculty whenever I can.	5	4	3	2	1
8. I gossip about faculty's shortcomings.	5	4	3	2	1
9. I see myself as a colleague with faculty.	1	2	3	4	5
10. I learn a lot from faculty.	1	2	3	4	5
Calculate the sum of all circled numbers.	Total ____				

If the total of your answers is greater than 35, you probably have a growth mindset that serves you well in relating with faculty members on the job. Let's look more closely at the characteristics of this growth mindset and explore practical ways you can develop and maintain it.

Value Strong Relationships with Faculty

I'd like you to meet Tom. He prepares the budgets for grant proposals submitted by faculty in the Urban Studies Department. Because he has done this for the past ten years, faculty rely on him to put budgets together with relatively little involvement on their part. It is an especially simple process for grant renewals: they give Tom pertinent information for the various line items, he creates the spreadsheet, and they sign off on it. But then there's Dr. Reed. She's in the habit of giving Tom incomplete information. Dr. Reed states that she "hates to be bothered" with budgets, and when pressed, tends to get flustered.

If Tom has a fixed mindset, he may grumble behind Dr. Reed's back about the missing information. He might feel chronically irritated at the time spent to do Dr. Reed's budgets relative to other faculty's budgets. Tom may feel Dr. Reed is ignoring him or disrespecting him or purposely making his job more difficult. He may believe he has no way to get Dr. Reed to provide the necessary information.

Then one day a crisis occurs in which Dr. Reed's proposal is almost submitted without a travel budget. Tom finds a note on his desk saying only "Tex site visit = 1st week Feb." He feels like calling Dr. Reed and yelling, "The proposal you sent me didn't include any site visits! And you didn't have any last year. How on earth was I supposed to know you needed a travel budget?"

However, Tom does not act on his frustration. Because he values their relationship, he feels confident they can work out the problem together. He decides to call Dr. Reed and propose they sit down and discuss the travel budget.

Staff, like Tom, who have a growth mindset value strong staff-faculty relationships. They put consistent effort into developing good, clear communication; awareness of one another's goals and activities; and an atmosphere of mutual respect. As I have already noted, faculty may not go out of their way to build relationships with staff. But if your mindset places a value on relationships with faculty, you can take the steps to build those relationships and make them strong. This includes both formal and informal communication.

Here are some other things you can think about to forge strong staff-faculty relationships.

Know your faculty. Faculty differ as individuals and they differ by department and school culture. So, become familiar with the particular faculty group(s) with which you are involved and the politics of working with them. For example, if you're working with tenured full professors in a small college, tailor your approach to them. If you work with adjunct faculty, consider their situation. Tenured faculty may be worried about their research funding, while adjunct faculty may be concerned their class will be cancelled if enrollment is low.

Avoid stereotypes. As we discussed in Chapter 2, faculty members are a varied group. Nevertheless, stereotypes about faculty abound. For example, I recently heard a staff member say about her work with faculty: "They're so inconsiderate. I can't stand it!" That comment reflected her frustration, but did it help her build stronger relationships with faculty? I suggest approaching each faculty encounter with an open mind and a willingness to work together in a professional manner.

Be accepting. If you are frustrated with faculty members, you may be harboring some unrealistic expectations or taking their behavior personally. Part of finding balance and equanimity in your work is accepting the way people are and doing your best to build strong, positive relationships. Check to see if you are mind-reading their thoughts, impugning their motives, or criticizing their personalities. This most likely will not help either you or them.

View Faculty as Colleagues

A colleague is an associate or partner one views as and relates to as an equal. Most faculty see other faculty as colleagues. And I have seen that staff who are successful are able to think about faculty as colleagues, as well.

When staff have a fixed mindset, they often perceive faculty as superior, privileged, or intimidating. This creates distance in their work with faculty. It's difficult to partner with faculty if they have been defined as unapproachable.

As a new consultant to executives and faculty members, I initially adopted a deferential stance. Then I attended a consultants' conference where I learned to "look clients straight across"; that is, to see them as equals. When I put this into practice with faculty and other clients, I found them more responsive, respectful, and collaborative. In fact, with a growth mindset, it doesn't matter that faculty may have more power, we as staff can value the contributions we make to our partnerships with them.

I'm not suggesting, of course, that staff should try to establish the same kinds of extensive formal and informal collegial relationships that faculty share with one another, or that staff share with other staff. We are talking here about a mindset, the attitude you have toward faculty while working with them. It's more subtle. For example, consider what happens when Tom (from our earlier scenario) finally sits down with Dr. Reed. Let's look in on them again.

Finding time to get together was tricky, but they're finally able to do so three days before the grant has to be submitted for review. Tom senses the tension in the air and does his best to defuse it. He offers Dr. Reed a soda and begins by saying he knows that preparing budgets isn't her favorite activity. He stresses that they are doing this as a team and points out their respective skills. He does this with a nonthreatening, collegial tone that puts Dr. Reed at ease.

Dr. Reed admits she added the site visits in her last draft of the proposal and apologizes for forgetting to pass the information along. Tom asks Dr. Reed to stay while he makes the necessary changes in the budget. He asks her for the specific travel details and shows her how the expenses are calculated based on the university's travel rates.

As they work together, Dr. Reed's confidence in Tom's ability to prepare budgets is reinforced; at the same time, she sees the importance of keeping him fully informed. The mutual comfort and respect with which they work together is evident when they share a laugh as Tom accidentally enters a per diem rate of $3. Toward the end of the meeting, Dr. Reed reaps an unexpected benefit from Tom's accounting skills when they do some additional budget juggling and realize they can hire a second part-time data entry person.

Here are some things you can do or think about to make sure you maintain a mindset that supports collegial relationships with faculty.

Focus on your common purpose. You may find the following questions, suggested by Wendy Leebov and Gail Scott (2003, p. 322) in their work with hospital staff, helpful for focusing on a common purpose. When people who work together address these questions, they can define their common goals, develop trust and commitment, and clarify their roles in relation to each other.

• Why am I (staff) here?

• Why are you (faculty) here?

• What do we want to do together?

• How will we do it?

You don't have to read this whole list aloud to faculty, but you can take time to consider the questions before you sit down together. If you think about how the questions might be answered, you can bring that perspective into your dialogue.

Be friendly. This might sound obvious, but that doesn't make it any less important. Some cultures use a specific term to refer to adopting a friendly, welcoming attitude. For example, Hawaiian culture speaks of *aloha* (literally, "being in the presence of life spirit"). The word *namaste* (literally, "I honor you") is used in some South Asian cultures. Unfortunately, the English language does not have many words to describe the welcoming, open-minded attitude that works best for establishing collegial relationships.

In the spirit of aloha and namaste, you can project a positive, agreeable, can-do attitude with each and every faculty member. You can do this no matter how cordial he or she may be. Having a friendly, professional style does not mean you are a pushover. Setting appropriate boundaries is discussed in Chapter 9.

Hold the Big Picture

Holding the big picture grows naturally out of the ability to engage in systems thinking. In our example, Tom's choices in his interactions with Dr. Reed demonstrated his awareness of himself, Dr. Reed (other), and the budget process (context). Specifically, his big picture included:

- Acknowledging his own frustration and avoiding a knee-jerk reaction, such as judging Dr. Reed as irresponsible or gossiping about her to his coworkers
- Anticipating and empathizing with Dr. Reed's impatience and resistance to the budget
- Recognizing that Dr. Reed is generally a good communicator and is appreciated by staff for her collegial approach to most administrative issues
- Considering that the situation reflects the different priorities and skills he and Dr. Reed bring to the grant proposal process: his facility with numbers is quite different from her specialty as a poet

Here are some other things you can do or think about to make sure you are holding the big picture.

Focus on the vision and mission of your institution and department. Many groups and organizations of all sizes, including colleges and universities, have created vision and mission statements. These statements reflect the big picture and can help members of the organization keep it in focus. According to CEO coach Mike Myatt, an organization's vision is what defines its endgame, and its mission can be thought of as "the road map that will take it there."

Does your institution or your department have a vision and/or a mission statement? If it does, and you aren't already familiar with this material, I suggest you check it out. It can help you keep the goals and the well-being of all faculty, students, staff, and others in perspective.

Anticipate the practical implications of decisions and actions. With the big picture in mind, you can appreciate how one part of the system affects the other parts. While a fixed mindset is likely to see events in isolation and may lead to a quick fix with unintended consequences, a growth mindset is often able to anticipate consequences and avoid potential problems.

You can anticipate who may be affected by decisions you or the faculty make, as well as the impact on everyone involved. For instance, if you spend budgeted money one way, it won't be available for alternative uses. If a faculty member decides to speak at a particular conference, he or she will not be in town for graduation. You also can clarify any precedents that may be set by a decision you or a faculty member makes.

Share the big picture with faculty. Don't assume that just because they are faculty, all faculty members are looking at the big picture. In fact, in the midst of the day-to-day business of teaching and research, some are not focused on it at all. They may be so busy and feel stretched so thin, that they often do not take an extra moment to step back and consider the broader perspective.

You, as staff, can help faculty stay in touch with the big picture in a variety of ways. This means assuming a leadership role. Ask yourself, "What can I do to provide the leadership and support needed here? How can I provide the next steps toward institutional goals, toward the overall mission?" It may be a small leadership role, but it is important nonetheless.

For example, you can:

- Orient faculty toward a deeper understanding of the yearly academic cycle

- Point out what policies apply to specific faculty requests

- Explain the practical implications and unintended consequences of faculty decisions

- Inform faculty about how quickly they need to make certain decisions

- Anticipate who may be affected by decisions you or the faculty make

Balance Commitment with Healthy Detachment

In the scenario, Tom's decision to assume a collegial mindset resulted in a positive outcome for everyone involved. However, we can't assume that every attempt to adopt a growth mindset will result in automatic and instant success. Suppose Dr. Reed had been unavailable to meet with Tom. The grant proposal might have been submitted without travel expenses for the site visit. In that case, Tom could adopt a healthy detachment. Rather than blaming Dr. Reed or himself, he could have accepted and learned from the situation and worked to prevent it from happening again.

Detachment in this context means we don't take things personally or let ourselves become overly emotionally involved. We don't try to control situations or change people because that approach is unlikely to succeed. We don't get caught up in gossip or other pettiness. Instead, we stand back and take a more calm, objective perspective. When conflicts arise, we take an extra breath before reacting.

Former UCLA softball coach Sue Enquist once said, "I want my team to be more detached from the wins and losses and be more focused on doing the little things well." A growth mindset takes easy situations and difficult situations and treats them as equal. Tom might find working on Dr. Reed's budgets a challenge, while the other professors' budgets are a breeze. Yet he knows the bottom line—in this case, literally—for each situation is of equal importance to the department and the university. So he exercises detachment and does not get caught up in Dr. Reed's frustration or resentment. When it comes time to work with Dr. Reed, he focuses on getting the details of her budget worked out correctly.

Sometimes people say that feeling too detached on the job leaves them bored, disinterested, or insufficiently motivated. They look at detachment as somehow unhealthy. They're afraid they'll become unproductive on the job if they don't maintain a sense of engagement. So it is important to strike a balance between healthy detachment and commitment. Tom might tell himself, "I'm not going to let Dr. Reed's inattention to this task get me riled up. Her weakness won't distract me from doing a good job. I'm committed to doing my part to make this a successful research proposal, regardless of what anyone else might or might not do."

Here are some other things you can do or think about to make sure you achieve the right balance between commitment and detachment.

Develop a healthy detachment. Detachment is not usually recommended in our educational system, or in our society in general. So you may wish to consider this suggestion more closely—both in your relationships at work and in your personal life. Here are some ways to develop a healthy detachment.

• Accept that you cannot change or control others. You can, if you choose, control how you respond to what others do or say, or fail to do or say. Ask yourself: "When I look back on this a month from now, will I be proud of what I did?"

• Resolve your resentments. If you hang onto personal resentments, it is difficult to respond professionally rather than personally.

• Identify the triggers, or hot buttons, that send you into reactive mode or emotional spasms. When those buttons are pushed, take a deep breath and recognize the opportunity to practice detachment.

• Get out of situations that compromise your self-esteem or emotional and physical well-being. In other words, avoid situations in which you feel consumed by negative emotions or that lead you to disengage from the work itself.

Show your confidence. Detachment and confidence are strong partners. It is much easier to be detached if you are feeling confident, and confidence also tends to go hand in hand with commitment. Your confidence that you know how to get things done—"I've done this before; I know the ropes"—goes a long way toward getting faculty members and others to calm down and take on what needs to be done in a systematic way.

Focus on What Is Working

A positive mindset, in which you focus on what is working, can in and of itself invite success and satisfaction on the job. I'm not suggesting you sweep challenges under the proverbial rug. But often we do the opposite: we focus on challenges to the exclusion of good experience and opportunities.

In workshops, I like to ask staff to list what they like and appreciate about their work in academia. Here are some ideas they find have worked well. In each case, I provide quotes from workshop participants.

We share in important, cutting-edge work that makes a difference in the world. Consider everything your college or university contributes to the world: educating the next generation, pushing back the frontiers of knowledge, creating new leaders. Most staff draw

79

satisfaction from being part of this mission and find the work itself is engaging and interesting and full of opportunities. If your job is a good fit with your talents and interests, you probably feel this way, too. What staff have said....

- "We are always being exposed to exciting new ideas."
- "I have a chance to think out of the box, to brainstorm."
- "I plan conferences that bring together professors from all over the world."

Our role is a key to success for students, faculty, and the community. As staff, you may have contact with faculty, undergraduate and graduate students, staff peers, administration, consultants, the media, and community members, among others. In some cases, you may be perceived as a representative of your academic institution. Through these contacts, you have the chance to influence lives. What staff have said....

- "I have a role in hiring the right people."
- "I coordinate with different departments."
- "I get to work at graduation and see students and their families. This makes it all worthwhile."

We enjoy contact with the faculty. Faculty can serve as mentors and advocates for staff. Staff and faculty have the opportunity to join in exciting work partnerships, which in some cases turn into lifelong friendships. What staff have said....

- "I love the faculty and the work, the daily interactions with faculty."
- "Faculty show appreciation for our work. I know my opinion is valued."
- "The department chair is warm and welcoming. She invites program assistants to social events, department meetings, and yearly retreats."

We have a part in creating the vision and infrastructure for this department. Staff can play important roles in long-range planning as well as in the daily running of a department. Some faculty are more comfortable than others when it comes to empowering staff in this regard. Even if you aren't given a voice in setting rules and policies, you may have opportunities to set the office tone and take a lead in interpersonal dynamics. What staff have said....

- "I am a consistent, calm presence for them. It is my job NOT to be stressed."

- "We have a chance to educate the faculty about how to get things done in the invisible world of administration and in the real world."

- "We create mutual understanding, help faculty and staff communicate better, decrease and defuse conflict."

The university environment is stimulating and interesting. Most academic staff have memories of campus life from their student days. Working at a college or university provides some of the same benefits. Intellectual stimulation is in the air, even if your job does not directly involve teaching or research. Savvy staff can plan their careers and transfer to different positions when a job is not working out or they feel they have outgrown it. What staff have said....

- "I like to attend lectures, concerts, and basketball games."

- "We have a chance to take classes, both academic classes and staff development trainings."

- "I enjoy having access to a university library. The wellness program also is a big plus."

Adopt an Experimenter's Mindset

A growth mindset is about learning, about trial and error. It's about adopting what Wendy Leebov and Gail Scott call an experimenter's mind-set. We have the choice to approach any situation, however challenging, as an opportunity to learn something new. If you've ever been involved in any form of experimental research, you know how important this attitude is. You start with a question, and an open mind about the answer. And then you conduct an experiment to learn what you can. Based on the results, you make adjustments and design a new experiment.

The same applies in staff jobs. In fact, often the best you can do is to research the possibilities available at any given juncture. You can follow hunches, build on successes, seek new resources, and learn from mistakes. When the going gets tough, if you think you won't be able to make a move until you have a guaranteed outcome, you may wait forever.

In Tom's scenario, when he found it difficult to complete the budget for Dr. Reed, his first move was to phone and suggest a time for the two of them to work in person. Dr. Reed responded to that. But if she had not, Tom could have tried emailing with his request for a meeting or with a specific question about the budget. And so on, until he found a process that worked.

Here are some other things you can do to maintain an experimenter's mindset.

Be flexible. When we are flexible, we are not wedded to a single way of doing things. We maintain an open mind and are willing to try new approaches. You may find yourself working with faculty members who are not so flexible in certain areas, even if they are open-minded from an intellectual perspective. In that case, you can be the one to demonstrate flexibility.

Stay learning. If you are feeling stymied, don't stay that way. Try something else. I think Franklin Delano Roosevelt said it best: "It is common sense to take a method and try it. If it fails, admit it frankly and try something else." Sometimes it helps to learn from others' successes with similar tasks and then adapt what works for you.

How to Develop a Growth Mindset

"But," you might say, "I can't just switch off one mindset and turn on another. I tend to react in the heat of the moment. When things get rocky in the office, I fall back into a fixed mindset. A growth mindset sounds good, but I'm not sure I can adopt one under every circumstance." Many people say they revert to old patterns during stressful situations and do not think they can change.

Carol Dweck describes a four-step process for developing a mindset that addresses this dilemma. In essence, these steps involve— (1) acknowledging our fixed mindset, (2) recognizing we have a choice, (3) having an internal dialogue between our fixed and growth mindsets, and (4) taking action based on the growth mindset. Let's look at how these steps might play out for a staff member in the academic setting.

Apply Dweck's Four-Step Process

Acknowledge your fixed mindset. Suppose you find yourself getting annoyed at work, sometimes for no apparent reason. Basically you like your job, so you take the time to examine your reactions and get a better understanding about what is going on. Perhaps your first inclination is to blame faculty: they aren't available when you need them, they don't appreciate your hard work, and so on. Looking deeper, ask yourself what your own mindset is. And you may realize you are approaching work with the underlying belief that "interacting with faculty is the worst part of this job!" You may see that you hold this as a fixed mindset, believing nothing can be done about it and feeling powerless. This very acknowledgment can be the first step in creating space for a different attitude to emerge.

Recognize you have a choice. This step involves taking a leap, based on the understanding that we don't have to hold onto a particular mindset. You recognize it is possible to look at your interactions with faculty in different ways, that this is a choice you can make. In fact, you may not know at first what the most appropriate growth mindset would be. For instance, you might assume you should adopt the mindset "I am powerful, and interacting with faculty is the best part of this job." However, you may feel that adopting this view simply wouldn't be honest for you.

Here are some questions to consider as you clarify your choice:

- Am I blaming someone? Am I making a mountain out of a molehill?

- Am I placating? Do I think I have no choice but to do as I'm told, even when that doesn't feel right?

- Am I feeling imposed upon when it's not about me personally? Do I have to take this personally?

- Am I seeing myself as less than capable? Am I believing my doubts about myself or about faculty?

- How can I look at the situation differently? How are the faculty member and I caught in mindsets that put us at cross purposes?

Asking questions such as these can lead you to formulate a growth mindset you can sincerely adopt. For example, it could be "some faculty interactions are satisfying and empowering and others are challenging. I want to find out what I can learn from each."

Create an inner dialogue. Simply recognizing you have a choice may not be sufficient to turn a fixed mindset into a growth one. Every mindset—whether fixed or growth—makes itself known in our mind through an internal voice. The first thing your old mindset might say is, "Here we go again, this is what I hate about my job."

According to Carol Dweck's model, what you can do at this point is talk back to your familiar inner voice with a new voice. You can create an inner dialogue between the two voices.

> Fixed mindset: "Dr. Butcher dumped a report on me when she knows I leave at 5 p.m. Here we go again."

> Growth mindset: "If you do what you've always done, you'll probably get what you always got. Placating is not working. Let's find a new approach."

> Fixed mindset: "Nothing will work with Dr. Butcher."

> Growth mindset: "I'll find a way to talk with her about these last-minute requests. It's worth a try."

Ideally you could hold an inner dialogue like this while the situation is happening. But most of the time it will be more realistic to do it afterward and to apply it at the next opportunity.

Take action. As you deal with similar situations over time, you learn to hold a growth mindset and to put it into action. In the chapters that follow, we discuss in greater detail how to put a growth mindset into action and develop alternative approaches to familiar staff-faculty interactions.

Remember, Your Mindset Is In Your Mind

We usually act outwardly in accordance with what we feel and believe. We may choose to "speak our mind." It does not, however, diminish a mindset to hold it in our mind rather than put it into words or action, if that is called for in the situation. The mindset will not lose its power.

For example, a staff member who has been asked to take notes at a faculty meeting may be out of line if he or she tries to participate actively in the meeting. Even if the staff member believes his or her opinions are of equal value to those of the faculty, it probably is not appropriate to speak up. One staff member told me she uses the phrase "strategic deference" to refer to her nonverbal style when she works with faculty. Her deference is designed to show respect and create rapport, not to be subservient.

Practice Adopting a Growth Mindset

As with any form of personal change, it is helpful to practice adopting a growth mindset. Here are two scenarios that describe staff-faculty interactions. Each is written from the perspective of a fixed mindset.

Your task is to evaluate the initial mindset and to reformulate it as a growth mindset. [Possible responses are given at the end of the chapter.]

First scenario. You work in the college's IT Department. Two faculty members leave you voice mails at the end of the day with urgent requests. Both say their computers just crashed, insist you show up at their office first thing in the morning, and imply that you might not fix their problem fast enough.

Your knee-jerk response would be to call back and say, "Chill! You aren't the only one with a problem, you know. I'll get to you as fast as I can." However, you focus instead on your mindset. Your fixed mindset thinks, "Faculty are so self-centered. They expect me to drop whatever I'm doing and make their priorities my priority."

How might a growth mindset view this situation? _____

_____

_____

Second scenario. You are coming out of the grocery store on Saturday afternoon, on your way to your mother's birthday party. Your husband and brother are waiting for you in the car. You run into the chairperson of your department. She says, "I'm so glad you're here! I won't be in the office Monday, and a memo *has* to go out to all department faculty. Why don't I just give it to you now? It's really short. Do you have a pen?"

You feel like saying, "Yeah, I've got a pen. What's the message you want me to send out?" However, you focus instead on your mindset. Your fixed mindset is "Faculty are so arrogant. And I'm supposed to do whatever they want."

How might a growth mindset view this situation? _____

_____

_____

Faculty Mindset

So far we've considered the mindset you hold as staff. But there is another side to this equation: each faculty member also brings a mindset to the table. In some situations, the mindset held by faculty stands in contrast with the staff mindset. This can be a source of conflict.

One way to understand this dynamic is to review Table 2.2 in Chapter 2. In it, we compared faculty and staff characteristics, and the different perspectives of these two groups. For example, faculty tend to focus on abstract thought and take a big-picture view, while staff tend to focus on institutional processes; logistics; and concrete, practical details. Here is something interesting. Compare what you see in Table 2.2 with the growth mindsets we have just discussed:

- Valuing strong relationships with faculty
- Viewing faculty as colleagues
- Holding the big picture
- Balancing commitment with healthy detachment
- Adopting an experimenter's mindset

Do you notice something? Two of these five mindsets are typically held by faculty! Faculty characteristically hold the big picture and use an experimental approach. Therefore, as you adopt these aspects of a growth mindset, you may actually be helping to bridge the gap between yourself and faculty.

Possible Responses

1. "Working without a computer can be a real crisis for faculty. They don't like feeling dependent. I don't need to take their panic personally. Even though we're understaffed in IT, I'll do the best I can to help them."

2. "Faculty can be overwhelmed by their many responsibilities. I don't need to take on their feeling of overload. It's not appropriate for us to work together when my family is waiting. However, I can find another way to help her. I can ask her to email me her request by Monday morning so I can prepare the message and distribute it. I'd better watch my tone of voice as I suggest this to her."

Summary

Adopt a Growth Mindset

- A fixed mindset is rigid, while a growth mindset is geared to flexibility and willingness to learn.

- Staff who adopt a growth mindset are more likely than other staff to be satisfied and successful in their work.

- Growth mindsets for staff include valuing strong relationships with faculty, viewing faculty as colleagues, holding the big picture, balancing commitment with healthy detachment, focusing on what is working, and adopting an experimenter's mindset.

- The four steps for developing a growth mindset are acknowledging your fixed mindset, recognizing you have a choice, having an internal dialogue between your fixed and growth mindsets, and taking action based on the growth mindset.

SECTION III

Working with Faculty:
Practices and Suggestions

6. Communicating with Faculty: Basic Skills   91

7. How to Establish a Partnership with Faculty 111

8. How To Say No and Deliver Bad News   125

9. Continuing the Partnership with Faculty   137

10. Become Organizationally Savvy and
    Build Your Resources   157

www.WorkingWithFaculty.com

6

Communicating with Faculty: Basic Skills

- Active listening
- Questioning
- I-Messages
- Directing Others
- Giving Feedback
- Summary

Many staff members have told me with pride that their skillful communication has led faculty to treat them better than they treat other staff.

You have probably noticed, it's often in the moment that we open our mouths to speak with someone that the proverbial rubber hits the road. What we say and how we say it determine whether our work will proceed smoothly or not.

In this chapter, I offer you a series of communication skills I find useful for the interactions that take place in an academic setting. These include the basic skills of active listening and questioning, and the more proactive skills of I-messages, directing others, and giving feedback. I have drawn on the work of top experts who use a skills-based approach, as described in Owen Hargie's (1997) *The Handbook of*

Communication Skills. More recently, this approach has been adapted for use with people in all kinds of settings. *Leadership Effectiveness Training,* by Thomas Gordon (2001), is helpful to academic staff at all levels, and I recommend it as a good place to start.

If you are already familiar with these basic skills, you may want to skim through this chapter and proceed to the next chapters to see how the skills are specifically applied to staff-faculty relationships.

The skills approach breaks communication down into separate and distinct skills. We often use this approach when learning other things. For example, if you learn to swim, you might first practice your breathing, then learn the proper kick, and then get instruction on arm movements, before you put all the pieces together. Communication can be learned in a similar manner. Of course, it can seem a little artificial to practice one skill at a time because we don't speak that way in real life. But I've found people who practice the skills while keeping in mind that they will put them all together in a natural way at the end find this approach helpful.

Active Listening

Skillful listening allows you to communicate to the speaker that you have heard and understand him or her. You can also use it to gain information about the speaker's ideas and mood. Sometimes the easiest and quickest way to appreciate the value of a skill—any skill—is to take a good look at what happens in its absence. Here, to begin, is an experiment in listening that I suggest you try.

Don't Listen to Me!

You will need another person to help you here. It could be a colleague at work, a friend, or a family member. Tell him or her it won't take more than two or three minutes. The only requirement is that you do this in person, not over the phone.

Sit down next to your friend or colleague and give the following instruction: "I'm going to tell you something, and your job is *not* to listen to me."

Then tell the other person something you consider important. What you say could be true or a complete fabrication, it doesn't matter for the purpose of this exercise. As you speak, watch the other person's reaction. Notice how that reaction makes you feel. When you have finished talking, take a moment to debrief what happened.

So, how did your friend or colleague demonstrate not listening? Here are some classic ways: by refusing to look at you, engaging in a distracting activity, interrupting to say something to you about a different topic, humming, appearing bored. And I probably don't need to ask how *you* felt. It is amazing that even while doing an exercise and knowing it isn't a "real" communication, we can still feel slighted, insulted, or desperate to be heard. That only goes to show how essential it is to let others know we are listening when they speak.

I'm Listening to You

Now consider an example of how active listening, effectively practiced, might look in one university setting.

Karl works in the Office of the Dean and is about to make a phone call when Dr. Wilcox walks in. Dr. Wilcox just received a memo from the dean and wants to discuss it immediately. Karl explains the dean is unavailable. After a disappointed Dr. Wilcox makes an appointment for the following day, he sticks around to air some of his frustration to Karl.

Karl's first reaction after scheduling the appointment is to signal to Dr. Wilcox how busy he is by shuffling some papers or reaching for the phone.

But Karl decides to practice active listening instead. He intentionally turns his body toward Dr. Wilcox, who is standing to the left of his desk. He looks straight at Dr. Wilcox while the professor is speaking. He nods his head when Dr. Wilcox makes a point, even if he doesn't agree with it, to show he is listening. Karl is concerned Dr. Wilcox may try to pry information about the memo from him or ask questions he can't answer. So he is pleasantly surprised when the professor finishes speaking, gives a little laugh, apologizes for taking Karl's time, and walks out of the office looking more relaxed than when he walked in.

What happened? Although Karl didn't say anything to Dr. Wilcox, he communicated a significant message: I'm listening to you! Simple as it may sound, this is sometimes all we need to know. Of course, most of the time, active listening is part of a longer communication during which we also have an opportunity to speak.

By taking the time to listen attentively to faculty, you demonstrate your respect and put them at ease. Your ability to listen makes it clear you're a professional. It demonstrates you have the detachment characteristic of a growth mindset.

A skillful listener is able to pay attention to self, other, and context. In addition to listening to faculty, listen to (i.e., be aware of) what is happening in the larger context. In the case of Karl, this might have meant being aware the memo in question went out to all faculty, and that most of them were upset by it. Or it might have meant noticing that Dr. Wilcox has a pattern of demanding to see the dean at the slightest provocation.

Communicating *Without* Words

Listening is essentially a nonverbal act. Not only can you take in a lot of information, but you can communicate your understanding and responsiveness without words. Just let your body do the talking. In fact, our bodies are always talking, even when we are not consciously aware of it. The so-called Mehrabian Effect states that nonverbal behaviors account for a whopping 55 percent of the impact we have on other people when we talk with them. In a now-famous study, Albert Mehrabian (1981) found that voice tone accounts for 38 percent of the impact and words for only 7 percent.

When you get a chance, observe two people talking. It's best if you can't hear what they are saying, perhaps in a crowded restaurant. Watch for the cues about their relationship that you can pick up just from observing their body language. For example:

- Facial expressions
- Hand gestures
- How physically close they are to one another
- Whether one person is leaning toward or away from the other

And of course you can also observe these dynamics in your own conversations with faculty. Become aware of what you are saying with your own nonverbal behavior, and also of what you observe in the faculty member's behavior.

One important caveat about nonverbal communication: it is highly influenced by culture. Nonverbal cues can have different meanings, depending upon the culture of the individuals. For example, while maintaining eye contact is considered a sign of openness and honesty in the mainstream culture of this country, it is considered disrespectful in some other cultures. The acceptable distance between two people also varies by culture.

Practice Using Nonverbals

Next time you are talking with a friend or faculty member, practice the following techniques of active listening:

* Maintain eye contact (in a natural way, without staring)

* Lean toward the speaker

* Nod occasionally and say "uh-huh" (in a way that says "I'm listening," not necessarily "I agree")

* Allow for natural pauses, without jumping in to respond; wait until you are sure the person has finished before you speak

* Respond nonverbally (e.g., when you hear of a success, your eyes light up; when you hear troubling news, you furrow your brow)

* Avoid getting distracted by anything or anyone in the environment

* Avoid rehearsing what you are going to say next

Active listening also can be practiced on the telephone. In that case, your tone of voice and uh-huh's take the place of eye contact and body language.

Paraphrasing

Suppose you have listened carefully while a faculty member spoke, and now you want to let him or her know you heard and understood. What are some of your best options for accomplishing this? One way is to paraphrase what you just heard. A paraphrase is a restatement of what someone has said. You put the essence into your own words.

Here is an example of paraphrasing. Sarah, a new staff member in the Botany Department, is speaking with Dr. Paulin, a professor, who has just rushed into the office.

Dr. Paulin: "I left a master copy of the syllabus where I always put it, on top of my inbox. All the TAs were supposed to get their copy before the first class, like always. But they showed up at our meeting this morning with last semester's syllabus. Unbelievable! No one was prepared. Listen, this is impossible!"

[What Sarah might be tempted to say: "Don't blame me! I wasn't even here last semester."]

Sarah: "So the updated syllabus wasn't there when you needed it."

Dr. Paulin: "Yes. Do you think you could stop whatever you're doing right now and make copies of the right one?"

By responding with a paraphrase instead of automatically defending herself, Sarah was able to defuse the situation. In fact, it doesn't matter if it was Sarah or someone else who made the wrong copies. When Dr. Paulin felt his problem was understood, he was able to move quickly into solution mode. He was more interested in getting the right syllabus to the TAs than in assigning blame.

Paraphrases come in all shapes and sizes. On the minimal end of the spectrum are simple encouragers. These encouragers are brief interjections in a conversation that communicate you understand what the other person is saying. You avoid bringing up new ideas or asking questions. I call them *encouragers* because they encourage the person to continue talking. You allow the speaker to get out his or her full message.

At the other end of the spectrum are summarizing statements. These are relatively lengthy paraphrases that you might use at the end of a conversation to tie everything together. For example, you might list the action points that you and/or a faculty member are taking away from a meeting, so that you both agree about what is going to happen next.

Brief paraphrases, such as the one used by Sarah, fall in between encouragers and summaries.

Practice Paraphrasing

You can use paraphrasing to focus on two aspects of a person's statement: the facts and the feelings. In different situations, facts or feelings may be more central. Notice that Sarah focused on facts when she spoke to Dr. Paulin. She also could have mentioned the professor's obvious frustration with the mixed-up syllabi. When paraphrasing feelings, it is important to avoid making overstatements or analyzing why the person feels that way. For example, Sarah could have reflected the professor's frustration, but without overstating his anger (even if it seemed evident from his tone of voice or the way he rushed into the office). The key point here is that a paraphrase stays true to the other person's statement, without adding to it. In this way, it prompts the other person to provide more information or begin to move toward a solution. If your paraphrase is incorrect, the speaker usually clarifies and continues naturally.

Some communications experts suggest using lead-ins to paraphrases that let the speaker know you are trying to confirm their meaning. Examples include: "So, you're saying...." "Sounds like...." "I wonder if...."

"Would it be correct to say...?" "What I hear you saying is...." "Could it be that...?" However, these lead-ins can sound forced or formal, especially if they are overused. You may occasionally want to use a lead-in when you are not confident you understand the intended message or when a faculty member seems particularly sensitive or emotional.

You may find it works to use a tentative tone when paraphrasing. You can end with a questioning tone, as though saying, "So this is what you mean, correct?" In this way, each statement and restatement becomes a building block toward mutual understanding.

Try your hand at paraphrasing the following statements made by faculty who are expressing anger or frustration to a staff member. You can assume whatever staff position you think makes sense for the situation:

1. Dr. Howard Ornstein, chairperson of the Russian Department: "How come the office staff is suddenly sending all memos out only through email? No one consulted me about this. Now I'll have to print out all those emails. What a waste of time. And it certainly won't save any trees."

Paraphrase: _____

_____

_____

2. Dr. Lucille Spera, lecturer in the School of Business: "I have absolutely no intention of paying this fine. Someone sent me a sticker for the D parking lot. It's halfway across campus! I requested the C lot, and that's where I've been parking. And I'm going to keep parking there, right next to the Business School, even if you issue me a hundred tickets."

Paraphrase: _____

_____

_____

[Possible responses are given at the end of the chapter.]

Questioning

While paraphrasing can lead the faculty member with whom you are talking to volunteer more information, questioning more or less guarantees he or she will reveal more. There is, however, an art to asking helpful questions. The most basic distinction is between open-ended and closed-ended questions, sometimes simply called open and closed questions. Let's look at how you might use each of these in your work setting.

Closed Questions

Closed questions are those that can be answered with a single word. Usually, that word is yes or no. However, it could be a number or a name or another singular piece of information. Here are some examples:

- Did you get a response from the Human Subjects Review Committee?
- Is hiring a part-time assistant an option you've considered?
- What time does the faculty meeting start?
- How many times did you download the data file?
- Should I shut down your computer during the storm?
- Are you pleased with the way I wrote up the report?

Of course, someone could always decide to give an elaborate answer to a closed question. For example, "No, I'm not so pleased with your report, because you forgot to include important information about..." Or, "Yes, I've considered a part-time assistant, but that would require cutting something else in the budget and I don't see how we can do that." Nevertheless, the questions in this list are considered closed because a one-word answer would suffice.

Closed questions have advantages in some situations. They are especially useful when you're seeking a decision or clear-cut answer, when you want to avoid a lengthy discussion, or when you're gathering specific information or trying to pin something (or someone) down. They are not useful when you want to encourage the other person to speak openly and at length.

Open Questions

Open questions offer a broad invitation to talk. Here are some examples:

- How do you feel about the university's plans to remodel the Faculty Center?
- Why did you allow this student to take your class when it was already full?
- What are the next steps in creating better collaboration within this department?
- When you say hiring more people isn't the answer, what is your reasoning?

Open questions can be used to learn about someone's opinions or feelings, to brainstorm solutions, to clarify instructions, and to build a stronger relationship, among other things. They can be ineffective in certain situations. For example, if you are speaking with a faculty member, he or she may not wish to share an opinion or rationale in any great detail, and might consider your question intrusive. This makes it all the more important to understand the difference between open and closed questions, so you can make the best choice in any given moment.

Practicing Questions

Try your hand at creating open and closed questions in response to the following statements made by faculty. In each case, make an effort to come up with both open and closed questions, and compare them to see which would be the better response.

1. Dr. Leo Chang, assistant professor in the Art Department: "I think we should use the extra money in this grant to get rid of all those old wooden easels and buy some new portable ones."

Closed question: _____

_____

_____

Open question: _____

_____

_____

2. Dr. Jill Duncan, professor in the Mathematics Department: "I've been in the education business long enough to know it isn't going to happen. We simply aren't going to see more women and minority students flocking to sign up for the Applied Thermodynamics courses. There's just not enough interest."

Closed question: _____

_____

_____

Open question: _____

_____

_____

[Possible responses are given at the end of the chapter.]

I-Messages

So far, the communications skills you've been experimenting with in this chapter involve your listening to or obtaining information from a faculty member. Your primary focus has been on the faculty member's needs, thoughts, and feelings, not on your own needs, thoughts, and feelings. From the self-other-context viewpoint, you are paying attention primarily to the other, and secondarily to the context. And this is often appropriate. Focusing on the other doesn't automatically mean you are placating. The key is balance, that is, being able to shift your focus between self and other (and context) from moment to moment, not necessarily on all three at once.

Now then, let's say you want to state your own opinion or express your feelings during the course of a conversation. How do you shift the focus appropriately to self? The next three communication skills provide some ways to do exactly that.

Asserting Yourself

For our purposes here, asserting yourself means revealing something about yourself to another person. This could be anything from requests to simple facts or information to opinions or personal details. Our focus is on how to communicate your needs and thoughts and feelings in a way that is as nonthreatening as possible and that allows the other person to hear what you are expressing. It is a way to ask for what you want.

One technique that is helpful when asserting yourself is the I-message. That is, a statement that begins with the word "I" and that clearly describes what you are thinking, feeling, or wanting. This might sound obvious, but in fact we often avoid making I-messages. We avoid them unconsciously, out of habit. This can happen because we hesitate to take responsibility or because our immediate response is to say something about the other person instead, perhaps something accusatory.

Consider this scenario. Dr. Carlos Sanchez, a professor and chairperson in the Law School, has just announced he has called a meeting for faculty in the department and he wants you to take notes. There is only one hitch. The meeting is scheduled for 4 p.m. on Friday. You have plans for the evening, and you know faculty meetings tend to run well over an hour. Simply listening to him, paraphrasing what he has said, or raising questions isn't likely to help your time bind.

What this situation calls on you to do is to share your own needs about the meeting time. Instead of making Dr. Sanchez wrong about the time he has chosen, you could tell him your concerns. You might say, "I have noticed these meetings run late, so I just want to be sure you realize I can take notes only until 5 p.m. that day."

Here are three sets of statements made by a staff member to a faculty member. Each set demonstrates two different ways of expressing the same thing: either as an I-message or a you-message (which I am calling an other-message here, to be consistent with the system thinking terminology of self-other-context).

1. *Other-message*: "You're not expecting this project to be done today, are you?"

   I-message: "I need a little more time to complete this project."

2. *Other-message*: "You didn't give me the report I need to write up a summary for that proposal."

   I-message: "I don't have the report I need to write up a summary for the proposal."

3. *Other-message*: "Dr. Grieg doesn't know what he's talking about when it comes to voice-activated transcription."

   I-message: "I have a lot of experience with voice-activated transcription, probably more than Dr. Grieg does."

Notice, the other-messages tend to come across as critical of the other person. Most fit the kind of response Virginia Satir calls blaming. They let the faculty member know only indirectly what you are thinking or feeling or wanting. Rather than speaking for and about yourself, you may sound like you know what they are thinking or should do. In each case, imagine yourself in the faculty member's shoes, and how you might respond to an other-message.

Practice I-Messages

Each of the following three statements was made by a staff member to a faculty member, but without incorporating the principles of I-messages. Your task is to restate each so it takes the form of an I-message.

1. You work in finance and Dr. Edith Warren, a new professor in the Chemistry Department, is calling to request a reimbursement check. You say, "You haven't sent in any paperwork, no receipts, nothing."

I-message: _____

_____

_____

2. Dr. Qi Zhuo, a lecturer in Asian Studies, asks you to leave the feed-back forms for his lecture on a table at the back of the hall.

You say: "The evaluation forms? What evaluation forms are you talking about?"

I-message: _____

_____

_____

[Possible responses are given at the end of the chapter.]

Directing Others

Everything we say to another person has the power to influence him or her, one way or another. Even the things we choose not to say or that we neglect to say can have an influence. Nevertheless, there are times when, in order to do our job effectively, sharing information or our opinion may not seem sufficient. Rather, we may need to ask faculty directly for what we want or to give them instructions. We can do this in a way that is congruent, that balances their needs and point of view with our own.

Making Requests

In the previous section, we looked at one way to make a request: through an I-message. For example, if you say to a faculty member, "I need those forms by 5 p.m.," you are using an I-message. In this case, you expect the faculty member will understand you are requesting that he or she give the forms to you. Most requests, however, take the form of a question, typically a closed question. We want to know whether or not the person will comply, so we ask, "Can you please do such-and-such...?" However, an open question can be appropriate at times; for example, "How would you feel about doing this...?"

Here are some examples of requests. One of the following is not actually a request. Can you identify it?

- Dr. Levin, can you get the signed forms to me by 5 p.m. Thursday?
- I'd like your help in avoiding unnecessary service calls.
- Dr. Kidder, it's time to post the exam schedules.

- Can you please provide a translation, Dr. Aquero?

In this list, the comment directed to Dr. Kidder is not a request. It suggests the need for an instruction, which we will look at in the next section. Some situations require that you let faculty or other staff know what to do. In these cases, whether or not they wish to do it is not the issue.

Giving Instructions

Wendy Leebov and Gail Scott (2007) describe a multi-step process of communication that fosters relationship building. I find these steps to be very useful when it comes to giving directions or instructions. Here are four steps based on their model that you can follow, not necessarily in this order:

1. State your desired outcome—what you want to see happen

2. Name the behavior you would like to see—the actions that need to happen

3. Give your rationale, including the consequences—why you want to see this happen

4. Show understanding—make it clear you empathize with their situation or feelings

So, for example, in the case of Dr. Kidder, whose exam schedule needs to be posted, you might say, "I want to make sure all students have access to the exam schedule. Please print out your schedule and then post it on the bulletin board right outside the office. It would be helpful if you could do this by Friday so students can see it next week. We don't want to end up with students missing an exam, as happened last semester."

Additional do's and don'ts for giving effective instructions to faculty that you might find helpful include the following:

- Organize your thoughts ahead of time
- Be polite, not bossy or demanding
- Describe a specific action to be accomplished
- Be time-specific
- Keep it simple, leave out unnecessary details that could be confusing or distracting

- Use visual aids (e.g., drawings, tables, photos), when appropriate
- Get a clear commitment and follow up, if appropriate
- Check that the other person understood what you were explaining
- Be confident, don't apologize

Practicing Directing Others

In our previous example with Dr. Sanchez, the Law School professor who called a meeting at 4 p.m. on Friday, we considered I-messages as one way to handle the situation. But perhaps stating your availability until 5 p.m. does not address the whole situation. Perhaps you have observed that few faculty attend Friday afternoon meetings. You might find it appropriate to take a more assertive approach, to take responsibility for changing the way these meetings are scheduled. For instance, you might propose to Dr. Sanchez that you send out an email asking all the department faculty about their preferred meeting time, and use the responses as a basis for scheduling future meetings.

With the guidelines for making requests and giving instructions in mind, think of what you might say to Dr. Sanchez. Consider integrating some of the other skills we have already covered, just be aware of what they are as you use them.

Giving Feedback

Feedback and I-messages are closely related communication skills. While the focus of I-messages is on revealing your thoughts and feelings, the focus of feedback is on communicating your observation about the impact of what someone has said or done. I think of feedback as holding up a mirror for faculty to show them their behavior and the consequences. If they like the reflected picture, they are likely to continue or increase that behavior. If they don't like it, they will be more aware of their behavior and its negative impact. What they see in the mirror might come as a surprise. So you want to give the feedback in a way that helps them feel at ease and receptive.

In general, we may think of feedback as something delivered by bosses to their employees, or by faculty to staff, and not the other way around. In a job performance evaluation, that is usually true. But there are many other ways in which feedback is given and received among members of a working community. Frequently, giving feedback to faculty can prevent them from getting into embarrassing situations or trouble. Everyone needs information about the unintended consequences of their behavior. And giving positive feedback is an important part of building relationships.

Often we give feedback without thinking about it, or even considering it "feedback." At other times, we are asked explicitly to give our feedback. Either way, by learning skills to give feedback more effectively, we can enhance our communications.

Effective Feedback

In your work with faculty, effective feedback can be one of three types.

1. Positive feedback, or appreciation, for what he or she has done

2. Redirection, or feedback about what he or she has done and the consequences that prevent desired outcomes

3. Neutral feedback that may be helpful because it increases the other person's awareness, without necessarily suggesting appreciation or redirection

Simple feedback. If you want to give faculty simple feedback, in an uncomplicated context, it can be enough just to state your observation. This typically works well for neutral feedback. It also can be useful for conveying appreciation or redirection. Here are some examples of simple feedback for each of the three types, several of which take the form of I-messages:

- "Your filling out the paperwork really helps me out." [appreciation]
- "I was inspired by your presentation to the board." [appreciation]
- "I found some typos in the syllabus you sent for duplication." [redirection]
- "Since you have not provided me with the details, I can't start the new budget." [redirection]
- "Students at the back of the lecture hall can't see the bullet points on your PowerPoint slides." [neutral]
- "You've ordered fewer textbooks this semester than you did last year." [neutral]

Feedback in four steps. Often when giving feedback to faculty, you will be most effective if you are explicit and state the connections between their behavior, its consequences, and your appreciation or what you want. In this case, I suggest you give the feedback in four steps. The four steps are the same for appreciation and redirection, except for the final step, as shown in Table 6.1. Note that neutral observations are not included because they typically don't require a four-step process.

Table 6.1 Four Steps for Feedback

Appreciation	Redirection
1. My intention	1. My intention
2. Description of others' behavior	2. Description of others' behavior
3. Consequences of others' behavior	3. Consequences of others' behavior
4. What I appreciate	4. What I want or expect in the future

Let's look more closely at each of the four steps.

1. Begin with an opener in which you state your **intention**. For example, you might say, "I'd like to tell you about..." or "I thought you might want to know about..." or "I'd like to help you save time with your scheduling."

2. State your observation of the **other's behavior.** Here are some qualities to keep in mind when you hold up the mirror and share your observation with faculty:

   • Be clear and specific; state what you observed, not your interpretation

   • Focus on behavior rather than personality

   • Use I-messages to avoid sounding like an expert about the other person and what he or she should do

3. State the **consequences of the other's behavior.** Again, be specific so the person understands his or her impact on others or on the situation. It helps if the person can picture what he or she did and what happened as a result. Use descriptive, appropriate language.

4. For **appreciation**, say thank you and show your gratitude. For **redirection**, ask for what you want or what you expect in the future. Use an I-message and offer constructive suggestions.

The feedback you share may have a strong impact on faculty. They may feel vulnerable even if you have made a clear and objective observation. So you don't want to leave them hanging. You can end your feedback by asking about their reaction or opinion or by focusing on an action point.

Here are some examples of the four-step process. The first illustrates appreciation and the second two illustrate redirection.

1. Dr. Crowley used his contacts in another department to help you get an appointment to the Student Services committee.

   Your feedback:

   "I want to let you know I got that seat on the committee [intention]. The email you sent [other's behavior] to the committee chair about my work seems to have been a major factor in my getting selected [consequences]. Thank you. I appreciate your going out of your way for me [appreciation]."

2. Dr. Tam is facing a deadline to submit his grant budget. When you tried going over it with him, he became frustrated about the new regulations that are forcing him to make cuts. He tossed the papers back on your desk with a loud and caustic remark.

   Your feedback:

   "I want to be able to help you with this complex budgeting process [intention]. When you raise your voice and seem upset [other's behavior], I get upset, too, and can't think straight [consequences]. I'd like to find a way to sit down together and work this through productively [redirection]."

3. Dr. Jain frequently cancels his graduate seminars at the last minute.

   Your feedback:

   "I'd like to talk about what happens when you change the schedule [intention]. When you cancel ten minutes before the seminar [other's behavior], I get barraged by upset grad students [consequences]. If you could give me a few hours' notice, I could reach most of them with a text message. That would save us all the last-minute hassle [redirection]."

Practice Feedback

Each of the following scenarios allows you to try your hand at giving feedback to the faculty member.

1. Dr. Gary Snell is a physician and a professor of Internal Medicine. He asked you to page him when a call comes in from The National Science Foundation. But when the call came in and you paged him, he did not respond. This happened twice.

   Your feedback: _____

   _____

   _____

2. Dr. Joan Mann, a professor of Medieval Studies, comes to the library, where you work, and asks to see a rare book that is not available for loan. You catch her potentially damaging the book by trying to copy pages on the photocopier.

   Your feedback: _____

   _____

   _____

Possible Responses

The following are possible responses to the practice exercises in this chapter. Keep in mind that there are no single correct answers. What you say and how you say it are always matters of individual style. So treat these as examples of the respective skills, not as prescriptions.

Paraphrasing

1. To Dr. Howard Ornstein: "It sounds like you aren't pleased with the decision to send out memos via email. I can see that it isn't going to work for you."

2. To Dr. Lucille Spera: "Could it be there's been a mix up about your parking sticker? You'd like the Parking Office to cancel your ticket and issue you a sticker for the C lot."

Questioning

1. Dr. Leo Chang: "I think we should use the extra money in this grant to get rid of all those old wooden easels and get some new portable ones."

   Closed question: How many new easels should we purchase?

Open question: What criteria should we use to figure out which portable style will be most appropriate for our classrooms?

2. Dr. Jill Duncan: "I've been in the education business long enough to know it isn't going to happen. We simply aren't going to see more women and minority students flocking to sign up for the Applied Thermodynamics courses. There's just not enough interest."

Closed question: Have you seen this article in the *Chronicle* about more minority students in the sciences?

Open question: How can we recruit more women and minority students?

I-Messages

1. To Dr. Edith Warren: "In order to cut you a reimbursement check, I need your receipts and completed request form. I'll email you the form."

2. To Dr. Qi Zhou: "I wasn't aware you planned to give out evaluation forms today. I'm sorry, I don't know which one you need. If you tell me, I'll leave them on your table."

Directing Others

To Dr. Carlos Sanchez: "I understand how important these meetings are to you [paraphrase, show understanding]. And I want to provide the best notes possible [I-message, state desired outcome]. Do you see it as a problem that few faculty are attending? [closed question] If you do, I'd like to suggest something. I'd be willing to contact the faculty tomorrow and ask why they aren't coming. It could be because of the time of the meetings, or some other reason [give rationale]. When we find out this information, you can set the time for the meeting accordingly [name the behavior]."

Feedback

1. To Dr. Gary Snell: "I want to talk with you about how best to reach you [intention]. You asked me to page you in emergencies [other's behavior]. However, the last two times I tried, it seems you didn't get the page [consequences]. I think we need to find a better system so I can reach you with important information [redirection]."

2. To Dr. Joan Mann: "I'd like to help you with that rare book [intention]. When you open it wide like this [other's behavior], the binding

can easily break [consequences]. For this reason, I'd like to ask that you only take notes [redirections]."

Summary

Communicating with Faculty: Basic Skills

- You can improve communications through a skills-based approach that allows for practicing distinct skills and carefully combining them to meet your needs.

- Active listening includes nonverbal responses and paraphrases that demonstrate you are listening to faculty; closed and open questions can be used to gather information.

- I-messages allow you to reveal something about yourself or assert yourself in ways that are likely to influence others. Directing others allows you to make requests or give instructions.

- The focus of feedback is on communicating your observation about the impact of what someone has said or done. Feedback can take the form of appreciation or redirection or can be neutral.

7

How To Establish a Partnership with Faculty

- How do I convince faculty I can be of help?
- How do I get (and hold) faculty's attention?
- How do I address faculty?
- How can I get faculty to respond?
- Summary

Communicating with faculty in academia presents a unique set of challenges. Consider the situation Amy faces as a staff member who has daily contact with faculty in three separate departments at a large university medical center. She described to me how she maintains communication with all the players involved. Not only does she work closely with three professors holding department chair positions, but each professor manages his or her own respective fiefdom. Thus, she needs to interact with many of the downstream faculty members, fellows, managers, supervisors, researchers, students, and other staff. Does this scare or intimidate her? No! She said, "This unique opportunity has allowed me to learn how to do 'the impossible.'"

She told me that how she organizes her approach to faculty is the key. "With each new task, I must be prepared and have facts and figures," she said. "References help, too. I go in with a well-thought-out plan. This forethought must be quick as well as accurate, with a Plan B and a Plan C ready at any time. It might sound like I'm preparing for big ideas or big change, but actually this approach is effective with even the most minuscule of issues. If I'm successful, faculty will depend, rely, and count on me for the same level of results with each new task." In fact, she said, sometimes her approach is so effective, and so many faculty are turning to her, that she jokingly asks herself, "Now what have I done?"

Amy could be described as a systems thinker, even if she isn't familiar with the term. She plans ahead, tunes into the needs of each professor (other) and each situation (context), and then organizes herself to provide resources and congruent communication. In a nutshell, what she's done is effectively apply the communication skills we studied in the previous chapter in her practical, everyday job encounters with faculty. It isn't enough to be able to practice these skills in a vacuum. We need to—as the expression goes—"walk the talk." We need effective ways to get into the conversation with faculty and to keep it going in a smooth and productive manner. In this chapter and in Chapters 8 and 9, we look at a variety of situations and contexts in which you as staff can put these skills to use.

Here are some specific challenges that may call forth your expert communication skills:

- Faculty who do not share your priorities
- Faculty who are not oriented to administrative issues or interpersonal communication
- Faculty who expect to be treated as special
- Faculty/staff power imbalances that lead you to feel vulnerable
- A decentralized environment, with departments using different systems

I have organized this chapter and Chapter 9 around specific questions staff members frequently ask during my workshops. For example: How do I convince faculty I can be of help? How can I get faculty to respond? How do I say no or deliver bad news? How can I engender respect?

Note that one question I do *not* address in this section is how to communicate in situations involving stressed or difficult faculty. Because these issues are so complex, they are covered separately in Chapters 11 and 12. Keep in mind, however, that many of the situations you encounter in this chapter won't have simple, straightforward solutions. I can't give you an easy formula to manage all conditions.

Some of the examples I discuss may not apply to you, your job, or your institution. Instead, think about how you can shape my suggestions to fit your own situation and style. For example, if you don't work in a medical school, or you only relate closely with one faculty member, you may need to adapt Amy's example to your circumstances.

How do I convince faculty I can be of help?

As staff, a main focus of your job is to help faculty members, to provide them with information and resources, and generally to make their work easier. How you can help them may be obvious to you, but not to them.

Why might some faculty not be receptive to these intentions? Some new faculty were recently graduate students, and in that capacity were not accustomed to having assistants. They got used to doing things for themselves. Then, after becoming faculty members, they kept that mindset. These faculty may actually welcome staff help, but simply not be expecting it. You may need to assert yourself and show them how you can be helpful.

Other faculty may not have experience working in collaboration with staff. Perhaps over the years, staff in their departments have not challenged their independent mindset or tried to engage them in a collaborative mode. These faculty may resist help because they are unaware of the experience and specialized training staff bring to the job. They may be unfamiliar with the kinds of resources staff can offer them, and in general may know little about staff roles and responsibilities. In fact, they may be unaware of some of their own roles and responsibilities as faculty. In that case, they may resist your help because they sincerely believe they don't need it.

In Chapter 2, we took a close look at some basic faculty characteristics. Some of these traits predispose faculty to thinking they don't need staff help. Because of their independent and solitary work style, for example, they tend to keep ideas to themselves too long. They don't bring staff in on their thinking or get them involved in projects until late in the process. They tend to be very last minute when it comes to preparing class materials or grant proposals or planning a meeting. Your offers to help may be perceived as interference, as making a project more complicated, even as an invasion of their territory.

Other faculty may want staff help, but just not know how to go about getting it. They may assume staff can read their minds and get annoyed if staff do not automatically assist in all the ways they want. In this case, resistance to your help comes in the form of "Why didn't you already take care of that?"

So how do you convince faculty you can help them?

To begin with, you need to educate faculty about what you can do to help. You may have to sell them on the idea. In my consulting work, I have found that administrators, staff, and faculty respond positively when I tell them I have handled the same kinds of issues on other campuses. To be convincing when you make your case to faculty, explain how your help will benefit them. Offer specific examples of ways you can be of help. You will need to use your best influencing skills, so I suggest reviewing that section in Chapter 6.

Here are some additional ways you can convince faculty to accept your help:

- Explain that staff are available to handle the logistics and other practical details so faculty are free to concentrate on teaching and research.

- Say, "I have done [this type of task] with other professors before." Give examples of professors you have helped and how you helped them (e.g., conferences you organized, articles you edited, brochures you designed). Say, "Here's how we usually do it, working together."

- Orient faculty to your role; explain how things are done and how long specific tasks take.

- Show faculty samples of what you have done so they can get a sense of the quality and kind of work you do.

- Be on the lookout for any erroneous assumptions faculty may have about your role or theirs. Don't be afraid to bring these up for discussion.

- Make it clear you will not nit-pick details and that your help will focus on what the faculty member needs to know.

How do I get (and hold) faculty's attention?

Making the effort to convince faculty you are there to help, as we just discussed, can go a long way toward getting their attention. But sometimes attracting their attention is less about general relationship building and more a matter of negotiating the nitty-gritty practical details of the situation. For example, you have specific information to share with them and you need their response. To do this, you must attract their attention, but you also must be able to sustain it. In fact, this question might be stated as "How can I get information to faculty if I can't even get their attention?"

Consider what it is like to work for Dr. Welchek, in his second semester in the Department of Molecular Biosciences. He is overwhelmed with his research projects and collaboration with several non-profit organizations, not to mention the new course he is teaching. He has been assigned a half-time research assistant. Gloria has worked in a biotechnology company and finds the campus inefficient and confusing by comparison.

Dr. Welchek is booked solid and has not sat down with Gloria to give her the big picture of his projects or needs. Sometimes days go by without Gloria even seeing him. When he does stop to communicate, he stands in her doorway, gives her a few details to handle, and seems hurried and distracted. Because he has so much to do, he is usually in reactive mode. For example, he drives across campus to pick up a box of materials, rather than asking her to do it. He waits until the last minute, too late to delegate a task to her.

Gloria would like to help, but finds it difficult to connect with him. Her frustration is beginning to show. Her talents are not well used, and she needs more connection and perspective and planning to be effective. She wants to know, "How do I even get his attention?"

Many faculty are like this; they're in a state that one effective and compassionate manager told me she likes to call "beyond swamped." They are so bogged down with their work, they can't see what is going on around them. Most of us have this experience when we're engrossed in a project, caught in an emergency situation, or threatened by something that triggers our personal vulnerabilities. Usually we avoid staying swamped long term. But some faculty find themselves mired in the mud. They might be running as fast as they can, but the mud is too deep to get out. The fact that this "mud" comes with the career they love doesn't help the situation.

Opening the Channels

To get and hold the attention of faculty—especially those who are beyond swamped—can require ingenuity on the part of staff. It requires you to make the effort to open the channels of communication.

When you hear the word *channel*, you might think of a place in a river or harbor where the water runs deep and boats can pass more easily. Just the opposite of a swamp! In the case of communication, instead of boats, it is our words that can move more freely through the open channels. To open the channels with faculty when you're finding it difficult to get their attention, consider these suggestions:

• Say their name to interrupt their train of thought.

• State specifically what you want them to know. Don't go into a long story leading up to your point.

• Use open-ended questions to gain their trust.

• Make strong eye contact and use other skills of active listening.

• Approach faculty with confidence, as an equal doing your job.

• Walk with faculty in the hall, on their way to or from class.

• Find creative times to stay in contact. For example, every day while driving to campus, one professor calls the admin with whom she works closely to get updates and a perspective on the day.

• Develop signals you can use, and that they will recognize, when you need to connect or get their attention. For example, tape notes to their monitor or leave notes on their keyboard or on their chair.

• If faculty make complex requests on the fly, say you'd like to ask them a few questions. Ask to sit down for a few minutes to clarify exactly what is being asked and plan to meet at greater length if necessary. Say, "How can I best reach you when I have information for you or need your response?"

The Flow of Information

In its most essential form, all communication involves the transfer of information. These days, we have a wide and growing variety of means at our disposal for conveying information. And the academic setting is no exception. However, not everyone uses the same means. For example, students may be using instant message or twitter, while some faculty scarcely know what these technologies are. Young and old faculty may use their university email accounts in vastly different ways.

Therefore, as staff, if we want to get their attention, it is important to learn about and keep track of each faculty member's preferences for communication. Here are some of the main options:

- Phone call (to the faculty member's office phone or cell phone, to his or her administrative assistant's phone)
- Text message
- Email
- Voice mail
- In-person meeting
- Hardcopy memo

With so many options available, some staff find it helpful to create a database with contact information for those faculty with whom they communicate regularly, as well as for those they only contact infrequently. Table 7.1 illustrates one way to do this.

Table 7.1 Faculty Means of Communication

	Professor X	Professor Y	Professor Z
Email (university)			
Email (personal)			
Phone (office)			
Phone (home)			
Phone (cell)			
Fax			
Pager			
Instant message			

In addition to the means of communication, you also may want to find out the time of day or what days of the week each faculty member prefers to be contacted. This is especially important when you work closely with faculty and need to deliver timely information to them. It also is important when trying to contact faculty who are part time, who work at a satellite campus or research center, or who for one reason or another come to campus less frequently. Something else to be aware of is that faculty may prefer different means for different types of communication. For example, a doctor may prefer cell phone for most contacts, but want to be reached by pager for pressing matters while in the medical center (yes, pagers are still used in many medical centers, at least as of this writing).

The Special Case of Email

Email is a relatively new technology. As a result, its use can pose complications. For example, an email culture has developed whereby we assume people pick up and respond to their emails very quickly. Emails themselves travel very quickly, and we tend to expect a reply within 24 hours. However, some faculty may not check their emails with consistent frequency. Other faculty may only read what they consider priority emails. Thus, staff might assume a message to faculty has been received and read when it still is sitting in their in-box.

Further complications arise because faculty (like other people) typically have several email addresses. They may not have linked their addresses to forward their email, and may check some addresses more frequently than others. Suppose you work closely with Dr. Eng in the Music Department, and he has responded to your question about preferred means of communication by saying he wants you to contact him by email. You may need to get more specific. For example, it might work to use his university email for routine communications. But you may need to send a last-minute scheduling update about a concert to his home email.

Here are some other points to consider when using email:

- Make sure the subject line of an email is meaningful and will attract the faculty's attention.

- Use good grammar, appropriate capitalization, and complete sentences in all emails.

- Copy (cc) faculty or staff managers to whom you report on emails that are relevant to them. However, first check about what they want to be cc'd on so you don't overload them with emails.

- Find out how faculty wish to archive their emails, whether in hard copy, digitally, or both.

How do I address faculty?

Sometimes staff ask me, "Is it okay to use their first names?" In our twenty-first century world, it isn't always clear whether formal address is expected, preferred, or considered unnecessary. These aren't the kinds of rules or expectations academic institutions typically put in writing. They are cultural norms, and they can be difficult to determine because they vary by school and region.

Consider the case of Valerie Teaneck, who was a graduate student at a large university science center. After she completed the program, she was appointed to the faculty. As part of her new job, she was to supervise a laboratory in which she had worked as an assistant two years earlier. This put her in charge of some staff members who previously had been her supervisors.

When she stopped by the lab just after getting her appointment, Valerie was greeted by one of the administrators, Lee Wong, with whom she had worked closely. In a joking way, she let him know she now expected him to call her Dr. Teaneck. She made a joke about it, but they both knew it was a serious request.

Lee congratulated her and talked with her about her new role. Then, as they were parting, he gave her a hug and said, "Glad to have you here, Valerie." He made a point of using her first name to let her know that this was the appropriate way for staff to address faculty in that setting.

We might speculate that Valerie wanted to be called by her formal title because she felt insecure in her new position. This would be understandable, given the fact that she was stepping into what was essentially a role reversal. But her personal preference wouldn't be sufficient to change the customary use of first names by the staff with whom she would be working.

In general, the trend is increasingly toward the use of first names in higher education settings. Some institutions even encourage students to call faculty by their first names, although this practice is not widespread. Interestingly, McDowell and Westman (2005) found that graduate students who called faculty by their first names saw them as more approachable and helpful, while grad students who used formal titles felt more valued and respected by faculty.

What I recommend is familiarizing yourself with the norm at your institution and following it. Here are some suggestions:

- Use faculty members' formal titles at your first meeting or until you have been invited to interact on a first-name basis.
- Find out what the preferred form of address is (e.g., Dr. or Professor, or first name).
- When in doubt, use a formal rather than an informal form of address.
- Use titles when speaking to or about faculty in the presence of students.
- Use titles when speaking to or about individuals who hold high positions in the institution hierarchy (e.g., deans, president).

How can I get faculty to respond?

So, you have found a way to get faculty's attention. Now you know how they like to be contacted, and you have every reason to believe they are reading your emails and listening to the messages you leave for them. Perhaps you have had some productive conversations. But how do you get them to give a timely response to your email or message? How do you get a faculty member to send you the document he or she told you during a conversation would be sent right away? How do you get faculty to make a decision you need in order to move forward?

Faculty priorities and the demands on their time can vary greatly. On any given day, they may be caught up with last-minute requests, deadlines they are trying to meet, students who show up unexpectedly with a problem. All these things—and more—can result in their pushing your request to the bottom of their list. They may have every intention of responding to you, but suddenly they find themselves beyond swamped. What you see as an emergency, they don't see as an emergency at all.

And yet there you are, knowing that the form you asked the faculty member to fill out is due across campus tomorrow. Or that his signature is needed before 5 p.m. Or that her membership in an organization will be cancelled if the dues aren't sent in...yesterday.

In situations such as these, staff must use their communication skills to provide outstanding customer service to faculty. If they fail to respond when you need them to (and also when it is in their own best interest to do so), it isn't helpful to make them feel in the wrong. Even if you are fairly certain a faculty member has made an error or failed to follow up, practice active listening and try to understand what is needed from his or her point of view. When you need a response, see how you can make it easier for faculty to give you that response.

Here are some tips. In this case, it's a long list! This is an issue with which many staff have struggled. During workshops, participants have offered great solutions, so I want to include some of them here.

- Be sure a response is really needed. For example, you may be able to sign for faculty in some instances. Clarify when this would be okay. Signature stamps may also be appropriate in some cases.

- When you need a signature(s), arrange the papers on a clipboard, then mark the signature lines with sticky notes that say "sign here." Stand in front of the faculty member, hand him or her a pen, and flip to the pages that need attention. You will get what you need very fast!

- Batch your requests. If you have a range of items, such as needed information or phone messages requiring a response, plan a regular time to meet with the faculty member to deal with everything at once. Arrive with a checklist, then check off each item as it is completed.

- Make things easy. Tailor your request to minimize the time and effort it takes faculty to respond. For example, "I've sent four emails and left two phone messages to arrange to get your signature. Can I meet you tomorrow, after your 2 p.m. class, outside Room 602?" A clear and concise closed question like this may motivate the faculty member to respond without your needing to go so far out of your way.

- Build in extra time by establishing a false deadline that is ahead of the given due date. Ask faculty to respond by this deadline, with the understanding that you need time on your end to keep things running smoothly. Some people set their clocks a few minutes ahead for the same reason.

- Leave a trail of messages (as described earlier) on the faculty member's monitor or chair or in other preferred locations.

- Follow up a conversation in which faculty agreed to do something with a confirming email. You could copy other faculty members if you will need a response from all of them.

- Ask how faculty prefer to be contacted (e.g., by email, phone, in person) and at what time of day. And ask how best to get their attention (e.g., taping a note to their monitor, leaving a note on their chair, catching them in the hall after class).

- Use the subject line of an email to make it abundantly clear you expect a response: "Action needed!" "Urgent!" "Decision needed!" Note: you may be tempted to use all capital letters, and on occasion this may be okay, but be aware this is considered "screaming" in the cyber world, and some people may take offense.

- If you feel strongly that faculty might respond better if you showed a bit more clout, preface your message by indicating the particular individual (e.g., department chair, the registrar, or other person of authority) who has asked you to make this request.

• Give all faculty an annual annotated calendar indicating when they will need to get various responses to you (e.g., class materials, student drop class forms, exams to be duplicated, grades, travel arrangements for yearly conferences). You can add periodic updates for special events (e.g., visiting fellows, papers to deliver, critical meetings) as they arise.

• Know which faculty are likely to be late in responding; for example, turning in their grades late or asking for last-minute help with a PowerPoint presentation. Set up a special system ahead of time to remind them; that is, a more individualized system than the annotated calendar.

• Keep track of when faculty will be away at conferences or on vacation, and anticipate what will be needed so you can get any signatures or information from them before they leave.

• Stick to your guns. Follow procedures instead of making a lot of exceptions. If you go out of your way to accommodate faculty who are not responding, they will expect you to continue to do so.

• Respond more quickly to requests by faculty members who respond reliably to you. Always communicate in a positive and professional way with those who respond more slowly, but give their needs a lower priority. You never know—over time they may catch on and respond more quickly.

• Thank faculty when they respond appropriately, and reinforce the behavior you want to encourage.

Still haven't received the response you need? Here are some additional strategies you may wish to try:

• Make the consequences clear. For example, "If you don't RSVP, the chair will expect you to be there even if you don't plan to go." Use your feedback skills to address the effects of their actions (or inactions).

• Engage the help of other faculty. For example, if Professor X has responded to your request, ask him or her to talk to Professor Y, who has not responded.

- Try going through their administrative assistants and support people (e.g., TAs, course coordinators).

- Spell out the consequences of an action. For example, tell a faculty member that if you don't have his or her signature today, Professor So-and-So's application for promotion will be late. Or even, "Professor So-and-So won't get the appointment because of you!"

- If you have sent an email to a group of faculty, and several did not respond, send a follow-up email to all the non-responders. This way, they can see who else has not responded, and be motivated to take their names off this list.

- If a faculty member's unresponsiveness becomes egregious, consider bringing the issue to the attention of the department chair or the dean. Of course, you need to have a conversation with the faculty member about this before you go over his or her head.

I'd like to close with an example illustrating the creative ways staff have found to entice faculty to respond. Doyle works in the Office of Resource Management, and one of his responsibilities is to promote energy efficiency and conservation on campus. He noticed that faculty didn't like being bothered by his requests to turn out light bulbs in empty rooms, or close the fumehoods in their laboratories to prevent hot or cold air from escaping on nights and weekends. Faculty were more focused on and invested in their own academic career than in the broader goals of the institution's cost savings plan. Because utility costs come out of a budget that does not affect faculty, they had no personal incentive to comply with Doyle's request. It was seen as just one more thing for them to do. And more often than not, they didn't do it.

So Doyle put a little extra thought into creating ways to appeal to faculty. For example, he used scientific language with the scientists; economic reasons with the economics professors; and when communicating with English professors, he wrote a memo that referenced Charles Dickens's carbon footprint. That caught their attention! By invoking their values and interests, he convinced these faculty to do something that otherwise seemed too bothersome. He turned what was forgettable into what I like to think of as a "sticky idea"—one that can't easily be ignored.

[See Summary—How to Establish a Partnership with Faculty on the following page.]

Summary

How To Establish a Partnership with Faculty

- As staff, you may need to convince faculty you can be of help; for example, by educating them about your role, special skills, and past experience in supporting faculty.

- You can get and hold a faculty member's attention by communicating directly, learning about his or her preferred mode of communication, and asking how you can best work together.

- A common staff concern is getting faculty to respond to their needs. I list a wide array of creative techniques to increase the likelihood faculty will respond to your requests.

- The trend is toward use of first names to address faculty in higher education settings, but make sure to familiarize yourself with the customs at your institution.

8

How To Say No and Deliver Bad News

- ◆ Establishing Healthy Boundaries
- ◆ Delivering Bad News
- ◆ Summary

No! Arguably, no is one of the scariest words in the English language. We usually don't like it when someone says no to us. And we don't like having to say no to someone else either. When that someone else is a faculty member or supervisor at work, the experience can become even more of a challenge. We may avoid saying no for a variety of reasons, including:

- ◆ Fear of hurting the other's feelings
- ◆ Fear of the other's anger
- ◆ Fear of negative repercussions
- ◆ Fear of rocking the boat
- ◆ Fear of being seen as selfish
- ◆ Fear of feeling guilty

In this chapter, we look at two types of situations that require you as staff to say no to faculty: situations that call for you to establish healthy boundaries, and situations in which you have to deliver bad news, negative feedback, or criticism. Instead of letting these unpleasant situations "get to" you, consider them opportunities to apply a growth mindset and to operate from higher ground so you avoid getting caught in the drama or emotion of the moment. It helps to use systems thinking, to consider the context and what you know about the particular faculty member to whom you have to say no or deliver bad news.

Establishing Healthy Boundaries

In the workplace, as well as in other areas of our lives, our relationships are defined by the interpersonal boundaries we create. These boundaries help us define who we are as *self* in relation to *other*, and to set limits in relationships. They function like invisible walls between ourselves and others, much as the walls of a house separate its occupants from the outside world.

Healthy boundaries are ones that allow us as staff to maintain our privacy, take care of our own needs, prioritize in reasonable ways, defend ourselves when we need to, and generally feel safe and secure. David Richo (1991) talks about the importance of acting out of agreement and negotiation, rather than out of compliance or compromise. Of course, not all boundaries are healthy. Flimsy or nonexistent boundaries that allow us to be pushed around by others can be considered unhealthy. Likewise, fortress-like boundaries that stand in the way of meaningful relationships are unhealthy.

Unhealthy boundaries often lead to a survival stance. Tuning out your feelings and needs and focusing only on the faculty member's requests, behavior, or needs easily leads to a placating stance. In this context, placating can reflect a lack of boundaries. To someone who discounts himself or herself, it can seem safer than simply saying no.

Often staff do not give much thought to the boundaries they need to set at work until something happens that specifically challenges them to do so. They may not recognize the importance of drawing a line between doing professional tasks assigned to them and doing purely personal work for faculty. In the moment, it may seem easier to placate faculty by agreeing to a personal request than to "lay down the law." They don't realize that each time they comply with an unreasonable request, they set a precedent. If they don't say no the first time, it becomes harder to say no the next time.

In fact, one of the main challenges that motivate staff to establish healthy boundaries occurs when they find themselves dealing with what appear to be unrealistic expectations on the part of faculty members. Here are some examples staff have shared with me of situations in which they felt faculty had unrealistic expectations. Some involve taking care of personal business for the faculty member. Others unrealistically expect staff to shift their work priorities or sacrifice their own personal needs. You may recognize these various examples from your own situation, and may want to add some of your own:

• She often calls me at home at 6 a.m.

• He asked me to pick up his dry cleaning.

• She wants me to give her the best classroom at exactly the times she has requested, regardless of who already has booked the room.

• He expects me to do library research for him.

• She expects me to give up my lunch break whenever she has a tight deadline.

• I always get his home mail when he and his wife are out of the country.

• He asked me to go to the Post Office on my lunch break.

• She asked me to help with fundraising, but when we planned events to meet potential donors, she would not come.

• He thinks I have the power to override university policies and deadlines.

Let's look more closely at how best to handle situations such as these. Consider the following four scenarios in which staff felt the need to set boundaries and say no to faculty. As you read each scenario, and before you read the suggested response, think about how you would handle the situation. What specific communication skills (see Chapter 6) would you use in each case?

1. It's 9:15 a.m. You are working intently on a project for Dr. Brown in the Economics Department that is due in ten days. The time line is tight and your time is committed. Dr. Ramirez comes to you and demands in a frenzied tone that you drop what you're doing and prepare a report she needs by 4:30 this afternoon. The report will take you all day. You doubt this short-term project is the best use of your time, not to mention that Dr. Brown will be upset if you do not follow

through with your commitment to complete his project in a timely fashion.

You might say: "Dr. Ramirez, I would like to help you with this report. Actually, I have already agreed to work on a project for Dr. Brown today. Perhaps you and he can discuss priorities and decide the best use of my time." [Starts with and maintains a sympathetic tone that indicates active listening. Sets a clear boundary with respect to taking on new work. Uses I-messages.]

2. Dr. Bickford is going to the Bahamas for a two-week vacation. When he went on vacation last year, he forwarded his and his wife's home mail to the office, you sorted it, kept it in a special folder, and put it on his desk the day before he returned. His wife also received a special delivery package during that time, and you stored the box behind your desk for a week. You anticipate he is going to forward his mail to the office again this year.

You might say: "I know, Dr. Bickford, you appreciated my handling your home mail while you were away last year. However, I won't be able to do it again this time. It simply isn't fair to other faculty. And clearly I can't offer that service for everyone. I happen to have a U.S. postal service forwarding request form, in case you'd like to use it to forward your mail to a friend or neighbor." [Starts with an I-message. Sets boundaries with respect to taking care of faculty's personal mail. Offers a positive solution.]

3. You were hired by the Ecology program to do data entry. Dr. Riley finds out that you are bilingual and have worked as a translator in the past. She starts asking you to translate some documents. First it is just an email. Then she wants you to give her a synopsis of an article in a Spanish journal. Now she is asking you to write up the translation of another article. All of these tasks are in addition to your regular data entry responsibilities. Moreover, you get paid less for data entry than you did when you worked as a translator.

You might say: "I wanted to help you out, so I translated that email. My job here is data entry. And this translating is time consuming and a higher level skill. If you really want me to do this, we'll need to reexamine my workload and job description." [Starts with an I-message. Sets boundaries with respect to job responsibilities. Offers to work out a solution.]

4. You are the head nurse on a surgery ward in a teaching hospital.

You have just overheard a young professor yell at another nurse in front of a patient. You didn't want to create an even more uncomfortable situation for the patient, so you didn't say anything, but you do want to set boundaries.

You might ask the professor to come into an empty room and say: "There are very sick people here. I am responsible for maintaining a healing environment in this unit. Yelling is not okay here. If you have a problem with anyone here, please come directly to me to talk about it." [Starts with an I-message. Sets healthy boundaries with respect to yelling. Offers an alternative way to communicate anger.]

Setting healthy boundaries also refers to how we separate our professional and personal lives while at work. This is discussed in Chapter 14.

Delivering Bad News

In addition to situations calling for setting healthy boundaries, staff often have to say no in the context of delivering bad news. Bad news comes in different forms. It may involve informing faculty they must follow policies and procedures they either are unaware of or have chosen to ignore. Or it may be that you find yourself needing to deliver negative feedback or criticism to a faculty member. Being the bearer of bad news like this can be tricky. It can raise emotions. And it can lead to conflict, especially if the faculty member receiving the news blames you, the messenger.

The most effective way to deliver bad news is not necessarily the same as the best way to deliver good news. One rule of thumb is to put good news in writing, but to deliver bad news in person and confirm it in writing. The rationale behind this guideline is the need for extra attention on a personal level when it comes to bad news. Of course, good news can be delivered in person, too.

Here are some suggestions for delivering bad news:

• Choose an appropriate private place and time to avoid embarrassing the professor or initiating a loud verbal exchange that will disrupt others.

• Phrase the bad news in a way that creates a positive picture in the mind's eye. For example, instead of saying, "We close at 6 p.m." (which creates an image of the office closed), say, "We are open from 8 a.m. to 6 p.m." (which creates an image of the office open, with people working there all day long).

- If possible, ask questions so faculty can come to their own conclusions. For example, instead of saying, "You can't just fire that
research assistant without first going through the procedures,"
say, "Is Sandra clear about your expectations for her job? How
would you like to document her performance?"

- Discuss the rationale behind the bad news with faculty in a manner that does not make them lose their dignity or good will.

- Expect faculty to have a negative reaction, but retain your cool.
Don't let emotions trump the facts. And don't give in or let yourself be manipulated.

- Repeat your position as many times as you have to. You might
even say, "I know I sound like a broken record, but..."

- Address the issue of delivering bad news ahead of time. For
example, you might say, "As we work together, there may be times
when I have to deliver bad news to you. When that happens, how
would you like me to handle it?"

- Set the tone for collaboration so they understand you will work
with them to find alternative solutions to mitigate the consequences of the bad news. Spend time listening to what they
really want, identifying their legitimate interests, and then finding legitimate ways to get what they want.

- Look for win-win solutions.

The common response to being told no—in the academic setting, as
anywhere else—is to experience a loss. The faculty member didn't get
what he or she wanted or expected. As a result, they can experience
grief about this loss.

Elizabeth Kübler-Ross (1969) described five stages people generally go through in responding to loss. She was speaking about grief
experienced by terminally ill patients. However, other researchers have
discovered that these stages also apply more broadly when people are
affected by bad news. We can use this model to help us understand
how faculty react to bad news, such as an unexpected change in procedures. From their perspective, such a change complicates what they're
trying to accomplish and can hit them with the wallop of bad news.

The five stages named by Kübler-Ross are denial, anger, bargaining, depression, and acceptance (Table 8.1). I find that I, and others, go

through these stages when we don't get what we want or when something unexpected happens that we don't want. This can be something profound or something quite inconsequential. For the purpose of illustration, let's look at a small example. Yesterday I caught my fingernail on the door as I was walking into a meeting. Immediately I grabbed my finger, as if doing that could fix the nail. "Oh no," I thought (denial). I muttered, "You klutz, Susan!" or "Why was that stupid door closed, anyway?" (anger). Then I stared down at my clearly broken fingernail and thought, "Maybe I could just epoxy it back on" (bargaining). Of course, I knew I wouldn't really try that, so I felt bummed by the dismal appearance of my poor, torn nail (depression). Then it was time for the meeting to start, and I quickly forgot all about my nail because my attention went to something much more important (acceptance).

Table 8.1 Stages of Responding to Loss

Stage	Characteristic feelings and reactions
Denial	Trying to avoid the inevitable, acting as though the new information is not accurate
Anger	Frustrated outpouring of emotion, often avoiding one's own vulnerability, not ready to accept the loss
Bargaining	Trying to figure a way out, looking for alternatives, seeking some sense of control
Depression	Sadness, realization of the inevitable, settling into the new reality in a more healthy way
Acceptance	Finally accepting the reality of the loss or change, finding a realistic way forward with less emotional turmoil

That's a silly little example, but I like how it covers all the stages. Keep in mind, though, they don't always occur in the same neat and tidy order. It's not uncommon, for instance, for anger to resurface even after one has begun to accept the reality of a loss. Now let's move on and look at how faculty might progress through these same stages after receiving bad news, and how we as staff can help the process.

To begin with, our job as staff is to anticipate that faculty will experience loss and go through these stages when they are told no or get bad news.

Suppose Dr. Cole, a professor of Biology, has written an article he wants to get published in a particular journal. As his assistant, it is your responsibility to submit the article using the journal's new online submission process. However, when Dr. Cole realizes the process now includes a blind review of all articles, he asks you to hold off. Instead, he wants you to send the article to a colleague who is on the board of that journal, with a note requesting the colleague "just get it to the right person." In the interest of helping Dr. Cole, you politely let him know that trying to circumvent the official process is unlikely to help his prospects of publication.

Denial

Because he has used a personal route for submitting articles in the past, Dr. Cole is likely to move immediately into denial. He may say, "But I've done this a dozen times. What you're saying can't be so." Implying that you don't know what you're talking about, that he knows better, he may insist, "No, this is how it works. I don't have to do an online submission. I'll just phone my colleague and she'll take care of me." And he may go ahead and send the article to the colleague he believes can subvert the new process.

Your best response to denial usually is to give the faculty member some time to come to terms with the new reality. Be patient while he or she goes through the denial stage. You can tell Dr. Cole something like "I wish it were so" or "I'm sorry it has changed." These I-messages show you are engaged with him but are not stopped by his denial. You may choose to gently rephrase the new information.

Anger

Often faculty experience loss or not getting what they want as a personal affront. They suddenly have to deal with inconvenient new circumstances and they don't like it. They usually experience and express anger.

Dr. Cole may sound angry at you, but underneath he probably is really angry at the change in the submission procedures. He may criticize the new procedure or the people who changed the rules. He may be furious, for example, that it will take months for his article to go through the blind review process when he previously could have taken care of everything with one phone call to a friend. If he tries sending the article through the wrong channels anyway and that doesn't work, he may be angry with his friend. Dr. Cole might even use some colorful language during these first two stages of denial and anger.

When a faculty member is expressing anger, you will want to choose your responses and actions carefully. First, of course, consider the larger perspective. Realize that Dr. Cole is progressing through predictable stages on his way to acceptance. You can support him by staying calm yourself, not taking what he says personally, and acknowledging his loss and upset. You might say something like "How frustrating that they changed it," "Yeah, this is really upsetting," or "After all you've done to finish this manuscript, now there are new steps." When Dr. Cole senses you understand and accept his anger and difficult situation, he will likely relax a bit and be more ready to look at new options.

When we react to a faculty member's anger or deny the difficulty of his or her feelings or the situation, the person tends to stay stuck in anger rather than moving to the next stage. Of course, if you sense you are in danger, you must take care of your safety. You can do this by giving the five-stage process some time, taking a time out, or agreeing to talk later. This also helps the faculty member gain more perspective.

Bargaining

As it becomes clear anger will not resolve the situation, the faculty member usually turns to bargaining. In Kübler-Ross's stages, bargaining refers to an attempt to find a way to satisfy what we need for ourselves. As a step toward accepting the loss, we try to gain a sense of control in the situation.

In this case, Dr. Cole might follow up with his personal contacts and try to get them to make an exception in the case of his article. In fact, as staff, we need to be aware that faculty's attempts to bargain in this way often work. Our job is to inform them of policies and procedures, what they can and cannot do, and then see how things evolve, without taking their reactions and emotional expressions personally.

We can help them generate realistic alternatives and choices. For example, you might ask Dr. Cole, "Are there other journals with a more rapid review process?" Helping him bargain in this way, by defining his next steps, can make it easier to move beyond anger and feel less blocked.

Depression

With the depression stage comes the realization that the loss is real. In most cases, bargaining hasn't solved the fundamental problem. At this point, the faculty member is usually feeling disappointed and sad. It is often a quiet, inwardly emotional time that helps the person let go of the denial and anger and begin to come to terms with the loss. Dr. Cole may feel dejected that his article can't be instantly accepted for publication, or that his attempts to circumvent the system didn't succeed. He may feel like giving up. As a result, he may make no move to submit it.

During this phase, you might say something like "Yes, this is a lot to face." You can practice active listening and paraphrase what he is feeling. If he is stuck in non-action, this may not be the time to push him toward action. Rather, allow the genuine feeling of loss to lead him toward acceptance and problem solving.

Acceptance

The final stage marks a completion of the reaction to loss. Dr. Cole realizes he can't subvert the new online process or manipulate an exception for himself. Only when he has accepted the new reality—and not until then—will he be ready to move forward.

Eventually he will say, "Okay, so I can't do it the way I used to. Let's just move on and get it done. Please submit it online." The acceptance stage may include hope, as the realization dawns that "the old way may not work anymore, but that doesn't mean I have to give up. I can try the new process." This leads to seeking new solutions and effective problem solving. For example, Dr. Cole might consider submitting his article to alternative journals.

At the acceptance stage, you can get ready to move forward together, with a new plan. You may present the faculty member with some new ideas or resources and acknowledge the new beginning.

Practice Scenarios

In the previous section about establishing healthy boundaries, you practiced responding to sample scenarios. Here is an opportunity to respond to scenarios in which staff have to deliver bad news to faculty. As you read each scenario, and before you read the suggested response, think about how you would handle the situation. What specific communication skills (see Chapter 5) would you use in each case?

1. Dr. Fritz in the Archeology Department has purchased some items for which she wants you, her admin, to obtain reimbursement. In the receipts you find a $70 charge for Pampers, and you recall she brought

her family, including her 14-month-old son, to an archeological dig. When you start to question her about the item, she waves her hand to indicate it's not a big deal, and wants you to "just find some way to write it up" so it can come out of her grant budget.

You might say: "Dr. Fritz, we need to discuss this. This expense is not permissible within the grant guidelines, and will raise red flags for the auditors. I'm not comfortable trying to hide it in the budget."

2. Many students want to get into Dr. Hoeing's history of filmmaking seminar. They especially like that he shows lots of old movies. The seminar always has a waiting list. Often when students plead with Dr. Hoeing to let them in, he does. You work in the Registrar's Office, and are tired of fighting with students when they insist the professor has given them special permission, and you have to tell them he can't do that. You decide to speak with Dr. Hoeing about the problem.

You might say: "Dr. Hoeing, it's wonderful that students like your seminar so much. However, as you know, the college has a maximum enrollment for seminars. In fact, the way our computers are set up, they will automatically toss out any over-enrollment. Students get upset when they believe they can take the seminar, and then find out they can't. Is there a way you and I can work together to prevent this confusion?"

3. Dr. Newman is behind on her time line for creating a videotape of two-year-old children engaging in parallel play. This videotape, which she received a small grant to make, will play an important part in her Developmental Psychology class next semester. You find out that Dr. Newman is about to proceed without obtaining the necessary human subjects review. She tells you it will all be done in a single videotaping session, and no one will notice.

You might say: "Dr. Newman, I know you want to get this done in time for next semester. But obtaining human subjects' approval is required by the university. This is a legal issue. Really, I don't think we want to do the taping this way."

[See Summary—How To Say No and Deliver Bad News on the following page.

Summary

How To Say No and Deliver Bad News

- Establishing healthy boundaries allows you as staff to maintain your privacy, take care of your needs, prioritize in reasonable ways, defend yourself when needed, and generally feel safe and secure.

- Setting a clear boundary is especially important when faculty have unrealistic expectations of staff.

- Put good news in writing, but deliver bad news in person and confirm it in writing.

- When you say no or delivered bad news to faculty, expect them to experience the normal five stages of loss (i.e., denial, anger, bargaining, depression, and acceptance). It is helpful to support them through the stages to acceptance.

9

Continuing the Partnership with Faculty

- How can I orient faculty to university policies and procedures?
- How can I identify and work with a faculty member's resistance?
- How can I have more productive one-on-one meetings with faculty?
- Is there anything I shouldn't say?
- How can I engender respect?
- What should I do next? How do I follow up?
- Summary

Over the years, I have gathered an abundance of questions from staff about facilitating communication with faculty, as well as corresponding ways to address those questions. So far in this section, we have looked at some of the ways to get the conversation going, as well as at the particular issues of setting boundaries, delivering bad news, and saying no. In this chapter we cover additional situations that can arise as the conversation continues. Like Chapter 6, this chapter is organized around some of the questions staff members frequently ask during my workshops.

How can I orient faculty to university policies and procedures?

Dr. LaSalle is a new adjunct faculty at your small college. At the end of her first semester, the students from her classes come in droves to the Registrar's Office, where you work, complaining she has given them all pass/fail grades. The college does allow students to choose the pass/fail option for a set number of courses. Most courses, however, must be taken for grades. You tell the students you will contact Dr. LaSalle and do your best to correct the problem.

As it turns out, Dr. LaSalle previously taught at a university that used pass/fail exclusively. She is convinced this is a better system and argues with you: "I want students in my classes to be creative, to learn to think freely. Focusing on grades stifles this. I've taught for years in a pass/fail system with great success. Students who sign up for my course will just have to use their pass/fail option."

Like Dr. LaSalle, some faculty consider policies and procedures to be negotiable. When confronted, they may try to convince staff to make an exception in their case. Or they may just try to circumvent the system and hope that nobody will notice.

To understand why this happens, we need only to look again at the faculty characteristics we discussed in Chapter 2. Faculty tend to be independent creatures, more focused on their teaching and research than on the broader workings of the institution. Following policies and procedures may be low on their list of priorities. They may have received more rewards during their years of education for thinking outside the box than for following strict protocol, and continue that approach in their current position. And, as we saw in Chapter 1, one of the challenges for staff working with faculty members is that faculty often do not follow procedures. In this case, it falls to staff to be aware of policies and procedures and to orient faculty to them. This keeps everyone—faculty and staff—out of trouble.

All colleges and universities have established policies and procedures for their faculty and staff, though they may differ from campus to campus, institution to institution. These days, in addition to being printed in manuals, policies and procedures usually are posted on the school's Website. Of course, that doesn't mean everyone takes the time to read and become familiar with them. Have you done so?

In general, *policies* refer to the broader rules; *procedures* refer to the specific ways in which those policies are expected to be carried out. Table 9.1 lists some of the main areas covered in university manuals and on Websites.

Table 9.1 Policies and Procedures

Policy Area	Sample Procedures
Academic	Proposals for new courses, determination of credit hours, class rosters, course scheduling, exam scheduling, add/drop rules, reporting of grades, course cancellations, classification of courses
Business and finance	Purchasing and reimbursement procedures, records management, budgeting, allowable travel-related expenses, electronic information security, credit union
Ethics	Conflict of interest code, copyright, whistle-blower guidelines, political activities
Facilities and environment	Designated nonsmoking areas, alcohol sales on campus, health and safety procedures, use of protected areas, parking regulations, disaster preparedness
Personnel	Hiring procedures, promotions, terminations, performance evaluations, benefits, sexual harassment, family leave, misconduct, tenure track process
Research and development	Grant applications, use of human subjects, confidentiality, trademarks, intellectual property, copyright infringement/protection, human gene manipulation, patents

Staff can be involved in (1) educating or orienting faculty to university policies and procedures (i.e., in an ongoing way, after the official orientation offered by the institution) and (2) enforcing those policies and procedures. You may have one or both of these roles at different times. First, here are some strategies to use in orienting faculty to policies and procedures:

- Begin orienting new faculty when they arrive on campus. Prepare written materials and checklists related to relevant policies and procedures, and make these available for immediate use.

- Explain your role and resources to faculty.

- Realize policies and procedures may not be high on their list of priorities, and think of creative ways to get their attention. For example, preface a request to faculty with a statement of the relevant policy or procedure. (See "How do I get (and hold) faculty's attention?" in Chapter 7 for additional suggestions.)

- Look up policies and procedures on the intranet, and show faculty how to do this themselves. Talk them through the steps of finding the URL, bookmarking it, navigating the various documents, and so on.

- Double-check with faculty that they understand the policies and procedures you have explained to them.

- Anticipate the faculty's ongoing needs for information. For example, start two weeks before faculty will need purchase order numbers, and bring them into the process at that time.

- Don't assume faculty are aware of or intend to follow specific policies and procedures.

Here are some suggestions for enforcing policies and procedures, especially in cases in which faculty are resistant or noncompliant:

- When a faculty member is upset by or angry at a policy or procedure, provide backup information. Have the policy available on your computer screen or in print. Faculty are more likely to get angry at the procedure on the paper or screen than at you—the bearer of bad news.

- Provide faculty with the rationale behind the particular policies and procedures. Sell them on the idea, rather than merely demand their compliance. If you are unsure about the reasons, check with staff or faculty involved in establishing the policy or procedure.

- Explain who has established a policy or procedure. For example, if faculty object to the 52 percent indirect costs for grants, let them know the decision was made by the Office of the President or the provost, not by the dean or chairperson.

- Explain the benefits to faculty of using specific procedures. For example, keeping receipts will avoid delays when requesting reimbursement, submitting a grant application on time will prevent the possibility of needlessly being disqualified for funding, obtaining a permit will eliminate the worry about getting a parking ticket, providing required textbook lists will allow students to obtain the books and show up with them in class.

- Explain the consequences of not following procedures. For example, if medical faculty try to bring guests into the surgery arena without following protocol, those guests may find themselves scrubbed and ready but unable to enter, causing inconvenience and embarrassment to all involved.

- If possible, offer faculty an alternative way to do something that will still comply with procedures but that will make their lives easier. For example, Dr. Mulley comes by your desk at the Media Department to ask if you have a projector she can use for a presentation on microorganisms. She wants to practice using it before class next week. You explain that all media equipment is clearly described on the department Website, where she can choose the appropriate equipment for her needs, take an online tutorial, and place her order.

- Don't bend the rules, try to be consistent. This can be challenging if faculty become angry. Take a deep breath, use your best influencing skills, and stick to your guns!

- Remember that following policies and procedures applies to you, too. I am reminded of this whenever workshop participants talk about faculty who asked them to backdate contracts or break rules, but who did not come to their rescue when the breach was discovered. So, never let faculty persuade you to break a rule to help them out. You may be held accountable for your own behavior.

How can I identify and work with a faculty member's resistance?

Even if you've done your best to orient faculty and to shepherd them through procedures, you may find your efforts sometimes fall short. Certain faculty may resist your requests. This can happen in obvious and not-so-obvious ways.

Consider the many faces of resistance that Peter Block describes in *Flawless consulting: A guide to getting your expertise used.* Faculty may:

- Press you for more details
- Flood you with their own details
- Go behind your back
- Personally attack you or your request

- Ignore your request
- Tell you outright why they won't comply
- Offer tangential excuses
- Procrastinate
- Come up with a different solution, or ask you to do so

Whether or not the resistance is obvious, you can identify it by the evidence, or result. If faculty have not responded or complied with a procedure within a reasonable amount of time, they may be resisting.

So, what is the best way to handle resistance?

First, let me mention what is *not* the best way. Don't try to fight back. Any counter-resistance you offer to faculty is likely to amplify the problem. You can't get rid of resistance by applying more pressure. That only engenders greater resistance. Instead, you need to become more resourceful. Here are some suggestions.

- Understand that, as Peter Block says, "resistance is an emotional process, not a rational or intellectual process." Once someone is resisting, it is hard to talk that person down. Usually you can minimize resistance simply by refusing to butt heads.

- Don't take personally any resistance you encounter. In most cases, faculty are not resisting *you*. They are resisting what they perceive as a threat, something they feel will steal their time or force them to do something they don't want to do.

- Nothing takes the wind out of resistance like a little empathy and encouragement. Let faculty know you appreciate their frustrations and fears. Show them that you are genuinely interested in their goals and concerns.

- If faculty resist you by going behind your back and finding other staff willing to break rules, more often than not the wisest approach is just to let it go.

How can I have more productive one-on-one meetings with faculty?

John, a research assistant in the Psychology Department, is working on a grant proposal for Dr. Stratos. She gave him a draft she had started and asked him to get it in shape for the funding agency. He hasn't had a chance to speak with her recently because she was out of town at back-to-back conferences. On the day of her return, he catches her in her office at lunchtime and asks if he can run some questions by her. "The proposal is almost ready," he says. "I just need to check a few things, and I can have it on your desk this afternoon." He asks her for her updated CV, points out an inconsistency between the budget and time line, and asks her for a missing page number for a quote.

After Dr. Stratos has quickly responded to these questions, she shows John some handouts she picked up at a conference. She wants them adapted for students in one of her lectures. They spend the rest of the "meeting" discussing the handouts, before she has to run off to class.

As John is walking back to his office, he realizes he forgot to ask Dr. Stratos to provide three publication dates he found missing on the grant application's reference list. He kicks himself, realizing he now won't be able to get her the proposal as promised, which may jeopardize their chance for meeting the application deadline.

What is wrong with this scenario? One-on-one meetings offer a lot of advantages for staff-faculty communication. But the fact is, they also can lead to greater frustration if they aren't handled well.

Before we talk about how to make one-on-one meetings more productive, consider some of the benefits that can come from in-person meetings with faculty members:

- The opportunity for two-way communication and an exchange of ideas (e.g., a chance to explore each other's point of view)

- A venue for handling many items of business within a short period of time

- The ability to shut the door and focus without interruptions

- More in-depth discussion than possible in email or on the phone (e.g., a chance to look at materials together and a chance to observe the other person's nonverbal responses)

The key to making meetings productive is to prepare for them ahead of time. If John had (1) scheduled the meeting with Dr. Stratos and (2) come prepared with an agenda, he would have been better able to ensure they had enough protected time to cover everything that needed to be addressed. He could have scheduled the meeting by email or over the phone. Of course, Dr. Stratos still could have had an agenda of her own (i.e., working on the handouts). I've heard staff describe bringing an agenda to a meeting only to have faculty put it aside. In fact, many best practices for productive meetings commonly used in organizations are not familiar to some faculty members.

Buy-in to the agenda is always important when two or more people hold a meeting. John could have dealt with this issue in a number of ways. For example, when scheduling the meeting, he could have asked Dr. Stratos for her agenda items. If she mentioned the handouts then, they could have determined whether they would have time to discuss both the proposal and handouts in the time allotted or whether they needed a separate meeting. He could also have emailed her the agenda ahead of time. Alternatively, especially if the meeting was going to be relatively short, John could have said in his email that it would be about the proposal and could have asked at the outset of the meeting if she had any agenda items to add. They could then have considered whether they had time to discuss handouts in addition to the proposal. If Dr. Stratos had brought up the handouts in the middle of the meeting, John could have quickly brought the two of them back to the agenda.

Figuring out how long the meeting needs to last is an important aspect of scheduling and of setting the agenda. John could have said he needed a fifteen-minute meeting with Dr. Stratos about the proposal. If she only had fifteen minutes available at the scheduled time, that would have clarified immediately that an additional topic required a separate meeting or that they needed to reschedule when she could attend a longer meeting.

Assessment is especially important for longer meetings. I like to use a plus/delta format in which you and faculty write down the pluses (what went well) in one column and the deltas (what could be changed or improved) in the other (Table 9.2). These assessments help both of you focus on your roles in making meetings effective and improving the quality of meetings.

Table 9.2 Plus/Delta Chart

$+$ Works well. Continue.	Δ Needs to be changed. Suggestions.

Here are some suggestions for making one-on-one meetings with faculty productive:

- Make sure you have their attention. Take a moment to break the ice and establish rapport and a collegial tone.

- Refer to the section "How can I get faculty to respond?" in Chapter 6 for relevant suggestions, such as batching your requests, using a checklist.

- Stay focused on the agenda and avoid talking about university politics or your personal life.

- Maintain a calm, patient, and confident presence. If appropriate, reassure them, "It will get done. I'll take care of everything for you."

- Take good notes during the meeting.

- Together, go over your decisions or agreements and each person's to-do items at the end of the meeting. Tie up loose ends with more specific plans, who will do what, and time lines. Be sure you both understand everything and are on the same page.

- Remember, faculty may not see the implications of a decision for you. Teach them about how the system works, if necessary.

- Go over your notes and follow up with an email to document decisions, agreements, and unfinished business. Schedule your tasks on your calendar and plan follow-up meetings or communications.

- Establish a regular time for one-on-one meetings.

- If you are working with a faculty member on a complex task (e.g., helping him or her apply for promotion, convening a meeting with community leaders, creating a new concentration within an undergraduate major), plan a series of meetings. This requires a project plan rather than an agenda for a single meeting (some of the ideas in Chapter 9 may be helpful).

Is there anything I shouldn't say?

In this book and in workshops, I stress the importance of open and empowering communication with faculty. Staff can't be afraid, for example, to say no when the situation calls for it or to deliver bad news when necessary. But this often leads to another question. Staff want to know if there is anything they shouldn't say to faculty. Are there any clear no-no's?

In one sense, the only no-no's are the same types of things that any professional should avoid saying in a work environment. However, I think it is helpful to look at the general flavor and the particular nuance these kinds of words might take on in an academic setting.

Avoid Gasoline Words

We want to avoid what are sometimes called *gasoline words*. These are words or phrases (Table 9.3) that can bring up negative images, sound threatening, or make faculty feel blamed. They are likened to gasoline because their use can lead to an explosion. Another way to look at it is that these words violate the communication skills we covered in Chapter 5. For example, using them may indicate you are not engaged in active listening. Or they may fail to employ I-messages when an I-message is called for. You may want to review these parts of Chapter 5 now.

Table 9.3 Words and Phrases to Avoid

You have to . . .	You're confusing me . . .
You should . . .	Why didn't you . . .
You must...	It's not my job.
You can't...	I can't . . .
You always . . .	I'm just the technician.
You never . . .	Calm down.
Your problem is . . .	No (at beginning
You're wrong . . .	of sentence)

Here are some examples of statements that begin with gasoline words. The information may be correct, but the words can create negative inner images or emotional reactions. The gasoline words are bolded so you can make note of and avoid them. In each case, I have followed with an explanation for why the words can be perceived as inflammatory, and also with an alternative statement that is nonthreatening. Note that many of the alternatives include I-messages.

1. DON'T: "**You should** check your email more often."

   [When faculty hear you say they "should" (or "shouldn't") do something, they may feel you are being insubordinate.

You may sound bossy or parental.]

TRY: "I sent out an important email yesterday. Did you receive it?" Or "I'm not sure you received one of my emails. Could you check and let me know if you have received it?"

2. DON'T: "**You have to** respond to Dr. Wing by the end of today."

   [Saying faculty "have to" often brings up their resistance. They don't like being told what to do. The faculty member's inner voice may chime in, "You can't make me!"]

   TRY: "Dr. Wing at NSF indicated he expects to hear from you today. Do you need anything from me to make sure that happens?"

3. DON'T: "You **can't have** Room 6 on October 2."

   [Emphasizing the negative makes faculty feel unnecessarily obstructed or denied. The same information can be phrased in a positive way that sounds friendlier and more helpful.]

   TRY: "Sorry, on October 2 Rooms 2, 4 and 7 are available. Room 7 is the same size as Room 6."

4. DON'T: "**You always** (or **you never**...) talk to him first."

   [When people hear that they "always" or "never" do something, it can sound accusatory. Moreover, it is rare anyone "always" or "never" does anything; usually there are exceptions.]

   TRY: "Since I'm the one preparing the reports, I think it would be more efficient if you spoke directly to me first. I'll let Betsy know when the report is ready for her to proofread." Or "Since Betsy is in charge of the budget, I think it would be more efficient if you spoke with her first. I'll wait for her to get me the data."

5. DON'T: "**It's not my job** to clean up after a faculty lunch."

   [When faculty hear you say it is not your job, they may get the impression that you are unwilling or uncooperative, even if you aren't.]

   TRY: "I've noticed the conference room needs cleaning after faculty lunches. Would you like me to arrange for someone to come in and clean?"

6. DON'T: "**No**, it will never be approved without your signature."

    [When faculty hear "no" at the beginning of a sentence, they are hit first with the negative. Again, this can make you appear unwilling or uncooperative, even when you aren't.]

    TRY: "Your signature is required for approval." Or if you want to state it more clearly and strongly, frontload the sentence: "This request will be rejected without your signature. You will miss the deadline for submission unless it is signed and delivered by noon tomorrow."

7. DON'T: "**I don't know what to do.**"

    [Although of course it is appropriate at times to say you don't know something, often you can be proactive and find out what to do. Faculty will appreciate your effort.]

    TRY: "Interesting question. I will research this and get back to you by 4:00 this afternoon."

Avoid Being Overly Personal

This can be a fine line because we want to be ourselves and act natural at work. It's not fun to have to think about censoring ourselves in the place where we spend so much of our time most days of the week. However, when it comes to being personal, it is best to aim for a balance that is comfortable and appropriate for everyone involved. In other words, be personal in the sense of friendly, but not overly personal.

For example, it is only natural to share pleasantries at the beginning or end of a meeting or a day. It's the normal, human thing to do. You and faculty may ask each other, for example, about your health or your children or a vacation. On the other hand, going into detail about a family issue or a medical problem may be seen as crossing professional boundaries. Faculty may feel imposed upon, or more importantly, see you as wasting the already limited amount of time they have available to meet with you.

In general, I suggest playing it safe. Assume that most faculty members would prefer not to hear details about your family or your weekend unless they signal first that they are interested or have initiated the conversation with personal stories or details of their own. Let time, confidentiality, and professionalism be your guide.

In Chapter 8 we discussed how to set healthy boundaries. In the context of this chapter, the point is to stay focused on the academic work and not on yourself, your feelings, or your personal needs. Here are some ways to set this boundary:

• Avoid long stories, whether personal or about something you read or saw on the news

• Avoid getting emotional; if strong feelings arise at work, take a time-out

• Avoid complaining about your job, about faculty, or about other co-workers

• Avoid getting involved in office politics

You might ask, so what if faculty themselves do these things? And a few faculty will do them. But just because a faculty member with whom you work airs personal matters or wants to discuss office politics with you doesn't mean you should reciprocate with your own personal stories or getting into a discussion about theirs. I'm not suggesting you say to faculty, "I don't want to hear all the details of your aunt's surgery" or "I'm too busy to think about office politics." But you can avoid open-ended questions, such as "How is your aunt doing?" or "Why do you think Dr. Jenkins wanted to speak to her?" When faculty bring up these topics, you can practice active listening without getting involved. If you don't feed the fire, so to speak, they will probably get the message. Eventually they will probably stop trying to engage you in these kinds of conversations.

The Special Case of Social Networking Sites

One place where the personal and the professional intersect these days is on the Internet at social networking sites, such as Facebook and MySpace. Much has come to light about the potential impact joining Facebook can have on one's work relationships. In fact, some high-profile cases in which information on Facebook became the cause of embarrassment, or worse, for workers have appeared in the media. This issue is as relevant in academia as it is in the corporate and nonprofit sectors. Staff and faculty can have access to personal information about each other through networks on Facebook and similar sites. For this reason, some people opt not to join these sites. Perhaps the most sound advice if you do join is to be as careful as possible with what you post and try to monitor what others post about you. Ask yourself how you would feel if the people with whom you work read this about you.

How can I engender respect?

If we look at faculty-staff relationships from a historical perspective, the word *respect* is probably not the first descriptor that comes to mind. This is because our definitions for what constitutes respect have evolved in recent decades. The standards we hold for respectful behavior have been elevated. These standards have changed for working relationships in all settings, not just in academia, as well as for our non-work relationships.

Take the example of the secretary. In the mid-twentieth century, this was a catch-all term for many academic and corporate staff members. The secretary of years past often was seen by her faculty boss as "my girl." Typically, she served coffee as readily as she typed up memos. Male secretaries were an anomaly, and university faculties were even more predominantly male than they are today. The faculty-secretary relationship was defined by the gender-oriented hierarchy within which it existed. The secretary was at the beck and call of faculty, and often was rewarded more for her loyalty than for her professional skills. Even if she had training beyond high school, a secretary had virtually no career mobility.

However, it would be wrong to conclude all secretaries felt miserable and disrespected in this situation. In fact, people generally applied a different standard in those days. If her boss considered her "my girl," a secretary did not likely take offense. In her eyes, this did not mean her boss lacked respect for her. Nor did her boss consider this a lack of respect. Within the existing system, a secretary knew her place and learned to serve with a smile and to derive satisfaction within the confines of the job as she knew it.

I only go into detail in describing this piece of history because it illustrates something fundamental: our values are largely culturally determined. As culture shifts, so do our values. In the current culture, respect in the workplace is based on a heightened value for equality. Faculty and staff may not enjoy equivalent pay scales, but their equality on a human level translates into new expectations about how they communicate with one another. The use of titles such as administrative assistant to replace the more generic "secretary" is just one indication of this new level of respect.

These days, we have higher standards for respect, but this doesn't mean staff always feel faculty treat them with respect. Some faculty may be "old school" and communicate with staff in ways that do not live up to today's standards. Others may have more personal reasons, such as being focused on their own work to the exclusion of staff or being "beyond overwhelm," that cause them to speak to staff with less than full respect. Staff may also feel disrespected on account of their ethnicity, sexual preference, disability, or other characteristics.

As a staff member, it is helpful to find ways to communicate with faculty that engender respect. Here are some suggestions:

- One of the ground rules for receiving respect from others in any context is giving respect to them. Be sure you always treat faculty (as well as other staff) with the same level of respect, dignity, empathy, and professionalism you wish to receive.

- Be mindful of your body language and tone of voice day in and day out, hour after hour. Sit up and pay attention when faculty approach you. Smile and say good morning in a way that sets the tone. Avoid rolling your eyes, shrugging your shoulders, or slouching when they speak to you. Plan your verbal as well as nonverbal communication to get the results and treatment you prefer. I'm often surprised at how many high-level people in organizations are not aware of their inept nonverbal cues and tone of voice.

- The one who asks the first questions usually takes charge of the conversation and tone. When faculty approach or ask for your help or attention, I suggest asking, "How can I help you?" This suggests you are competent and confident and wish to know specifically what they want. It also tends to deter the faculty member from relating a long, rambling story that doesn't get to the point of what he or she wants you to do.

- Make visible signs of engagement with a faculty member's request or project, and move forward with what needs to happen next. Take notes. Copy the faculty member on an email that shows you are taking immediate action.

- Use phrases that convey respect, a can-do attitude, and commitment to results. Say, "Yes, I can help you with this," "First we need to...." and "I'll stick by you until we have this resolved." Keep in mind that your credibility with faculty comes, to a considerable extent, from your ability to get done without a lot of hassle the things that are important to them.

• Show interest in faculty's work and successes (if you are genuinely interested). Learn the terminology of their field. Tell them about recent newspaper or magazine articles that may be of interest to them.

• Dazzle them with your insights, observations, and suggestions. I don't mean you should flaunt your knowledge. Trying to make yourself appear right, and someone else wrong, certainly won't earn you respect. But you can find the appropriate moments to wow faculty with the depth of your knowledge and skill.

• Cultivate your own self-respect and self-confidence. If you have these qualities, it can be easier for faculty to respond in kind.

• Educate faculty about the importance of respect. Don't assume they are aware of whether or not they come across as respectful. Use your feedback skills to raise their level of awareness. For example, if a faculty member raises his or her voice and sounds critical, you could step back and hold up your hand, palm facing outward, near your body to show you are protecting yourself. Often, especially initially during a tense encounter, a nonverbal signal is more effective than a verbal signal.

• Sometimes it is easier to give feedback about faculty's treatment of another staff member than of you. For example, if you see a professor intimidating a staff coworker, you can signal your awareness of the offending behavior by moving closer to them. The intimidation is likely to stop. Alternatively, you could walk up and ask both of them, "May I help you?"

• Stand up for yourself when you feel disrespected. For example, if a faculty member refers to you with terms such as "my dear" or "honey" and you feel disrespected by it, state your feeling politely, calmly, and firmly. A sense of humor can be helpful in getting your message across. You might say, "Only my husband is allowed to call me that" or "You know, I respond twice as fast when you call me Chris."

• If you find yourself angry about a communication from faculty you felt lacked respect, wait until you are not emotional to deal with the situation.

- Getting revenge for lack of respect through retaliatory poor performance is not a helpful strategy. If you do poor work, you diminish your contribution to the university and lose the opportunity for job satisfaction. Ultimately, you stand to be the biggest loser if you end up with a poor evaluation.

- Avoid gossiping about faculty, using derogatory nicknames for them behind their backs, imitating them, and writing memos you would not want them to see.

- Rather than seeing yourself as a victim, take responsibility for changing the situation. Become a leader in the area of respectful communications.

What should I do next? How do I follow up?

Let's conclude these three chapters with a look at what you can do to follow up your conversations with faculty. Suppose, for example, you orient a faculty member to campus policies and procedures—how do you know whether he or she has actually implemented what you explained? Take the case from the beginning of this chapter about Dr. LaSalle, who gave students pass/fail grades. After your conversation with the professor, you could sit back and wait to see if more students show up with complaints. Or you could be more proactive. In this case, that might mean following up about the grades for the students involved, for example, letting Dr. LaSalle know you will send her an email when you receive the corrected grades.

Here are some suggestions for following up with faculty:

- Confirm any agreements you make. If you make a verbal agreement with faculty, follow up by putting it in writing. And don't wait to do this. Not only does putting it in writing help both parties remember to carry out the agreement, but it can bring to light any potential misunderstandings. If you have to make changes to clarify the agreement, put those changes in writing, as well.

- Create a paper trail to document what you discuss with faculty. If anyone questions you about a detail later, you will be able to easily point to the relevant documents.

- Follow up by reminding faculty about what they said they would do. Leave them reminder notes. Send them emails. Put due dates onto an office calendar. Keep following up until the task in question has been completed.

- Some things require repeated follow up on a regular basis. For example, you may need to follow up quarterly about budget information, weekly about conference room reservations, and so on. Organize a system for handling each situation so you are prepared to put it into action whenever needed.

- Sometimes, when the occasion arises, it is nice to follow up a meeting or communication with a thank you note. There's nothing wrong with offering purely positive, unsolicited feedback!

Summary

Continuing the Partnership with Faculty

- As staff you can be involved in educating or orienting faculty to university policies and procedures.

- You can minimize resistance from faculty by refusing to butt heads, and by not taking their resistance personally. One-on-one meetings with faculty will go better if you prepare ahead.

- Avoid using gasoline words (inflammatory language) with faculty; avoid being overly personal in your interactions with faculty.

- As a staff member, it is helpful to find ways to communicate with faculty that engender respect. I list many suggestions.

10

Become Organizationally Savvy and Build Your Resources

- Inform yourself
- Identify Stakeholders
- Assemble or Create Resources
- Get Organized with Your Computer
- Develop a Network of People
- Do as Much Behind-the-Scenes Work as Possible
- Conclusion
- Summary

Details, details, details. As we saw in Chapter 2, one strength that staff tend to bring to the job is their attention to detail and ability to focus on the practical. Staff members often describe themselves as well organized and detail oriented. However, I have noticed that these strengths do not always translate automatically and productively when staff members are working with faculty. There can be a number of reasons for this. For example, the staff member may have come from another setting and be unfamiliar with the way things are organized in academia. Or the staff member may underestimate the organizational needs of faculty. In this chapter, we look at some very practical ways to boost your organizational savvy.

From the systems thinking perspective, Chapters 7, 8, and 9 focused on communication between self and other. Here, we shift to the third element: context. Just as it is important to pay attention to your relationships with faculty, I suggest you attune to the organizational context.

Inform Yourself

To begin with, to become more savvy, inform yourself about the organizational structure, roles and responsibilities, and policies and procedures that are relevant for your job. If you are fortunate, you will be able to find all or most of this information on your institution's Website. However, all the resources you need may not be available in one place. Or the information you find may be incomplete.

Here is a list of some of the types of information I think are useful to have on hand:

- Job descriptions
- Organization chart showing the chain of command (i.e., hierarchical structure)
- Official procedures, strategic objectives and standards
- Written policies
- Annual reports; vision and mission statements for your department, institute, or center
- Manuals for machinery, equipment
- A history of past projects, including their outcomes and any setbacks
- Granting agencies
- Professional organizations
- Major conferences

When Kelly began working as an administrative assistant in the English Department of a local college, she was organized and organizationally savvy and wanted to get up to speed quickly. Because her predecessor had left suddenly, no one was available to give her much of an orientation. On her first day at work, she took the initiative to search in the office files and on her computer as well as online for the relevant documents. She knew she had an immediate need, for example, for letterhead and shipping labels. She also needed information about parking. However, her search didn't turn up much that was of use.

That evening over dinner, Kelly was complaining about the state of disorganization she faced in her new job to a friend who worked in another department at the college. The friend commiserated, and then added, "Too bad you're not working in Engineering. I've heard they really have it together over there."

That gave Kelly an idea. The next morning she checked out the Engineering department's page on the campus intranet. What she found was very helpful. Someone in that department had taken the time to identify forms, external vendors, and other resources, and had posted it on the intranet. Kelly was able to download and print everything she needed. Table 10.1 shows an abbreviated list of the documents she found on the Engineering department's page.

Table 10.1 Forms and Policies

Administrative Forms:
Letterhead
Shipping labels
Computer and network usage
   compliance form
Off-campus equipment
   verification form
Personal information form
Use of personal automobiles
   for university business
Data storage transmittal
Participant parking
   permits
Reserving a room,
   facility rentals

Financial Forms:
Purchase order
Human subjects' incentive
   purchases
Lost receipt form
Petty cash reimbursement
Independent consultant or
   contractor form
Request for quotation

HR Forms:
Hourly timesheet
Employee work schedule form
Request to hire form
Temporary and casual new hire
   form
FTE change memo
Position summary form
Employee performance appraisal
   form
Overtime slip
Staff development enrollment
   form

Policies and Procedures:
University code of conduct
Confidentiality statement
Setting up a contract
Responding to legal or media
   inquiries
Purchasing card policy and
   procedures
Minors in the workplace policy
Hot weather guidelines

Travel Forms:
Mileage reimbursement form
   (auto-calculation worksheet)
Request to charge travel form
Travel expense summary
Unused ticket affidavit

Like Kelly, you may be a new staff member who needs to inform yourself in order to get organized. However, many staff who have been on the job for a while also can benefit from paying attention to and improving their information base. Here are some ways to gather the information you need:

- Attend any orientation presented by Human Resources or by a department manager.

- Take time to learn how your academic institution (really) works. Don't try to fly blind, or to operate without a clear awareness of the relevant policies. You may think you know how things work, but it is better not to go on assumptions.

- Observe how things get done. See what is effective and what is not. Use the forms and procedures that are already in place. Don't waste your time trying to reinvent the wheel.

- Learn from other departments. Resources from another department may need to be adapted for use in your department. You also may be able to borrow resources from other campuses. Most academic staff are helpful to one another and willing to share resources, although I have seen this vary across different campuses.

- Seek out or create forums in which staff can come together, discuss work, and share their resources. If you work in relative isolation, don't let that limit you. Invite a colleague for a lunchtime walk or attend a brown bag lunch. Get to know colleagues from other departments with whom you talk on the phone.

- Make sure you get the most current information and use the most up-to-date resources. Beware of out-of-date binders that may contain misleading information. Veterans in your department may be good sources of information about how things are done. Then again, these staff may not be aware of the most current policies.

Identify Stakeholders

As you are getting organized, it is important to recognize all the different people, or *stakeholders*, who are involved in different aspects of your job. These are individuals who would benefit from being kept in the loop. Sometimes you will know right away who the stakeholders are; at other times, this may be less obvious. In general, consider stakeholders who:

- Have a point of view or opinion relevant to the task
- Have resources you can use
- Have an impact on the work you do
- Are affected by decisions you make (or are implementing)
- Have a need to know for political reasons (i.e., so they do not hear the news from others or feel blindsided later)
- Need something from you

For example, when Kelly makes a list of the stakeholders who need to be involved when she prepares syllabi for the fall semester, she will include all the English department faculty who teach undergraduate students, the TAs who work with those classes, and herself. Always remember, you are one of the stakeholders! When she helps to prepare the proposal for a grant submitted jointly with the Bilingual Education department, the stakeholders she will include are herself, the English faculty member on the grant, the Bilingual faculty members, the respective research assistants, and a contact person in the Contracts office, among others.

Table 10.2 shows a sample form you can create for each project or task you work on to make sure that you identify and stay in contact with all the important stakeholders. Be sure to add columns and rows that match your particular needs. In the *Communication Catalyst*, Connolly and Rianoshek observe that if someone thinks you are not aware of or do not respect his or her purposes, concerns, and circumstances, that person will see you as a threat. Moreover, that person "will actively avoid, resist, and undermine any significant threat" (p. 16). By anticipating the stakeholders' needs and concerns, you show awareness and respect. And you take away or minimize the potential for a perceived threat. [See Table 10.2 on the following page.]

Assemble or Create Resources

In some cases, simply identifying the relevant information is sufficient to get you most of the resources you need to be organizationally savvy. For example, if you locate a form on the institution's Website, you can bookmark that form so you can download and print it every time you need it. At other times, however, you will have to spend more time clarifying your particular needs and then gathering the resources. Or you may need to create your own resources.

Table 10.2 Stakeholder Checklist

	You	Faculty	Other staff	Other departments
Goals/ purposes				
Circumstances				
Concerns				
Resources				

Here are some tips:

• Know where to go. The resources you need may be available, but you may be looking for them in the wrong place.

• Ask for mentoring. If you are new on the job, partner with a staff person who knows the ropes and can direct you to resources you might not readily find on your own.

• Create job aids for yourself.

What are job aids? A *job aid* was defined by Allison Rossett and Jeannette Gautier-Downes (1991), authors of the classic book on the topic, as "a repository for information, processes, or perspectives that is external to the individual and that supports work and activity by directing, guiding, and enlightening performance." Job aids can take the form of templates, time lines, checklists, spreadsheets, flow charts, and/or other types of charts. Job aids are tailored to your particular needs and are distinct from tools you might use. For example, a mouse, a keyboard, and a pair of scissors are tools, but they don't contain information, so they aren't considered job aids. In fact, your computer itself is a tool, as distinct from the documents (including job aids) you create using it.

Let's look more closely at some examples of useful job aids staff members have created for their use. In my workshops, many staff have appreciated learning about others' created or adapted charts, checklists, project management forms, and so on. Templates for the various forms can be downloaded from my Website: www.WorkingWith Faculty.com. You're also welcome to send me other job aid forms you have created that you would like to have available for others to download and adapt as they see fit for their use.

Checklists

The checklist is a job aid that helps you keep track of the tasks you are performing. For example, it allows you to break down the parts of the task or the items needed to perform the task.

Tables 10.3 and 10.4 show two coordinated spreadsheets Lorna Groundwater, at Stanford University School of Medicine, created to help welcome, orient, and prepare new professors who will teach and practice medicine at the university. The first serves as a checklist for Lorna's own responsibilities, and the second gives the new professor a list of his or her responsibilities. The tasks are listed in order of priority. The left-hand column is used to record a checkmark and date when the action in that row has been completed. Although these examples are abbreviated, they suggest the many tasks required for a professor to be fully credentialed, registered, and equipped to begin his or her first semester.

Table 10.3 Sample Checklist for Staff Working with a New Professor

Done	Action	Description	Location	Person info.	Contact	Misc
	Meet with faculty affairs administrator	Obtain information about new physicians	Conference room	n/a	Name, phone, email	
	Hospital privilege packet	Fill out new applicant request form	Credentialing Dept.		Name, address, phone, email	
	Obtain off-site facility privileges	Fill out hospital privileges packet forms	Risk Management office		Phone, address	
	Business cards	Need medical license #, mailing address & code, phone number, email address	Address of printing company	Contact person	Phone, fax	Pay w/ credit card

Adapted from Lorna Groundwater.

Table 10.4 Sample Checklist for a New Professor

Done	Action	Description	Location	Person	Contact Info.	Misc
	Medical license	For out-of-state doctors	California Medical Bd		Website	
	Finger-prints	Taken by XYZ, to Dept. of Justice	Local police station or Dept. of Public Safety		Phone, make appointment online	Office hours
	Obtain I.D. #		HR		Phone, email	
	Obtain SUNet ID	Need employee ID No.	HR cluster		Phone, email	
	Set up email address	Eudora or Outlook	IT		Phone, email	
	Check Website for your personal info	Indicate if you want it on public or private view	Website		Phone, email	
	Access to Last Word med. records, IDX, Linx	Clinic manager(s) To fill out and sign necessary forms	Clinic	Clinic manager	Phone, email	
	HIPA	FAA will sign you up for level required	Faculty affairs admin		Phone, email	
	Phone, copier codes		Facilities manager	Facilities manager	Phone, email	
	Access to pay information	Website link to pay information	HR		University Website	
	Parking	Parking stickers	Parking services		Website	
	Community academic profile (CAP)	Update profile in CAP on a regular basis	Website	You or AA, if given authority	Website	

Adapted from Lorna Groundwater.

How could you apply or adapt these examples to your situation to help you clarify procedures and communicate more effectively with faculty?

Time Lines

The focus of a time line, not surprisingly, is on the timing of tasks. That information can be built into a checklist, like the ones in Tables 10.3 and 10.4, or it can be a simple list. Alternatively, a time line can be presented using a graphic format. Bettyann Hinchman, event coordinator at the University of San Francisco School of Law, created the time line in Table 10.5 to help her organize when she was working with a professor to plan a conference. Because the sample time line is so long and detailed, I have abbreviated the number of items and sections here. The actual time line breaks down activities for additional time intervals (e.g., 4 months, 3 months, day before, day of).

Table 10.5 Sample Sections from a Time Line

5 months out	1 month out
• Meeting to discuss preliminary plans and responsibilities	• Draft of program
• Determine date options, length of event (½ day, 1 day, 2 days)	• Reservations start coming
	• Follow-up with speakers, confirm travel plans and accommodations
• Reserve event space	• Submit ad info for release
• Discuss funding sources, fundraising opportunities, registration fees	• Confirm with publications all material received
• Initial speaker contact	• Finalize and confirm all logistical plans
• Reserve date with caterer	• Recruit volunteer staff
• Initial meeting with Publications to discuss marketing materials and their time line	• Meet with caterer; discuss floor plan, time line, menu
• Schedule additional meetings	• Contact all vendors to confirm requests

Final 2 weeks

• Finish program, send to printer
• Start compiling firm numbers for attendance
• Run through with IT and video people
• Prepare all materials
• Final confirmation with all vendors
• Develop time line for "day of"

Adapted from Bettyann Hinchman

Significant Events Log

A significant events log is a job aid sometimes used by police to track criminal activities, by doctors to track medical status, and by professionals in other settings to track events of special importance to the work at hand. You can use this kind of log to keep track of important events in the office. It is similar to a time line or the spreadsheets discussed in the previous sections, but shorter. Whereas a time line focuses on the dates and details, a significant events log focuses on the most important upcoming events. Linda, a secretary in the Mathematics Department, created the significant event log in Table 10.6 at the beginning of each month to keep track of the major events for that month.

Table 10.6 Sample Significant Events Log
(week of Oct. 28—sixth week of first semester)

1. Faculty meeting (when, where, what time, attach a tentative agenda)
2. Necessary training (name of training, who to contact, deadline)
3. Visiting faculty talks (name of the talk, where and what time, attach CV)
4. Other mandatory meetings (where and what time)
5. Graduate student interviews (where and what time)
6. Other department events (where and what time)

Linda sent emails and hard copies of the significant event log to each faculty and each staff member involved. She also posted a copy on the bulletin board by the front door of the department office. Over time, faculty, staff, and graduate students learned to inform Linda about upcoming events to add to the events log. Information that might be listed include deadlines for papers to be submitted for a major professional conference, holidays, birthdays, and personnel data (e.g., who will be on vacation). I have enjoyed watching workshop participants learn from one another and adapt these ideas to their department's needs and culture.

Color Coding

If you are juggling multiple tasks, consider creating a spreadsheet like the one in Table 10.7, in which the various tasks are color coded so you can more easily keep track of them. You can color code by type of task, by individual faculty member, or by any other meaningful category. Lorna Groundwater created this list with different color codes for each faculty member. She used corresponding colored email flags

Table 10.7 Sample Color Coded Spreadsheet

Assigned	Description	Completed
3/07/10	Finish editing XYZ Letter of Intent, get approval, create CD, make copies & Fed-Ex to Maryland. Make copies for PI, co-PI, file, and create file. E-mail PI and co-PI	3/07/10
3/07/10	Finish making edits to proofs for XYZ manuscript and e-mail to journal and co-authors	3/07/10
3/07/10	Find faculty appointment letter from April 1990 for XYZ	3/08/10
2/10/10	Proof-read, edit, complete, and submit promotion packet XYZ	3/08/10
3/09/10	Posted directions on how to make conference calls in Ob/Gyn conference room.	3/09/10
3/09/10	Sent University policy regarding pharm/industry reps to XYZ	3/09/10
3/09/10	Update medical staff profiles for Department and Division web sites	
3/05/10	Find migraine specialists XYZ. Contacted XYZ. Got names and faxed to XYZ	3/09/10
3/12/10	Find director of XYZ program and director of Communications and Public Affairs for XYZ	3/12/10
3/12/10	Scan graphs for XYZ's talk	3/12/10
3/12/10	Draft letter of sympathy to XYZ for ABC – get sympathy card and distribute it	3/19/10
3/12/10	Scan author's pages for AJOG for XYZ	3/12/10
3/13/10	Edit Osteoporosis slides	3/13/10
3/15/10	Contacted Printer about final proofs for XYZ 's cards	3/21/10
3/15/10	Fed-Ex package XYZ and Fed-Ex letter for ABC	3/15/10
3/21/10	Contact Printer about final proofs for XYZ 's cards	3/21/10
3/21/10	Review grant application for XYZ: "Title"	3/21/10
3/21/10	Three Fed-Ex packages for XYZ	3/21/10
3/21/10	Revise directions to all Administrative Offices, library and conference rooms	4/16/10
3/21/10	Faxed final approval to Printer re: XYZ's cards	3/21/10
3/28/10	Edit XYZ abstract	3/28/10
3/28/10	Edit XYZ paper	3/30/10
4/05/10	Edited and e-mailed edits to XYZ 's paper for submission	4/05/10
4/09/10	Completed and faxed/e-mailed Award application for XYZ	4/10/10

Adapted from Lorna Groundwater.

to code faculty emails so she could track their work. She grayed out tasks that were already completed so the other items would stand out more boldly.

Note that, although the sample in Table 10.7 uses shades of grey due to publishing constraints (and therefore is not so easy to read), you can use all the bright colors you want. The brighter the better!

Get Organized with Your Computer

These days, computers play a large role in how we organize around many job-related tasks. If you are using job aids such as those I just described, chances are you created them on your computer. However, depending on how you use it, your computer can be either a help or a hindrance in getting organized. To make the best use of it, I suggest developing some good habits in the way you work with your computer.

Here are some things to keep in mind:

- Keep manuals on hand for critical software. Even if the manuals exist online, hard copies can be a lifesaver when problems arise and you are unable to access them.

- Keep all passwords in a secure but accessible location (in hard copy).

- Always keep back-ups for all your important files. Back up documents frequently. Even if your institution performs this function for you automatically, you may find it helpful to create your own local back-ups. This way you don't need to depend on (or wait for) others to retrieve lost files for you.

- Pay attention to file names. Create names that will inform you about what is in the file and also indicate the last date the file was changed. Use underscores (_) rather than dots (.) in file names (except for .doc).

- Use some form of version control for your documents. Never work on more than one copy of a version at the same time!

- Develop a dependable system of file sharing so you can pass documents back and forth with faculty. You can create a shared folder on the network that is specifically for works in progress. Keep track of versions so you only have one "live" file and everyone knows what it is.

- Create a system of folders to store all your documents, or use a document management system. Organize files in nested folders, rather than keeping all files at the top level.

• Don't leave documents on your desktop; one of the main reasons computers (PC or Mac) run sluggishly is a cluttered desktop.

• Keep all open containers of liquid as far away as possible from your keyboard. One spill is all it takes to kill a keyboard.

I recommend Eve Abbott's *A Brain New Way to Work* (2009). Her book is designed to help people in the workplace take advantage of new insights into brain function and apply them toward stress reduction and improved efficiency and organization. Her article with more tips for organizing your computer is on my Website, www.WorkingWithFaculty.com.

Keep in mind, too, that you are likely to be more tech savvy than many of the faculty with whom you work. Become acquainted with each faculty member's level of expertise. If you see faculty floundering because of computer-related challenges, be prepared to step in and help or call in IT personnel who can resolve the issue.

Develop a Network of People

So far we have talked about organizing your work with faculty mostly in terms of job aids and other non-personnel resources you can assemble or create. But people can also be among your best resources. I suggest you network with people, including staff and others, who can help with different aspects of your job. If someone within the organization did your job before, he or she can be your prime support.

Information. Use networking to broaden your sources of information about how the organization really works. Get to know people in other departments with whom you can consult when you are not sure how something should be done. These may be staff members in other departments who are engaged in similar tasks. For example, someone in another department who is submitting proposals to the same granting agency might have useful information about working with that agency. You also can network with staff members who have complimentary responsibilities within the institution. For example, someone in the human resources department who processes the applications for staff positions in your department may be able to provide useful information about hiring and firing procedures.

Collegiality and mutual support. Several years ago I gave a presentation to a large group of university managers during which we were talking about the kinds of supportive relationships they needed. They identified three supportive relationships they felt all staff members need in the complex academic work environment.

1. They need the support of someone who is more skilled and savvy at their particular area of expertise (e.g., accounting, management, personnel issues, program coordination) than they are.

2. They need another person who understands the ins and outs of the university system and politics, and who can help them manage their career so they get the promotions and kinds of positions that fit their talents and goals.

3. They need a third person who can support them in a personal manner when they are overwhelmed, discouraged, or upset. This is a trusted ally who knows them well and who can remind them of their strengths and be there for them when they are vulnerable and emotional. This person does not necessarily have to work at the same institution.

You can find and build this three-person support system for yourself—on your own or with the help of more knowledgeable people.

In addition, some campuses have formal structures that allow staff members to get together and share experiences and resources or to meet periodically for staff development. One university I know has a robust organization for staff managers across campus, with monthly meetings, staff trainings and retreats, a mentoring program, and luncheons. These activities play a major role in the cohesiveness and resourcefulness of staff in this high-profile university.

On other campuses, formal structures have been developed at the departmental level. For example, one Engineering Department where I gave a workshop had an organized staff group. Some of the staff in other departments didn't know it existed, or even that it was possible to form such a group. After our workshop, they planned to convene similar groups in their departments.

I have found that discussion among staff from different departments and schools affirms the importance of staff roles, reveals similarities in their experiences, and provides new ways to handle common logistical and communication issues with faculty. Staff who have met one another during one of my workshops often continue to get together, share resources, and support one another.

Consider initiating a staff support group on your campus. Keep in mind that this kind of discussion or problem-solving forum needs a sponsor or champion to keep it going. Perhaps you can be that person for a group at your college or university.

Help with complex tasks. Projects that involve many complex tasks can be a challenge, especially if you don't have strong relationships with those involved in different aspects of the project. Through networking, you build connections that can help in big and small ways when you need them. It may be as simple as someone returning your phone call more quickly because he or she knows you personally.

The opportunity to exchange favors. Form mutually supportive relationships. Have you ever wanted to ask someone for a favor, but felt you couldn't comfortably do so because you didn't know one another well enough? The solution is to build relationships ahead of time. Then, when either of you has a need, you won't hesitate to ask for help, knowing the favor will be returned at a later date.

Stephen Covey and his coauthors (1994) suggest we think in terms of a metaphorical emotional bank account to manage our interdependence with others. With it, we get credit for favors done to others and debits for favors received from them. How is your balance? Are you the generous one with your emotional bank account? It is beneficial in many ways to be the "go-to" person for resources and advice. What goes around comes around.

Emotional support. Develop a supportive network of co-workers as well as personal friends who can help you be effective on the job and give you emotional support when you need it. Do not expect to get your emotional needs for approval and appreciation met in your relationships with faculty. That level of support may be available, but do not rely on it.

The network relationships you develop can cover a wide range of styles and types. Some will involve people with whom you interact frequently and get to know personally. Others may be with people, either inside or outside the institution, you choose to network with because faculty interact with them, and therefore relating to them allows you to better help faculty with logistics and communication. In the latter case, your interactions may be more infrequent and formal. Here are some of the activities that foster networking:

- Volunteer for committees or task forces
- Go to staff trainings

- Attend lectures and workshops

- Participate in brown bag lunch series

- Carpool

- Share exercise workouts or a lunchtime walk

- Share kayaking, hiking, theater, or a ballgame

- Tune in to faculty's professional organizations, granting agencies, etc.

- When meeting other staff or faculty members socially or incidentally (e.g., when picking up your daughter at a birthday party), introduce yourself and say how you might support their work. You may want to follow up with an email.

- Keep a database (i.e., a contact management system) with notes detailing what you learn about individuals so you can remember relevant details about their life and work.

- Send a note of congratulations or acknowledgment when colleagues on campus receive recognition for their accomplishments.

- Send articles or links to colleagues about information that may be relevant to their work or appeal to their interests.

Do as Much Behind-the-Scenes Work as Possible

Most of the strategies we have discussed in this chapter involve doing work behind the scenes or in advance of interacting with faculty. This is the nature of getting organized. When you are organized, you are able to anticipate faculty needs and address them in a timely manner. You are able to simultaneously focus on the big picture and the details. When you organize, plan, and prioritize behind the scenes, you are better able to juggle multiple requests and address urgent, chronic, and recurring problems.

One important tool for organizing behind the scenes is time management. In essence, this means making the most effective use of the time you have to accomplish your work.

Do you recognize yourself in any of the following scenarios?

- Many people come to your cubicle to ask for directions to the Bursar's office. You are aware there are no signs for the Bursar's office at the front of the building or on the list near the elevator.

This easily could be changed, but no one has taken the initiative to suggest a solution to the right people.

• You're booked with meetings through lunch four days this week. A colleague invites you to lunch on the fifth day. You say to yourself, "I just can't keep up this pace."

• A faculty member stops to give you yet another progress report on his charming two-year-old's antics the night before. You're feeling rushed with a report that is due by noon. He seems to have lots of time to chat. You don't.

• You are talking with a colleague in the hall. You think, "I don't have time for this." Later you can't remember what you talked about.

If you see yourself in any of these scenarios, chances are you have some of the symptoms of poor time management: impatience, stress, frustration, overload, fatigue, forgetfulness, among others. Entire books have been written about time management, so I won't try to cover everything here. However, the following tips can help you better organize your time:

• Begin by observing how you use your time. Discover where you tend to waste time and then change your habits accordingly. Identify and eliminate your regular intrusions and distractions whenever possible.

• Set time limits for tasks. For example, spend a set amount of time responding to emails at the beginning of the day. Don't allow that time to flow over. Don't feel obligated to answer every email the second it arrives. You may want to disable the sound that announces an arriving email.

• Create to-do lists. Use a daily planner, either an electronic one or a notebook.

• Write down appointments immediately upon making them. At the beginning of the academic year, log in every standing meeting and appointment through the end of the semester or year. Use only one scheduling system to avoid double booking.

• Leave a window of five to fifteen minutes between meetings so you can clear your head, review the main points of the agenda for the next meeting, and get from one location to the next.

• Take breaks when you need them. Go outside, get some fresh air.

You may feel tempted to try to push through on a complex task. However, taking a needed break may end up saving you time in the long run.

- Determine when during the day it is most effective to do particular tasks. Does it make more sense to answer emails first thing in the day? If you tend to feel sleepy in midafternoon, maybe that is not the best time to work on the budget. Pay attention to the impact of circadian rhythms on your body. Eve Abbott (2009) studied the best times of day for different work functions. Memory works best in the morning. Our mental speed and accuracy in mathematics and cognitive projects peak in early afternoon. Mechanical skills work best in the afternoon.

- Instead of procrastinating, break large tasks down into smaller tasks. Tackle them one at a time to avoid the sense of overwhelm that can come from facing a large and complex project.

- Reevaluate your time lines on a regular basis. Be open and flexible about changing them.

- Avoid asking people to stop what they are doing and respond to your urgent needs.

- Ask yourself, "Is this truly urgent now?" Let go of any sense of intensity or drama you have around urgency.

- Practice tolerance, especially with people who think or move more slowly than you do. They may have a different work style, yet be just as effective as you are. Allow them to go at their own pace.

- Block out open, unstructured time in your calendar. Protect it!

- Change your voice mail every day to include your schedule and information about when you are likely to be most available.

- Plan for a healthy breakfast and lunch. Don't skip meals. Keep a supply of energy bars and instant soup to perk you up when needed. Reduce caffeine and sugar, which contribute to sensations of physical stress.

- When you have to wait for something, make good use of that time. For example, proofread that report while you are waiting for your next appointment to show up.

- Don't take on unnecessary or unessential work, either because someone tries to pawn it off on you or because you feel tempted for one reason or another to do it.

* Prioritize, prioritize, prioritize.

Conclusion

With this chapter, we conclude our section on practices and strategies for working with faculty. Throughout the section, we considered how to apply the systems thinking approach of self-other-context in a variety of practical ways in the academic setting. In Chapter 6, we looked at the relationship between self and other as it manifests through the communications staff have with faculty. We identified basic skills staff can use when talking with faculty. Chapters 7, 8, and 9 got practical as we reviewed answers to questions staff frequently raise about their relationship and communications with faculty. Finally, in this chapter, we shifted to the aspect of context and looked at what it means to be organizationally savvy in academia.

In the next section, I invite you to meet the faculty in some new ways. We'll look at how faculty react under stress and at some types of faculty you may find especially difficult to encounter in your work.

[See Summary—Become Organizationally Savvy and Build Resources on the following page.]

Summary

Become Organizationally Savvy and Build Your Resources

- Your know-how improves when you inform yourself about the organizational structure, roles and responsibilities, and policies and procedures that are relevant for your job.

- Recognize all the stakeholders involved in different aspects of your job and consider their concerns and needs.

- Identify resources you need for your job; partner with a staff person who knows the ropes and can mentor you; develop a network of people across campus who can provide information and mutual support.

- Find, create, or adapt job aids (e.g., checklists, time lines, project management tools, event logs) for yourself; use your computer efficiently.

- Anticipate faculty needs and address them in a timely manner; do as much behind-the-scenes work as possible.

SECTION IV

Dealing with Individual Faculty Members and Their Stresses

11. Faculty Stress Reactions and
    What You Can Do   179

12. Strategies for Working Skillfully
    with Difficult Faculty   197

www.WorkingWithFaculty.com

11

Faculty Stress Reactions and What You Can Do

- The Toughest Part of the Job
- The Faculty Stress Cycle
- Faculty Stressors
- Faculty Perceptions
- Faculty Stress Reactions
- Consequences
- An Ah-Ha! Moment
- What You Can Do
- Conclusion
- Summary

Recently, while leading a workshop with staff in the university setting, I asked the participants to brainstorm and list the opportunities and challenges they had experienced in their work with faculty. Then I stood back and observed as they made their lists and shared in pairs with other staff members. I noticed the challenge lists were growing much longer than the opportunities lists. And I couldn't help but be aware of the sudden atmosphere of gloom and doom in the room. So I took the microphone.

I said to the group, "I can see this exercise is bringing up powerful memories for you. It's bringing up pain and resentments you might not have realized you were harboring. When painful interactions remain unresolved, they create unfinished emotional business that can have a big effect on our mood. In fact, according to psychologist John Gottman (2000), negative interactions in a relationship carry five times the impact of positive ones. It may be helpful during our workshop today to notice how you're feeling, to see the similar reactions others are having, and to look for better ways to handle these challenges."

When I said this, the whole room relaxed. The staff appreciated that their stress had been recognized. They were able to go on and complete the exercise in an even more productive manner.

We will discuss the issue of staff stress, and how to take care of yourself in general, in the final section of this book. In this chapter, I'd like to look first at the other side of the equation—that is, what triggers stress for faculty, how they typically react to stress, and how staff can deal with their frustration and anger in order to restore harmony in the office.

The Toughest Part of the Job

Often staff tell me that their task-related responsibilities aren't the toughest part of their job. They experience their greatest challenge when things go sour while relating to faculty. Most of the faculty are easy to work with most of the time, they say, but occasionally they hit a bump. And when they do, staff may not know what to do to repair the situation.

Here's an example.

I'd like you to meet Jeff. He's a secretary in the Psychology Department. He recently took this job because he majored in psychology and he's hoping to go back to school someday, get an advanced degree, and work as a clinical psychologist. In the meantime, he figures he can learn a bit here and there as he answers phones, types or edits correspondence, and does other routine office tasks.

Monday morning of his second week at work, Jeff encounters heavy traffic and is fifteen minutes late to the office. He starts to apologize to Dr. Dixon, but the professor cuts him off, saying, "Taking another fifteen minutes to explain won't make you on time."

Jeff sits down at his desk in a state of shock. What did I do to deserve this sarcasm? he asks himself.

He quickly reviews his first week at work. He was on time every day. Sure, he's been late plenty of times in his life. Sometimes his wife gets on him about it. But Dr. Dixon knows nothing about that.

Anger starts to boil inside Jeff. These professors are psychologists, he fumes to himself. And this is how they relate to people? What does Dr. Dixon do, just listen empathetically when he's the therapist in a therapy session and then act like his normal self with everyone else?

In the heat of the moment, Jeff completely forgets that Dr. Dixon took him to the Student Center for a cup of coffee on his first day at work and chatted with him for half an hour. Now all Jeff can think about is the sarcastic remark he should zing back at the professor—knowing all the while that of course he won't because it's not worth risking his job.

In the end, he settles for making an ugly little doodle on the margin of his notepad and says to himself, "I guess I'm not going to learn what I hoped I might from these psychologists. I'd better concentrate on managing my own stress levels so I can survive this job."

The Faculty Stress Cycle

I've noticed that staff—like Jeff—sometimes make the assumption faculty members do not experience a particularly significant amount of stress due to their jobs. Faculty, they reason, are in positions of power within the university or college, and such positions are unlikely to give rise to undue stress. Or if they think faculty do feel stressed, staff assume that stress will be essentially cancelled out by all the various perks that come with being faculty.

Nevertheless, stress is an important aspect of the faculty experience. And internal stress on the part of faculty can lead to a variety of behaviors that are challenging to you as staff in your work with faculty. You may not always immediately recognize the true source of faculty's challenging behaviors. However, I think it helps to begin by understanding what Walter Gmelch (1993) terms the *faculty stress cycle*. Although this model applies to everyone, not just faculty, Gmelch has conducted extensive research with faculty to find out what stresses them most. His book, *Coping with Faculty Stress (Survival Skills for Scholars)*, is a classic in the field and was written to help faculty learn to overcome stress.

Gmelch describes four stages that make up the faculty stress cycle (Table 11.1). Technically, it's not a cycle in the sense that stage 4 does not automatically lead back to stage 1. The first stage Gmelch refers to as faculty stressors. In this stage, stressors are present or implicit in the environment as events or expectations of the faculty member, whether or not he or she actually feels stressed by them. The second stage focuses on the faculty member's perception. In stage 3, a stress response takes place. This can involve internal thoughts and feelings, an internal struggle for control, or outward behavior. Finally, in stage 4, the faculty member experiences the short-term and long-term consequences of this stress response.

Table 11.1 The Stages of Faculty Stress

Stage
1. Stressors
2. Perceptions
3. Responses (internal and external)
4. Consequences

Adapted from W. Gmelch, 1993, 16.

Gmelch assumes faculty must learn to cope with these stages of stress on their own, and provides many helpful suggestions for doing so, including better understanding their personality and how it influences their reactions to stress, and balancing the demands of their personal and professional lives. I'd like to add that, while faculty can address their own issues, staff also can play a helpful role. Let's look at how best to do this by examining the process one stage at a time.

Faculty Stressors

Different things have the power to trigger stress in different people, including in faculty members. For example, for an introverted professor of economics, being asked at the last minute to moderate a panel of politicians who get emotional, interrupt one another, and try to hog the microphone could constitute a stressor. On the other hand, consider an extraverted junior faculty member working on a large research project directed by a full professor who communicates almost exclusively by email. For this junior professor, being expected to work independently, without personal contact, could be a stressor. In each of these cases, stress is the result of how the individual perceives the demands placed upon him or her by others and/or by self. The various demands, or situations—the stressors—are not necessarily inherently stressful.

Researchers have investigated the factors most likely to trigger stress for faculty in general. Gmelch's Faculty Stress Index (FSI) comprises 45 items derived from a national study involving faculty from 100 institutions and has been used to evaluate faculty stress in a variety of settings. Faculty take the assessment by rating each of the items according to how much stress they feel it generates for them. Of the 45 items in the FSI, Gmelch identified what he calls the top ten most common faculty stressors (Table 11.2).

Table 11.2 Top Ten Faculty Stressors

Stressors
1. Overly high self-expectations
2. Need for financial support for scholarship
3. Not enough time to keep up with developments in the field
4. Insufficient salary
5. Pressure to publish
6. Too heavy a workload
7. Job demands interfering with personal life
8. Slow career advancement
9. Interruptions (e.g., telephone, visitors)
10. Too many meetings

Adapted from W. Gmelch, 1993, 16.

Because Gmelch conducted his research in the 1980s, I phoned him to ask if he had more recent data. Although he hasn't formally updated his study, he told me he believes the sources of stress have not changed in a significant way (with the probable exception of new technology).

In his original research, Gmelch found that the stressors for specific faculty groups differed from those listed in Table 11.2 for faculty in general. For example, faculty whose first priority is teaching did not include "pressure to publish" among their top five stressors. Department chairs reported the same stressors as did other faculty, with the addition of "establishing compatibility among institutional, departmental and personal goals"; "completing paperwork on time"; "attending meetings"; and "dealing with university rules and regulations."

Gmelch further groups the various faculty stressors listed in the FSI into five major types of stressors for faculty. I have listed them here, along with my own comments and observations. I've added a sixth category to modernize the list.

Reward and recognition. Faculty worry their accomplishments won't receive adequate recognition, either from colleagues on campus or from the broader, international community of scholars. They know that without a sufficiently impressive resume of accomplishments, their chances for promotion are not good. This source of stress is less relevant for non-tenure-track faculty.

Time constraints. Faculty need time and quiet space to pursue their academic work. When they are trying to concentrate on the tasks that are most important to them, they can feel distracted or invaded by what they perceive to be administrative trivia. Faculty may perceive staff as a source of stress, to the extent that they see staff as pressuring them to take time to do administrative tasks.

The combination of teaching, research, and administrative responsibilities faculty face can feel like an unduly heavy workload. They may feel beyond swamped and complain they don't have enough time to keep abreast of research in their fields. Other faculty may resent courses that require them to spend more time on preparation than they anticipated, or classes with high enrollments or with many needy or demanding students.

Departmental influence. Often administrative decisions are made by department chairs or deans who are themselves faculty members. To other faculty, however, this administrative function may be seen as a complication, as unnecessary or poorly conceived rules and procedures that get in their way. They may feel constrained within the academic hierarchy from voicing their opinions and may view staff as representing the administration. Departmental politics can turn the academic environment into a virtual minefield of stressors.

Professional identity. Faculty tend to have high self-expectations when it comes to meeting their career goals. Thus, some of their stress around professional identity is internally generated. In addition, stress can arise as they interact with others in ways they perceive as threatening to their professional identity. For example, many faculty do not like to admit they don't know something, even if it is not within their area of expertise (e.g., setting up a conference or managing a large project that involves several people). They especially don't like to feel they are powerless or that their credentials are being impugned in some way. Because they identify strongly with their work, they may take any criticism personally and feel threatened.

Student interaction. Faculty can encounter stressful conflicts with students in the context of advising and grading. Although faculty are in the power position vis-à-vis their students, the personal intensity of these interactions can be stressful to them as well as to the students. In particular, because faculty relate to others (i.e., students, staff, and faculty) from within an intellectual comfort zone, dealing with strong emotions (theirs or others) can be stressful. Faculty may find it stressful to work with students who have learning disabilities or attention-deficit disorder, or are not motivated to learn. This is especially true if these conditions fall outside the faculty member's area of expertise.

Although Gmelch did not find interpersonal tensions and conflict between faculty and staff to be among the top stressors for faculty, I think these dynamics are also important for staff to consider.

New technology. As I mentioned, technology most likely would appear on Gmelch's list today. Some faculty, especially older ones, are not familiar with the mechanics of using new software, databases, online courses, and computer-assisted instruction. They can find themselves easily stressed when required to function in this arena without adequate technical support.

Faculty Perceptions

In the second stage of the stress cycle, the faculty member becomes aware he or she does not have the inner and outer resources to meet the demands implied by a particular stressor or combination of stressors. This creates what Gmelch calls a *stress trap*. The individual is trapped between the demands and the lack of resources to meet those demands, unable to "get out." The only way to escape the trap at this point is to perceive the situation that is triggering stress in a different way. If this doesn't happen, the faculty member is likely to experience a stress response.

Faculty Stress Reactions

Initial Reaction

At times, the initial response—by faculty or anyone else—to a stress trap is to go into an inner state of overwhelm. I'm sure you're familiar with what that feels like. We all experience it at some time or other. Faculty's overwhelm can be characterized as follows:

- Feeling disorganized, disoriented, confused
- Either flooded with feeling or feeling nothing
- Either caught up in frantic activity or paralyzed

In addition, faculty may have the following initial emotional reactions:

- Angry
- Feeling out of control, helpless
- Afraid, anxious
- Inadequate
- Ashamed
- Guilty
- Frustrated, blocked
- Disappointed

You cannot count on a faculty member caught up in emotions at this stage to communicate them directly to you. He or she may feel too vulnerable, or the feelings may not be at the level of conscious awareness. If they are not emotionally expressive in normal situations, faculty may become even less expressive under stress. If they are adept at hiding their reactions, it may not be obvious to you that they are struggling with inner control. However, other faculty—even those who are usually rational and unemotional—may have unexpected outbursts of emotion when their stress level becomes intense. Like a dam bursting, their emotions come spewing out—at you or anyone else who's around.

If faculty are sufficiently stressed, their reaction may manifest in visible behavior. They may:

- Refuse to listen to you or to comply with policies and procedures
- Make personal insults, be abrasive
- Be demanding; make unrealistic requests with inadequate information for you to respond appropriately

- Fail to respond to your requests or give you vague answers
- Be easily distracted or engage in repetitive tasks, rather than move ahead with a major project
- Be disorganized, or more disorganized than usual
- Make threats, use intimidation (verbal or nonverbal), humiliate
- Make sarcastic jokes, tease
- Send withering emails
- Interrupt you when you are obviously busy
- Give dirty looks
- Treat others as if they were invisible
- Go behind your back if they don't get what they want from you

By learning to recognize these signs and symptoms of stress, as well as the patterns of faculty with whom you work, you may be able to avoid triggering additional stress and help them lessen or deal with their stress.

Coping

Often faculty are able to cope comfortably with a single stressor or one that is relatively mild. They may be able to distract themselves or find ways to perceive the situation so they don't become overwhelmed. For example, they may tell themselves, "This is time limited," or I'm disappointed I didn't get that promotion, but I've got a really excellent shot at it next year." However, when faculty are hit by more serious stressors or multiple stressors all at once, like everyone else, they may not cope as well.

Consider Dr. Friess. He has to grade exams the same week the final report for his main research project is due. Having faced this situation before, he copes by telling himself, "If I need to, I'll file for an extension and finish the report when exams are over." But then he finds out that asking for an extension on this report could jeopardize funding for another project he's seeking from the same federal agency. He is angry no one told him about this before. In fact, rightly or wrongly, he regards this as your responsibility as his project manager. Nevertheless, Dr. Friess considers it unprofessional to reveal his anger, so throughout his conversation with you he manages to suppress his feelings. Even though his level of stress has increased, he still is able to rely on his coping mechanisms.

In the end, Dr. Friess misses the deadline for his report. The future of his research is in danger, and he becomes overtly anxious. He is no longer able to cope with the intense pressure he feels and becomes demanding, makes unrealistic requests, and exhibits some of the other behaviors described in the previous section.

These types of behaviors can be extremely challenging if you encounter them in your work with faculty. And if you haven't encountered them, you may be shocked to learn that some of these behaviors are tolerated in the academic setting. Unfortunately, it's true. Don't take my word for it. As Stanford professor Robert Sutton has written, "Leadership research shows that subtle nasty moves like glaring and condescending comments, explicit moves like insults or put-downs, and even physical intimidation can be effective paths to power."

After I finish discussing the stages of the stress cycle, I will offer my suggestions for dealing with these behaviors.

Consequences

The final stage described by Gmelch is that of consequences. As we know, all our behaviors have consequences. In the case of stressed faculty, there can be many, both positive and negative, consequences including:

- Getting what they want as the result of their demands or manipulation
- Feeling powerful because others placate them or are intimidated
- Feeling embarrassed
- Justifying their behavior by attributing the cause of their reaction to the situation or other people (e.g., "She should have known what to do").
- Harming their relationships with others (e.g., causing others to avoid them).
- Damaging the self-confidence and self-esteem of staff, students, and others.

An Ah-Ha! Moment

In the workshop exercise, I begin by asking staff to list the behaviors they observe in faculty that they find most challenging. They typically write down things such as "demand," "act condescending," "expect you to read their minds," and "insult." In other words, their lists resemble the list of external reactions by faculty I cited earlier in this chapter. Then I ask staff to create a list describing how they imagine the faculty who exhibited these behaviors were feeling at the time. In this case, their lists look like the list of internal reactions I gave earlier in this chapter (e.g., out of control, afraid, anxious, inadequate).

Finally, I ask staff to make a list of their own feelings while interacting with these faculty members in challenging situations. As it turns out, this third list almost always includes the same feelings as the previous list: out of control, afraid, anxious, inadequate, and so on.

At this point, staff compare their lists and discover that the feelings they attribute to faculty and the feelings they have themselves are very similar. An important emotional commonality is revealed, and this leads to a big ah-ha! moment.

As we discuss this further, staff realize that when they see faculty being unreasonable or making demands, they need to look a bit deeper. Because underneath that unreasonable or demanding behavior lies a very human vulnerability. And that vulnerability is not so different from their own set of feelings when dealing with difficult faculty behavior.

So, I tell staff, the key is to avoid reacting the way some faculty do—the way they find particularly challenging. Even if faculty are struggling to gain a clear perspective in stressful situations, staff can rise to the occasion, maintain calm and perspective, and "be the bigger person."

What You Can Do

Yes, you can help faculty alleviate their stress, and you also may be able to help them prevent future stress. Here I offer ten practical strategies. See which ones you find most appropriate for your situation, both in terms of your staff role and of the needs of the stressed faculty members with whom you work.

Self-Assess

Before you work with the strategies, you may find it helpful to take the following self-assessment. Table 11.3 is adapted from Rebecca Morgan's (2002) book, *Calming Upset Customers*. Rather than total your scores, it may be more helpful to take note of which items need your attention and how you can apply them to your work.

[See Table 11.3 on the following page.]

Table 11.3 Self-Assessment: How Well Do You Serve Upset Faculty?

	Key: 1 = Never 2 = Rarely 3 = Sometimes 4 = Usually 5 = Always
	Never ... Always
A. I feel I can calm most upset faculty	1 2 3 4 5
B. When I'm with an upset faculty, I	
1. stay calm	1 2 3 4 5
2. don't interrupt	1 2 3 4 5
3. focus on his/her concern without getting distracted.	1 2 3 4 5
4. respond to personal accusations without getting defensive	1 2 3 4 5
5. have attentive body posture	1 2 3 4 5
6. have appropriate facial expressions	1 2 3 4 5
7. have confidence eye contact	1 2 3 4 5
8. listen completely before responding	1 2 3 4 5
9. show empathy	1 2 3 4 5
10. support other people's goals and ambitions	1 2 3 4 5
11. have a confident/helpful tone of voice	1 2 3 4 5
12. use words that don't inflame his/her anger	1 2 3 4 5
13. avoid blaming my fellow workers or another department for causing the problem	1 2 3 4 5
14. avoid distractions of paperwork and telephone	1 2 3 4 5
15. take notes when appropriate	1 2 3 4 5
16. know when to call my supervisor to help	1 2 3 4 5
C. After meeting with the upset faculty, I	
1. am in control of my emotions	1 2 3 4 5
2. don't repeat the story more than once	1 2 3 4 5
3. analyze what I did well and what I'd do differently	1 2 3 4 5
Which areas need your attention?	

Adapted from Rebecca Morgan

Strategies for Dealing with Stressed Faculty

The following strategies are not listed in sequential order. I suggest you become familiar with all of them and decide what will be most effective for each situation. In general, if faculty members are flooded with feeling, they won't respond if you try to move to problem solving too fast. You need to acknowledge their feelings first. When they feel heard and understood at an emotional level, they will be more ready to take on the rational aspects of the problem at hand.

- **Don't react.** The most important thing to keep in mind when working with faculty who are in the middle of a stress reaction is not to react! Instead of falling into the stress trap yourself, stop and do the following:

    - Take a deep breath. Slow down.
    - Identify the challenging faculty behavior, assess the situation.
    - Recognize the faculty member's underlying feelings that motivate the behavior.
    - Respond to his or her inner feelings rather than to his or her behavior.

- **Show that you understand their point of view.** Listen to faculty who are feeling stressed. Lend an ear and let them tell you whatever they feel comfortable disclosing about the situation. Respond in a way that conveys you have heard and accepted their feelings. As we discussed in Chapter 7, showing faculty you understand them can go a long way toward improving communication; it also can help lower stress levels.

    You may feel tempted to judge faculty members based on the behaviors they exhibit while under stress. This may be a natural reaction, especially if you think you would react differently to the same set of stressors. However, such judgments only exacerbate the situation. Instead of judging, take the time to step into the shoes of a faculty member and learn how he or she views the situation.

- **Help reinforce their inner equilibrium.** Even if you are focusing on providing administrative support and problem solving, there is a time for attending to the whole person, including the realm of emotions. Faculty react to stress much as everyone does. They can be thrown off balance emotionally, physically, mentally, and socially. You are in a position to help them maintain or reinstate their inner balance. Your calm presence can serve as a buffer between faculty members and their external stressors. I'm not suggesting you're responsible for faculty's emotional well-being, but you can serve as a positive influence.

- **Provide validation and reinforce the positive.** Faculty who feel stressed find themselves in a vulnerable position. They may be facing challenges they think they won't be able to successfully meet. You can help by providing validation. Validate the fact that this is a difficult challenge for them. Let them know you understand.

    A stress reaction may be their reaction to a fixed or negative mindset. Faculty who fall prey to this kind of reaction feel they cannot do something, that they will fail, that others will view them as unsuccessful. Providing validation is one way to reinforce a more positive mindset. Other ways include alleviating their stress by providing encouragement. If a faculty member is worried about a negative outcome, present a case for the opposite if realistic and appropriate.

- **Be professional.** Don't take personally what faculty may say to you when they are under stress. If they become angry or unreasonable, you keep it professional. You cannot help another person when you are losing your cool. Instead, provide a calm, confident presence, a container that helps the stressed faculty member feel safe, not pressured or blamed, and helps him or her focus on the issue.

    Cultivate the mindset of detachment, as we discussed in Chapter 6. Focus on coping with your own feelings and emotional reactions, rather than becoming sucked into theirs. If you don't like the manner in which faculty are dealing with you in a stressful situation, don't stoop to their level. Rather, commit to your level of professionalism. You can look at this as a process of gentle reeducation in which you're the teacher.

- **Provide administrative support.** Faculty who are under stress may need your extra support. They need to feel they can count on your help in practical ways. They may be looking to you to provide support so they have the time and space needed to "shovel out."

    Be proactive. Assess the tasks at hand and see how you might step forward to relieve a faculty member's burden. Lighten his or her schedule and take some pressure off, if you can. Often, it may be through doing something small, such as returning a phone call or obtaining specific supplies the faculty member needs. Expending extra effort during stressful times can make the difference between a deadline that is met or funding that is not lost (perhaps including the funding for your position).

As much as possible, look at the stress-inducing situation as time limited and assume you are providing extra support to faculty within a specific time frame. If you find yourself operating in high-stress mode on a constant basis, reassess the situation. In that case, it may be necessary to reexamine your priorities and options.

It may be appropriate to bring someone else in temporarily to provide support in your place. This can give the faculty member an opportunity to cool down and self-reflect. Often, stressed faculty will treat the next person better, or will treat you better after taking a break.

- **Problem solve.** When faculty are experiencing a stress reaction, you can help them by focusing on practical solutions. Rather than getting caught up in the emotions of the moment, talk about concrete actions. Take the lead in problem solving. When faculty see you are being practical and offering solutions, or facilitating them in coming up with solutions of their own, they may start to calm down.

- **Be up-front in setting expectations.** As we have seen, expectations play an important role in the faculty stress cycle. As a staff member, you may be in the position of communicating expectations to faculty, particularly around departmental policies and procedures. Be realistic. Define the next steps in the particular process in question and what they can expect will happen. When you communicate with faculty, be clear from the start about these expectations. Doing this can prevent stress reactions down the line.

  Also set expectations about their behavior with you. Let them know what is okay and what is unacceptable.

- **Follow up with reminders.** Whenever you set expectations with faculty or devise an action plan intended to alleviate a stressful situation, be sure to follow up. In Chapter 10, we talked about the importance of following up whenever you have a conversation with faculty about specific action steps.

- **Don't try to change them.** Last but not least, avoid trying to change faculty. That's not your role. How anyone reacts to stress is a function of that individual's personality, and personality is not something that can be easily changed by another person. Moreover, if faculty sense you are trying to change them, that will only heighten their stress level.

Conclusion

Academia can be a stressful place to work. As Gunsalus (2006) points out, "The academic environment has some special aspects that can complicate an already fraught set of problems. These include the star system, academic freedom, the general reluctance of those in academia to be managed, and disdain for those in management positions." Moreover, stress appears to be on the increase among faculty as a result of recent financial, technological, and other developments in the higher education setting. And it's unlikely to let up anytime soon.

In this chapter, we turned to Walter Gmelch's research for clues about how to help faculty overcome stress. And I offered a wide range of practical strategies I have found effective. If Jeff, the secretary you met at the beginning of this chapter, were aware of these strategies, chances are he wouldn't be so frustrated in handling Dr. Dixon's stress.

Keep in mind, too, that we all have bad days and get stressed at times. And faculty are no exception. Although you might feel on bad days that all faculty are a challenge to work with, the reality is that only a small fraction of faculty present a severe challenge. In the next chapter, we look at this subset of faculty and consider strategies you can apply to make it easier to work with them.

Summary

Faculty Stress Reactions and What You Can Do

- The main faculty stressors include reward and recognition, time constraints, departmental influences, professional identity, and student interactions.

- The faculty stress cycle has four stages: faculty stressors (events or expectations in the environment that affect faculty), faculty's perception of these stressors, faculty's stress response, and the consequences of that stress response.

- In stressful interactions, the feelings faculty have that underlie their behavior and the feelings staff have themselves often are similar. When you look a bit deeper at both faculty and staff vulnerabilities, you often can avoid reacting to faculty in unhelpful ways.

- When working with a stressed faculty member, assess your own stress level, listen without reacting emotionally, respond thoughtfully to his or her underlying concerns, remain professional, and provide support.

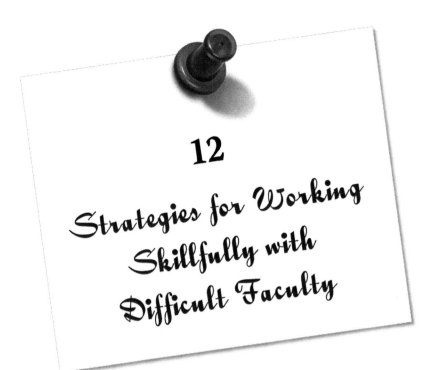

12
Strategies for Working Skillfully with Difficult Faculty

- Who Is Difficult for You?
- Characteristics of Faculty Who Are Difficult
- Faculty Who Are Self-Centered
- Faculty Who Are Aggressive
- Faculty Who Are Manipulative
- Faculty Who Are Unresponsive
- Conclusion
- Summary

In the last chapter, we considered what it is like to work with faculty when they become stressed. Anyone can experience stress, depending on the day or the circumstances or any number of factors. It is often difficult to work with someone if one or both of you is stressed, but that doesn't mean either of you is what I would call a *difficult* person.

Difficult people often are hard to work with, whether or not stress is involved. They have personalities and ways of acting that continually challenge those who have to work with them. These traits or behaviors are relatively consistent day to day, although added stress can make them worse. The strategies we have covered in previous chapters are geared for the 95 percent of faculty who respond to what works for most people. But a small number of people have behavior patterns that makes it truly difficult to work with them—not just for you, but for lots of others, too. In his article *Dealing with Troubled Faculty*, Howard Altman (2003) estimated that 5% of faculty are troubled to the extent that their relationships with other faculty, staff, and students suffer. These faculty require special handling, and that's what this chapter is about.

Of course, not everyone will experience the same set of characteristics or behaviors as equally challenging. Still, when it comes to dealing with difficult faculty members, most staff will agree it is hard to work with these individuals.

Who Is Difficult for You?

Take a minute and think about all the faculty with whom you work. Does anyone stand out as being particularly difficult? If so, it could be that you often feel bad after you interact with this person. Or perhaps it's someone you simply prefer not to work with, so you do your best to avoid him or her.

If you can identify someone you consider a difficult faculty member, you might want to jot down a list of some of his or her difficult behaviors. What specific feelings does this individual express that make him or her seem difficult? Is he or she angry or anxious or insecure? Does he or she feel entitled to special attention? Note that I'm not asking you to play therapist or guess what is in the person's mind; you can't know that. However, you can clarify the impressions you have. These impressions are important because they can influence how you relate to this faculty member.

Sometimes staff choose to handle difficult faculty by suffering in silence. Instead of complaining or trying to change the situation, they change their own expectations and learn to adapt to the faculty member's dysfunctional behaviors. Some version of this strategy can be useful as a survival tactic, if you can tolerate it. However, this must be done with keen awareness and detachment, while staying alert to the level of your resentment, discouragement, loss of energy, or depression. Be alert to signs that you are feeling victimized or disempowered, and consider trying some of the strategies discussed here. I have placed this chapter late in the book because these staff-faculty interactions are the most difficult. I think you will find them easier to approach after you have developed some more basic skills.

Characteristics of Faculty Who Are Difficult

I have noticed that people who are a pain to work with often are them-selves in pain. In other words, difficult people usually have underlying problems that contribute to and explain why they are difficult. They may have developed ways of relating to others during childhood that do not serve them well as adults. Sometimes their behavior actually does serve them well, in that they get what they want. The squeaky wheel gets the grease. Faculty who are difficult may be brilliant in their academic field, but lacking in self-awareness, interpersonal sensitivity and social skills. Ben Bissell (2003), who has researched and written about working with difficult faculty, lists some of their common char-acteristics (p. 121):

- They have a predictable, abrasive style of behavior.

- Nearly everyone finds them difficult—not just you.

- They usually try to keep all blame outside themselves. It is never their fault.

- They rob you of time and energy. Furthermore, they do not even have to be present to affect you.

- Their behavior is almost always out of proportion to the problem.

- They are usually terrible problem solvers. They know best, and are blind to both the positive possibilities in other options and the negative consequences of their own actions.

I would add that they may lack respect and empathy for staff and gener-ally do not seek to partner with staff for mutual benefit. They tend not to know how to bring out the best in others.

While these common characteristics apply across the spectrum of difficult people, Bissell and others have come up with categories that can help us identify specific types of problem people in the workplace. For example, in a book intended as a resource for administrators who work with difficult faculty, Bissell talks about six types (the bully, the com-plainer, the procrastinator, the guerrilla fighter, the expert, the icicle). Alan Cavaiola and Neil Lavender (2000) take a more psychological ap-proach in their book aimed at helping people deal with toxic coworkers in the workplace. Their categories (e.g., histrionic, antisocial, narcis-sist, obsessive-compulsive, passive-aggressive) are based on personality traits and personality disorders, as defined by the *DSM-IV model*.

I prefer to avoid categorizing faculty in ways that may sound judgmental or critical. Their behavior may be painful for staff or prevent them from getting their jobs done, but typecasting or name calling isn't helpful. Instead, I prefer a method of describing difficult faculty that borrows from Bissell's and other models in the literature, but that emphasizes behaviors. For staff working with faculty, I have found most of the difficult individuals you will encounter fall into four categories:

- Faculty who are self-centered
- Faculty who are aggressive
- Faculty who are manipulative
- Faculty who are unresponsive

In Table 12.1, I have listed behaviors typical for each of the four categories, as well as feelings (conscious or unconscious) that can lead to these behaviors. You may find this table helpful in identifying the faculty who are problematic for you. [See Table 12.1 following page.]

Working with difficult faculty members takes the utmost sensitivity. You may need to wear kid gloves. That is, you need to maintain your awareness of self-other-context, exercise self-control, and practice your best communication skills to handle both your interactions with them and your own internal world. The strategies we discussed in Chapter 11 apply to working with difficult faculty, as well. You need to maintain your own inner balance first. Keep in mind once again that you are not trying to psychoanalyze them. Rather, use the list of feelings in Table 12.1 to help you better understand why a faculty member is exhibiting a particular behavior. Responding to the underlying feeling may be your best strategy.

For example, ask yourself: could this professor's self-centered or aggressive behavior hide an underlying insecurity? If you think that is plausible, instead of responding to the behavior, you can respond instead to the underlying insecurity. This will alter the basic tenor of your response. It also will be more likely to draw a positive response from the faculty member.

Let's look more closely at each of these categories of difficult faculty. I begin each section with an example of a difficult faculty member, including his or her effect on staff members. Then I suggest how you as staff can work most effectively with these faculty.

Table 12.1 Categories of Difficult Faculty

Behavior	Inner Feeling
Faculty who are self-centered	
Act entitled to special treatment	Self-important
Seek admiration	Entitled to special treatment; nothing exists except their needs
Make unreasonable requests	
Devalue others	Superior to staff; staff exist only to serve them
Exploit staff, don't give credit	
Are critical, difficult to please	Insecure
Do not show empathy or concern for others	Afraid of failure, rejection, or looking bad
Appear charming when they want to, vindictive when they are not pleased	Threatened by others' success or recognition
Faculty who are aggressive	
Make demands and unreasonable requests	Entitled to special treatment, superior to staff
Express anger and hostility, go on the attack	Self-righteous
	Out of control or powerless
Blame others	Frustrated or blocked
Criticize others	Insecure
Demean or put others down	Anxious
Are sarcastic	Overwhelmed
Humiliate staff and others publicly	
Faculty who are manipulative	
Try to control staff's behavior without taking responsibility	Afraid of not getting something through direct communication
Use indirect communication or deception	Ashamed or guilty for their motives and/or actions
Go behind staff's back to get what they want	Afraid of being held accountable
	Anxious, out of control
May make staff look bad to others to serve their own purposes	Frustrated
Use passive-aggressive behavior	Inadequate, unable to get what they want
Faculty who are unresponsive	
Do not follow through	Afraid of failure, criticism, or rejection
Put off what is unpleasant or difficult	
Make excuses for inaction	Afraid to admit not knowing something
Are preoccupied or easily distracted	
Keep busy with unimportant matters	Anxious
Appear shy, detached, aloof, preoccupied	Overwhelmed
	Uncomfortable setting limits
Stay in their own world	Afraid to ask for help
May placate staff	
Ignore needs of staff	

Faculty Who Are Self-Centered

Dr. Dudley Turner, a professor in the Political Science Department at a mid-size private college, is sometimes interviewed by the local radio or TV station about current political issues. When this happens, he mentions the media exposure to almost everyone he meets. He seldom misses an opportunity to talk about his conference presentations, community speeches, or contacts with famous people. He seems to be saying that each event is but another indication of his expertise and celebrity.

Some of his faculty colleagues resent his name dropping and self-aggrandizing behavior. At the same time, Dr. Turner seldom gives them or the staff credit for their contributions and good work. He has even questioned the legitimacy of the academic credentials of another faculty member who is well known and received a prestigious award. Sometimes it seems as if he not only needs to be the star, but feels compelled to put others down if they shine too brightly.

Cynthia, a staff member in the department, has had many experiences with Dr. Turner that left her feeling unappreciated or defeated. She told me about one experience in particular that demonstrated his preoccupation with his own needs.

Cynthia was asked to serve on the board of directors for a local classical music radio station. She accepted with pleasure because she'd enjoyed listening to this station for years. She considered it an honor and mentioned it in the office when staff were speaking about their hobbies and interests.

When Dr. Turner heard about Cynthia's radio station board position, he immediately made it clear he thought she should resign. He indicated it posed a potential conflict of interest. This made no sense to Cynthia, and she was shocked at his unreasonable request. She tried to dissuade Dr. Turner by assuring him the position would not interfere with her staff responsibilities. In fact, except for evening meetings several times a year and some involvement in an annual fundraising event, the position required very little from her.

Dr. Turner responded by relating an anecdote about his own position on a volunteer board that had become very time consuming. He implied that Cynthia didn't really know how much time a board position would require, and that she wouldn't be able to manage the extra responsibility along with her heavy workload in the department.

As Cynthia listened to him, she saw no relationship between his anecdote and her own situation. She was infuriated by what she saw as his invasion of her private life. Moreover, this reminded her of how often Dr. Turner belittled her and other staff in front of other people. She had a hard time keeping quiet. But she didn't want to say anything because, as she later told herself, "How do you argue with someone who always thinks he's right?" On the way home that evening, she had a headache and couldn't get the conversation out of her mind.

Typical Self-Centered Behaviors

It could have helped Cynthia to understand she was dealing with a faculty member who was self-centered. Faculty in this category are often smart and talented, work hard, and find it easy to land leadership positions. They can be very charming. Yet they usually also are self-absorbed and self-involved, and can come across as arrogant. Much of their hard work is focused on gaining recognition. Often these faculty have grandiose ideas about their accomplishments and the recognition they feel they deserve. They consider themselves special and feel entitled to special treatment.

They generally lack empathy and are unable to see another's perspective. They inflate their own self-worth, while deflating the worth of others. Often they are critical of and demeaning to others, and can sound contemptuous or condescending. These faculty make unreasonable requests of staff and exploit staff for their own ends. If you do something for them, they will not give you credit or appreciation or help you look good or get ahead. If you work for a faculty member who is self-centered, you can expect to work overtime and give up chunks of your private life. You may end up feeling inadequate, frustrated, and that nothing you do is good enough.

These faculty are more interested in staff's loyalty and admiration than in staff's input or feedback. If you try to give these faculty feedback, they are more likely to blame you than to become self-reflective or introspective. When they feel criticized, their first impulse is to prove themselves right. They have a huge investment in seeing themselves as good, right, and valuable. For this reason, Cynthia did not try to discuss her issue with Dr. Turner.

In their book about toxic coworkers, Cavaiola and Lavender use the term *narcissist* for these faculty. This term is based on the narcissistic personality disorder, or individuals who are overly self-centered. The authors say, "Because narcissists feel they are far above the norm, they will often violate boundaries of authority, making decisions they are not qualified to make or taking on tasks that they really aren't trained to do" (p. 33). Faculty who are narcissistic do not respect authority and may commit ethical violations. For them, the most important thing is being admired as special, being right and getting their own way.

Strategies for Working with Faculty Who Are Self-Centered

Here are some suggestions:

- Avoid getting entangled in their problems. Try not to take their behavior personally or buy into their reality in a given situation.

- Avoid taking on unrealistic amounts of work because self-centered faculty won't look out for your legitimate needs and limits.

- Avoid looking to them for appreciation, approval, or credit. Find other ways to meet your emotional needs (e.g., from supportive coworkers and friends outside of work). If your family background includes parents who were not emotionally supportive, you may find it especially challenging to work with faculty who are self-centered.

- Avoid placating or trying to please them. It is easy to get hooked into trying to please someone who never seems to think you are good enough.

- Try to distance yourself emotionally and ignore their fault finding. If a faculty member tries to block your success or promotion, be realistic and don't imagine you can get his or her support. Remember, he or she doesn't really want to help you be successful or give you credit. Look elsewhere for support.

- Avoid confronting or challenging their opinion or expertise because they may view your challenge as an attack and will not reflect on their own motives. If you try to set a boundary, they are likely to feel threatened and counterattack. Even the communication skills described in Chapter 6 can backfire with these faculty members.

- If you feel it is important to assert yourself with these faculty members, use I-messages and set appropriate limits. Practice active listening and paraphrasing when you speak with them. Take notes.

- If you want something from them, choose an appropriate time and place, be specific and ask directly ("I'd like to take a vacation day next Thursday" or "I'd like to sit down together and go over your request for new equipment"), follow up, and document your request and their response. Clarify their expectations, ask "what-if" questions, and get them to anticipate the consequences of their ideas and plans.

* Comment on their real strengths (e.g., their intelligence, instances when they showed genuine charm, or concern for someone).

* Don't try to change them because they probably won't be open to your feedback or requests. They readily feel criticized and may lash back, rather than listening to or collaborating with you.

* Avoid them in general when you can. Notice if other staff members have found it difficult to work with them, and ask if these staff have discovered positive strategies that might also work for you.

* Stay attuned to your own needs. Keep in mind that you're unlikely to be anymore successful than were other staff who tried and failed when working with these faculty members.

Faculty Who Are Aggressive

Dr. Louise Harding, a professor in the Microbiology Department, asked Roberto, a lab assistant, to check on the status of the grant application she was preparing. Roberto was confused when she handed him a slip of paper with a name and phone number as she was running out of the lab and asked him to phone "about the grant," and to do it right away. Calls like this had never been part of Roberto's job, but when he tried to get clarification, Dr. Harding was already running out the door and snapped, "You're smart. Figure it out!"

At first, Roberto thought it would be better not to make the call until he had a chance to talk to the professor. But he also knew Dr. Harding would be irritated if she came back and discovered he hadn't gotten the information. She acted annoyed before, and it had been very uncomfortable for him. Now he was afraid of incurring her wrath again. So, after wasting an hour of lab time, he finally made the call. The person on the other end of the line was friendly, and after several awkward minutes of clarification, gave him the dates she said "Dr. Harding needed."

Roberto left the information in a note for Dr. Harding. She never thanked him, but he figured everything was fine, until about a week later, when she came into the lab and blew up at him. As it turned out, she had given him the wrong name and number to call, and Roberto had gotten the dates for a different grant application. As a result, Dr. Harding missed her deadline. She was furious at Roberto because she expected him to figure out the mistake on his own and correct it.

Typical Aggressive Behaviors

If the motto of faculty who are self-centered is "I'm the star," the motto of faculty who are aggressive is "I'm powerful." Staff who work with these faculty can feel bullied, intimidated, controlled, unappreciated, unworthy, afraid, and even threatened or victimized. Roberto was operating out of fear in a situation that could have been resolved readily if he and the professor had open channels of communication.

The idea of a predominant "bully culture" in academia has been discussed by numerous authors. According to Twale and De Luca (2008), the hierarchical structure of academia, the stiff competition over status and awards, the influence of corporate culture, and the increased tensions resulting from the economic pinch, all contribute to the establishment of a bully culture. Notably, bullying in this environment takes place as much among faculty peers as it does between faculty and staff.

C. K. Gunsalus (2006) describes faculty bullies as "people who are willing to cross the boundaries of civilized behavior that inhibit others. They value the rewards brought by aggression and generally lack guilt, believing their victims provoked the attacks and deserve the consequences. Their behavior prompts others to avoid them, which means that, in the workplace, bullies are likely to become effectively unsupervised" (p. 122).

Bullying, demanding, and intimidating behaviors often mask underlying feelings that are very much the opposite. Some faculty act aggressively to cover for their hidden insecurity, feeling of powerlessness or inability to deal with people who do not understand their "importance" and complex work. It is incumbent upon staff to learn to see through this façade and not allow themselves to become victims. Likewise, when faculty get away with behavior that would be unacceptable in other work environments, staff are encouraged not to give in to intimidating demands or break the rules to keep the peace. Staff have told me they have learned not to expect all faculty to take responsibility for their requests or to come to a staff member's rescue when the staff member is caught doing something illegal, unethical, or inappropriate.

Strategies for Working with Faculty Who Are Aggressive

Here are some suggestions:

• Try to emotionally disengage yourself from the behaviors and attitudes of angry and aggressive faculty. Difficult as it may be to do, don't succumb to feelings of guilt, sympathy, responsibility, or anger in response.

• Remain calm, confident, and assertive. Be non-defensive, non-judgmental, and respectful. Listen and give them time to blow off steam. You may be able to sense a faculty member building up steam to the point where it peaks and begins to run down. Then, when he or she takes a breath, look at the person directly, say his or her name, and acknowledge the difficult situation. Then paraphrase your understanding of what he or she wants and explain what you can do.

• Address the business at hand, not the faculty member's tone of voice or personality. Ask focused questions, such as "What specifically are you asking me to do?"

• Don't give in to outrageous demands or break the rules.

• If faculty take a cheap shot at you, such as saying, "What is this crap?" (referring to your work), ignore the remark and ask an open question to clarify what they want.

• If a faculty member becomes accusatory or aggressive in a way that is unacceptable to you, distance yourself by stepping back or putting your hand up (palm facing outward). Say something along the lines of "I'm uncomfortable with this conversation" or "I need a time out. Let's talk this afternoon."

• If possible, bring another person into the conversation. It's surprising how quickly an aggressive person can change his or her tone when a third person is present.

• Avoid a fight. Threatening or arguing with aggressive faculty is likely to backfire on you.

• If you are confident you have a strong case, stand up for yourself and assert yourself. Look directly at the faculty member with the feeling that you are equals. Use respectful, even deferential, language. Use I-messages. Even difficult faculty usually respect this and are likely to shift their tone.

• Be ready for faculty to be friendly when you establish respect as a worthy colleague. However, don't expect a more productive relationship immediately following a confrontation. He or she may need time to adjust to what has happened.

• After the encounter is over, give yourself time to recover. Take a break and nurture yourself. You may find it helpful to tell one person whom you trust about what has happened. Express your feelings fully. Avoid telling more people because it doesn't help to spread negative energy to others on your team or to be unprofessional.

• Don't let faculty's ego (and abusive behavior) destroy yours. If you find yourself too frightened or shutting down, take care of yourself (see Chapter 13).

• Be a friend to other staff members whom you see being pushed around or blamed by aggressive faculty. Show the person you care; acknowledge what you see happening.

Faculty Who Are Manipulative

Dr. Weill overheard Lisa, manager for the International Law program, speaking on the phone one day at lunch. She was telling a friend that she had worked there for five years and was thinking of a job change. "A change of pace" was how she phrased it. Dr. Weill didn't think too much about it at the time. But shortly thereafter, he learned that the dean of the Law School was losing her special assistant and was interested in Lisa as a replacement.

This irked Dr. Weill. Why should the International Law program lose Lisa to the dean? Not if he could stop it, he thought. So he mentioned this issue to two other law professors at the end of a meeting the next day. They agreed Lisa was easy to work with and did a fantastic job. They were all equally irritated. "Listen," Dr. Weill said, "we need to protect Lisa, and prevent her from leaving us." His colleagues concurred.

Annual staff performance reviews were held the following month, and the three law professors all purposely gave Lisa mediocre reviews. In effect, they sabotaged her career plans. Lisa didn't find out about the poor reviews until after her application for the position of special assistant to the dean had been rejected. And she was never able to figure out why she had gotten poor reviews, especially when everyone always praised her performance. This left her angry, resentful, and distrusting.

Typical Manipulative Behaviors

In contrast with faculty who are aggressive, faculty who are manipulative use passive aggression. They accomplish their aggressive acts through indirect or subtle means. They may conclude that the end justifies the means. This can be tricky, as Lisa discovered. The faculty who gave her poor reviews attacked her covertly for their selfish purposes. Probably, Lisa would have preferred they talk to her directly about their desire that she not change positions.

Bissell calls the manipulative person a *guerrilla fighter*. He says, "Guerrilla fighters use an insidious sarcasm and criticism to browbeat their 'enemies' into feeling that they were stupid to even have raised the issue. They 'shoot' from trees and bushes, attacking with no warning and catching the unarmed colleague unaware.... The guerrilla fighter believes that he can feel smart if he makes you feel dumb" (p. 120).

These faculty may feel powerless, insecure, angry, or guilty. However, they have learned to disguise their insecurities so they don't have to be accountable for their behavior. Trying to talk with them directly about their manipulative behavior may only provoke more passive-aggressive behavior. Because they have made these tactics work for them, and because others often are unaware of what they are doing, they have little motivation to change.

Faculty who are manipulative may use sarcasm, act confused, forget or miss deadlines, use delay tactics, be forgetful, laugh off others' comments or feedback, ignore rules and policies, joke with you in a hurtful way, change the subject, spread rumors, or outright lie. These faculty can be intolerant of frustration and feel entitled to what they want. They may perceive any request you make as intrusive and react with resentment. Because they have difficulty expressing their feelings appropriately, they may become more resistant if you are confrontational.

Staff reactions to manipulative faculty include anger, frustration, confusion, and self-doubt. Staff sometimes find themselves working harder than the professor. I consider the manipulative faculty member to be one of the most challenging for staff.

Strategies for Working with Faculty Who Are Manipulative

Here are some strategies:

- Learn to recognize the manipulation in faculty members' behaviors, especially when the dynamics are subtle.
- Listen without agreeing. Clarify their expectations. Be aware that communication skills that usually are effective may not work.
- Stay on top of any request you make and do so in a nonthreatening, non-aggressive way.
- Whenever possible, attempt to move toward joint problem solving. Get faculty to make clear agreements, then document what has been said and follow up. Include other staff members when possible.
- Get out of any entanglements with manipulative faculty in as tasteful a manner as possible. Focus on protecting yourself. Be careful not to hold a grudge because that will only hurt you.
- Don't try to change them.

Faculty Who Are Unresponsive

I have noticed two main characteristics of faculty who are unresponsive: some appear to be withdrawn, while others are noted for their procrastination. Let's look at cases that represent each characteristic.

Dr. Singh, a physics professor, is an example of a withdrawn faculty member. He tends to be missing in action when staff attempt to work with him. Dr. Singh asked Theresa, an artist in the Media Department, to create a slide show with some imaginative special effects for his presentation at an international conference. When they initially met about the project, Dr. Singh was a bit vague about the special effects he wanted. Now every time Theresa tries to contact him with a question, he does not respond. She has tried going to his office during the posted office hours, but he never seems to be there during those hours. In fact, the other day Theresa encountered a frustrated student who thought he had an appointment with the professor, but who arrived at the office and found it locked.

Theresa is upset because this project is taking longer than it should because she is lacking direction. Her other responsibilities are suffering as a result. Finally, more than a week later, she runs into Dr. Singh in the corridor and stops him to ask for help. He tells her that when she did not show him a draft of the slide show, he prepared the presentation himself without any special effects. He tells her not to worry about it. But as Teresa walks back to her desk, she is fuming.

Now let's visit an unresponsive faculty member who procrastinates. Although no one would ever say Dr. Huen, professor in the Department of Food Science, is withdrawn, staff find her difficult to work with because she is involved in too many projects and her thinking is scattered. This semester, Dr. Huen asked her assistant, Thomas, to manage the planning of a conference on nutrition education, a task he had done before. When Thomas met with Dr. Huen at the beginning of the process, the professor appeared animated and involved. Thomas thought they were off to a good start. But now he finds himself bogged down in the details, and Dr. Huen is not responding.

For example, Thomas knows the menu for Saturday night's dinner, when the keynote speaker is scheduled, is especially important. In two emails and a couple of voicemails, he has asked Dr. Huen to choose among several recommended menus from the caterers. She has not sent him an answer. He recalls having a similar problem last year, when Dr. Huen didn't respond until the day before the event.

Thomas is afraid Dr. Huen is going to leave everything to the last moment again, so he decides to send a stronger email. In it, he says, "The caterers need to be informed about the menu by Monday. Just to let you know, I plan to email you for this information every day for the rest of the week! And if I don't have the information by Monday morning, I will select the menu myself—even if it's hot dogs!"

Typical Withdrawn Behaviors

Bissell's name for withdrawn faculty is the *icicle*. This is because, as he points out, these faculty freeze up whenever they run into confusion or conflict of any sort. He describes the typical interactions of this group: "When confronted about where they stood, they replied, 'Not sure yet.' When asked if anything was wrong, they said, 'Not now. Everything is fine . . . just fine.' The icicle believes that whoever is the quietest wins: If you say nothing, you cannot be attacked" (p. 120).

These faculty are not heartless, as the image of an icicle implies. Rather, they may be shy and reclusive. They are likely to be introverts who may have grown up spending most of their time in the world of books and computers, and as a result have underdeveloped self-awareness and interpersonal and organizational skills. They often don't understand the emotional and communication needs of others, respond to social cues, or require social rewards (e.g., approval and appreciation). Some faculty who are unresponsive had negative experiences in the bully culture early during their academic career. A single damaging incident with a faculty bully may have left them living in fear of further trauma, and led them to retreat into their own intellectual world as the best means of protection.

Staff often find withdrawn faculty members' communication disjointed and lacking in focus. A staff member can feel stymied by their apparent indecisiveness. At times, withdrawn faculty may have provided all the pertinent information, but the staff member does not sense any emotional contact. This can put a strain on the staff-faculty partnership and lead to miscommunication.

Typical Procrastinating Behaviors

We all procrastinate at some time or other. Either we don't like the task or we have too much on our plate and don't get around to it. Hammer and Ferrari (1999), who studied procrastination rates among adults, report that 20% of people in this country considered themselves chronic procrastinators. Rates of procrastination among college students are much higher; estimated by Ellis and Knaus in 1977 to be as high as 95%, and unlikely to have decreased since then.

The faculty procrastinator, like others with this problem, avoids making decisions and commitments, puts things off, wants to be sure, fears failing or disappointing others. Ackerman and Gross studied (2007) faculty procrastinators and defined the essential problem as "knowing that one needs to carry out a task or undertake an activity, yet failing to motivate oneself to do so within the desired or expected time frame" (p. 97). This, they state, can be the result of:

1. The perceived importance of the task (the consequences of failure would be significant)

2. The lack of appeal of the task (too mundane, too time consuming, or too remote from the faculty member's area of expertise)

3. The difficulty of the task (lack of skills could lead to failure)

Faculty who procrastinate for these reasons can feel intense discomfort, stress, and guilt. Furthermore, their stress is accentuated by the effort required to keep track of many unfinished tasks and projects. Faculty who organize their many projects and define and prioritize their next steps don't experience the same level of stress and seldom procrastinate. Nevertheless, some faculty members have so many pressing priorities that their behavior can appear as procrastination to staff who are seeking a response to what staff see as important but faculty regard as a relatively low priority.

Ackerman and Gross distinguish between faculty who procrastinate primarily around starting tasks and those who procrastinate primarily around completing tasks. Their research indicates that a wider variety of factors affect starting tasks. This can be a helpful distinction for staff when working with faculty who procrastinate. For example, Dr. Huen's procrastination became a problem to Thomas only when he needed to finalize the details of the conference.

Procrastinators may be motivated by fear. They may hide behind their inaction as a means of protecting themselves. Although faculty who procrastinate may not offend staff as much as do other types of difficult faculty, their behavior (or lack thereof) can be maddening for staff. When faculty disregard crucial tasks or deadlines, staff can feel demeaned or disrespected.

Strategies for Working with Faculty Who Are Unresponsive

Here are some strategies:

* Approach unresponsive faculty carefully. Ask how you can be most helpful to them.

* Help faculty build confidence. Recognize when they are decisive. Acknowledge their good ideas and intentions.

* Try to draw out withdrawn faculty, even if it's hard. Be gentle but persistent. Ask open questions and wait for their answers.

* Beware of intruding on withdrawn faculty's space. Let them know when you will be coming to talk with them.

* To get faculty's attention, call them by name. Approach them in a businesslike and nonthreatening way. Be direct about what you need and give them reasons to work with you. Use logical, technical language and avoid becoming emotional or referring to feelings.

- If a problem arises, go to unresponsive faculty and suggest a solution. Be specific and state how resolving the issue will prevent future difficulties. Partner with them; identify small victories and build on them.

- Do as much behind-the-scenes work as you can. For example, if you ask faculty to do something that involves them contacting a dean, you could offer the draft of an email they could send from their computer with little effort or interpersonal contact.

- Help procrastinating faculty clarify goals and desired outcomes. Create a time line with interim deadlines. Use false deadlines so you have a chance to recover if they are late.

- Help faculty prioritize alternatives and problem solve. Stress the importance of task completion and articulate the consequences of inaction. Help them define their next steps. Explain the importance of not trying to do everything all at once.

- Put commitments, time lines, and deadlines in writing. Put your request in writing before you meet with faculty so they have time to think about their response. Or ask them to think about an issue and arrange to discuss it later, then get back to them and ask specifically for their input. They may prefer to communicate by email. Keep control of the process by following up and providing reminders.

- If appropriate, help faculty uncover the underlying reason for their procrastination. Invite them to think through how they can address their issues, and explore how you can work together to get things done.

- When unresponsive faculty do talk, listen and be attentive and supportive.

- Don't embarrass faculty in public or private, or make them appear wrong.

- Be direct about what you need and give them reasons.

- Be supportive and provide safety.

- Remember, unresponsive faculty probably are not ignoring you because of anything you have done.

Conclusion

In the first chapter in this section, we discussed what happens when faculty become stressed and how you can support them. Stress reactions are a normal aspect of work in the academic environment, just as in any other work setting.

In this chapter, we looked at a very small subgroup of faculty: individuals who have well-established patterns that make it difficult to interact or work with them. I described four categories of difficult faculty. Each of these categories presents challenges to staff that go well beyond the challenges involved in dealing with faculty who might be stressed or having a bad day.

My general suggestion when faced with difficult faculty is to avoid being reactive. Stop and identify the specific difficult behavior. Assess the situation. Try to recognize the underlying feeling that could be motivating the difficult behavior. Then respond to that feeling, rather than to the faculty member's behavior. Your best strategy may be to collaborate with other staff to validate your experiences and to learn better ways to work with these individuals. Whether or not the faculty with whom you work are difficult, it is always important to take care of yourself. In the next section, we look at ways to take care of yourself and your career.

[See Summary—Strategies for Working Skillfully with Difficult Faculty on the following page.]

Summary

Strategies for Working Skillfully with Difficult Faculty

- Very few faculty members are likely to be difficult. Their behavior patterns can make it difficult for you to maintain composure and be successful in your work.

- Faculty who are self-centered act as if they deserve special treatment. Faculty who are aggressive can be critical and make unreasonable demands. Faculty who are manipulative try to control staff without taking responsibility. Faculty who are unresponsive may be withdrawn or procrastinate.

- Each of these faculty behaviors requires that you have understanding, compassion, artful communication, and a thick skin. Consider the strategies suggested for building relationships, getting the job done, and protecting yourself.

- Trying to change challenging faculty members is unlikely to be successful.

SECTION V

Take Care of Yourself
and
Your Career

13. Be Resilient and Recover from Being
    Criticized, Beaten Up, or Worn Down   219

14. A Career That Works for You   241

www.WorkingWithFaculty.com

13

Be Resilient and Recover from Being Criticized, Beaten Up, or Worn Down

- ♦ How Resilient Are You?
- ♦ Warning Signs
- ♦ Know Your Stress Cycle
- ♦ Stand Up for Yourself
- ♦ Know Your Rights
- ♦ How To Recover from Being Criticized, Beaten Up, or Worn Down
- ♦ Become More Resilient
- ♦ Conclusion
- ♦ Summary

I have a little confession to make. If you met me earlier in my life, you might have found me to be what is called a Type A personality. I was rather driven to achieve and too centered on being successful in other people's terms. I was quite critical and demanding of myself. As part of my desire to change these qualities, I chose to write my dissertation about self-loving. I asked the men and women I interviewed to tell me the story of their self-loving. In the process, I learned a lot that was personally relevant, as well as securing a doctoral degree.

Based on my research, I was able to define self-loving. Perhaps you are familiar with this experience. Self-loving often emerges when you have inner tension, doubt, or conflict, and begin to take responsibility for their resolution. You recognize that taking care of others, trying to live up to external standards, or adopting someone else's perspective will not work for you. Instead, you learn to be more accepting, respectful, and nurturing toward yourself. You shed limiting patterns from childhood so you can live in accordance with your deeper values and express yourself authentically. In this way, self-loving becomes an ongoing process of finding vitality and meaning in life, through noticing and responding to what is true for you.

My research on self-loving has served me well through the years, and it informs the last section of this book. In the previous two sections, we focused primarily on the other and context aspects of the systems thinking approach. In this section, the focus is on the self—on *you*. Remember, we each can see ourselves as a dynamic, ever-changing system. Our intentions, beliefs, behavior patterns, and emotions are important interdependent components.

Although it might sound paradoxical, working successfully with faculty depends on your ability to take care of yourself. Being aware of their needs, paying attention to the context in which your interactions with faculty take place, and having the skills to communicate effectively with them—all these are important, as we have seen. However, it isn't enough. If you try to do all this while at the same time ignoring your own needs in the situation, chances are it will come to naught. I see too many staff who are burning out or feeling fed up.

So, although it often may go unspoken, taking care of yourself is one of your most important job responsibilities. I'm here to remind you: don't forget this! In *First Things First* (1994), Stephen Covey and his colleagues refer to the need for self-care as "sharpening the saw." It is like the lumberjack who is careful to sharpen his saw and axe before he cuts down a tree. If we don't make it a priority to take care of our personal tools, we're likely to become dull and worn out when the next demanding situation arises.

Don't let anyone persuade you that looking out for yourself is selfish, self-centered, a luxury, or for some reason unnecessary. Days or weeks—or longer—may go by during which nothing happens that calls your attention to the need to take care of yourself. That's fine. You're fortunate if your relationships with faculty are comfortable and productive, your job is free of undue stress, and you're feeling in balance. However, you never know when a difficult situation at work might trigger your stress response. If you know how to take care of yourself, you will find it easier to deal with stress when it arises.

In this chapter, I discuss the meaning of resilience and the warning signs that suggest a need to take better care of yourself. We also cover how the stress cycle can affect you; stress management (when and how to protect or stand up for yourself, knowing your rights); and ongoing self-care (how to recover from a crisis, and strategies to maintain your vitality).

How Resilient Are You?

When I think of resilience, one of the images that comes to mind is of the flowering plants in my garden after a heavy rainstorm. The leaves and blossoms can get so weighed down while it's raining that they bend almost to the ground. Then the sun comes out, the water evaporates, and they bounce right back. Stems and branches have a resilience that allows them to be weighed down for a while without snapping.

Staff need this kind of resilience—the ability to shake things off, to cope and adapt in the face of adversity, threats, or significant sources of stress. Fortunately, unlike plants, we don't have to wait for the sun to come out. If we encounter a storm, we can serve as our own sun. We can dry ourselves off and stand up straight once again.

Resilience can be considered one aspect of what some psychologists refer to as emotional intelligence. Daniel Goleman (1995, 1998) equates emotional intelligence and ego *resiliency*. He speaks about the importance of recognizing what we feel in the moment, and using that to guide our actions; making sure our feelings support rather than hinder the task at hand; tuning in to others' feelings; and having the skills to handle interpersonal relationships. An organization in which people have emotional intelligence, he says, will itself exhibit resiliency.

Research has shown that a variety of specific factors foster resilience. Our early life experience is one key factor that can influence how we react to change and stress as adults. In particular, having loving and supportive relationships when we're young gives us a foundation for withstanding what life throws at us. Of course, enjoying an easy, stress-free life at any age doesn't guarantee resilience. In fact, researchers such as Kathryn Conner (2006) report that some people become more resilient when forced to face difficult challenges. Some of the characteristics of a resilient person, described by researchers, are listed in Table 13.1.

Table 13.1 Characteristics of Resilience

Adaptability
Commitment to self
Goal-oriented (personal or group goal)
Internal locus of control (the belief that we, not
    external sources, control our lives)
Optimism
Patience
Purpose and meaning
Secure attachment to others
Self-efficacy
Self-esteem
Sense of humor

Regardless of what might have happened before, we can develop the qualities of resilience at any point in our lives. In *Building Resiliency: How to Thrive in Times of Change*, Mary Lynn Pulley and Michael Wakefield (2002) identify nine components they say determine our level of resilience. Each component can be nurtured and developed:

- Acceptance of change ("I see change as an opportunity")
- Continuous learning ("I like learning new things")
- Self-empowerment ("I seek to be in greater control of my destiny")
- Sense of purpose ("My work reflects my values")
- Personal identity ("I know who I am; my job doesn't define me")
- Personal and professional networks ("I'm connected to others")
- Reflection ("I think about my decisions and actions")
- Skill shifting ("I can try another approach")
- Relationship with money ("I use money wisely")

I would add that the following abilities are especially relevant within the academic setting and are associated with a staff member's resilience:

- Having confidence, self-esteem, and compassion for oneself
- Handling strong emotions and impulses (our own and others')
- Handling ambiguity
- Being flexible

- Communicating well
- Problem solving
- Planning, and following through on plans that have been made
- Recovering from mistakes

If you are working with a stressed or difficult faculty member, it is especially important to have confidence ("I know how to handle this challenge") and be able to handle your own emotions so you don't get overwhelmed or inflame the situation. Communicating, problem solving, and planning give you the upper hand so you can stay in control, taking into account your needs as well as those of the faculty member. Of course, as long as we're human, mistakes will happen. What really counts is not a mistake-free record, but how you handle the situation when you do goof up. Are you able to stay calm, acknowledge your error to yourself, communicate appropriately with others, correct the mistake, and learn from it? If you can, this is probably what others will remember most, not the fact that you made a mistake.

Warning Signs

When it comes to taking care of ourselves in the workplace, it is helpful to know when we're not doing enough. Usually, there are warning signs. Table 13.2 lists some the typical warning signs you might experience if you aren't looking after your own needs. Put a check next to the items that describe you.

Table 13.2 Warning Sign Checklist

❏ I feel cranky and irritable.
❏ I find myself responding rudely to faculty, snapping back, or giving them the cold shoulder.
❏ I feel resentful.
❏ I feel criticized, put down, blamed, or disregarded by faculty.
❏ I complain about certain faculty members when I'm at home or with coworkers.
❏ My coworkers are avoiding me.
❏ I'm avoiding my coworkers. We don't socialize any more.

❏ I stopped caring about my work. I take no pride in it.

❏ I'm exhausted. I feel physically sick.

❏ I wake up in the night worried about work or wishing some-one at work were different.

❏ I recently gained or lost weight, or changed my eating or sleeping habits.

❏ I don't eat right, exercise, get together with friends, read, meditate, or engage in my personal interests the way I used to.

❏ I'm bored.

❏ I feel pressured.

❏ I can't concentrate.

❏ My work area is a mess.

❏ I keep forgetting or losing things.

Total number checked: _____

If you have checked more than four of these potential warning signs, chances are you may need to do more to take care of yourself on the job. In the sections that follow, let's look at how you can do this, both during a time of crisis and in an ongoing manner.

Know Your Stress Cycle

Mira, a lab supervisor at a large university veterinary hospital, told me her job was filled with stressors. To make matters worse, the hospital cut its staff of twelve small animal supervisors down to five. The staff had to vie for the available positions, and tensions were sky high. Mira was amazed to learn she was one of the five selected.

When Mira told the faculty overseer, Dr. Nelson, about her surprise at being chosen, he looked puzzled. "Why not?" he said. "You're so calm and level headed, while everyone else is crying and carrying on. Of course we were going to pick you."

Mira told me she took this as welcome confirmation of her own process of learning how to manage stress. Years earlier, she had been known for her hot temper. She used to explode at people at the slightest excuse. Then one day she heard the echo of her father's voice in her angry outburst. He had been an angry man, and she had unconsciously picked up his behavior. "When I heard Dad coming out of my mouth," she told me, "I knew I had to change."

Over the next dozen years, Mira examined her perceptions and responses to stress. She became more self-secure. Instead of identifying with her job, she was able to step back and calmly collect her emotions. She would allow herself to feel frustrated and angry for five minutes, but then she would let those feelings go. Dr. Nelson confirmed that Mira's transformation was visible to and appreciated by others.

In Chapter 11, we examined the faculty stress cycle and its effect on faculty members. To recap (see Table 11.1), the four stages of the stress cycle are stressors, perceptions, responses, and consequences. This cycle is not unique to faculty, or for that matter to those who work in academia. Although many of the stressors that trigger you as staff are likely to be different from those that trigger faculty, the same basic four-stage stress cycle can help you understand your experience and manage your stress.

Stage 1: Your Stressors

Stressors are those things in our environment that have the power to trigger a stress reaction in us. According to Gmelch (1993), the number one stressor for faculty is overly high self-expectations. What are the main stressors for staff? I'm not aware of research that ranks the stressors reported as most important by staff at institutions of higher education. It's likely that high self-expectations head the list for staff, too. We'll look at this in Stage 2. However, a wealth of studies about stress in the workplace in general suggest the following stressors (not listed in any particular order) are potent for many staff members:

- Workload (too much to do, too many or unclear responsibilities)
- Time pressure (tight deadlines)
- Interruptions (phone calls, spur-of-the-moment demands from faculty)
- Lack of control (not enough say over your job)
- Uncertainty, ambiguity (lack of role clarity, insufficient information, unclear delegation by faculty)
- Lack of appreciation (feeling undervalued by faculty)

- Poor communication (faculty unavailable to talk, unclear communications)
- Lack of feedback (negative or positive)
- Social support (no one to turn to for collegial advice)
- Office politics (unfairness)

I suggest you use this list as a jumping-off point to identify your own stressors while working with faculty. Create your own Stressors List. Remember, as we discussed in Chapter 11, stressors can be present in the environment as events or expectations of us, whether or not we actually feel stressed by them. So, look over the list and think about which ones are inherent in your work setting.

Don't be limited by this list. Think about times you felt stressed. What in your environment served as the stressor for you in that instance? You may be tempted to list individuals with whom you work. No! To be congruent with a systems thinking approach, we want to avoid blaming others for our stress. Instead of personal blame, consider the specific behaviors involved.

For example, suppose you are making your list, and Professor Domas comes to mind. Stop and think about what specifically he does that stresses you. Does he fail to appreciate the work you do? Frequently interrupt you when you're speaking on the phone? Ignore you when he walks through the office? These factors, not Dr. Domas himself, are your stressors. List the specific behaviors, not Dr. Domas by name.

Stage 2: Your Perceptions

After you have identified stressors at work, consider how you actually see them. Listen to your self-talk; that is, what you tell yourself within your own mind about what is happening. Notice what pushes your buttons. What are your triggers? What kinds of interactions set you off and cause you to overreact? How you perceive these stressors is key to whether they will have an impact on your level of stress.

In the case of Dr. Domas, there are a variety of ways you could perceive the situation. If he never compliments your work, you might have one of the following interpretations:

- "It's just his style to voice criticism but not compliments. If he says nothing about my work, I know he has no complaints."

- "I can't stand this. If I don't get any appreciation, I lose interest in doing a good job. I'd rather quit."

- "I wish Dr. Domas would be more vocal with his praise. But ultimately it doesn't matter. I know when I'm doing a good job."

Only one of these three perceptions is likely to lead to a stress reaction. Which one is it, and why?

I suggest you review the stressors you identified in Stage 1 and take a close look at how you perceive them on a daily basis. I'd be willing to bet you have more than one way of perceiving each of your stressors. In our example with Dr. Domas, it might be harder to view his paucity of compliments as "just his style" on a day when he has offered several serious criticisms. So consider the various ways you perceive each stressor and see if you can come up with the perception that, in general, rings true for you and is less likely to throw you into overwhelm.

Remember that ultimately how you view your stressors is up to you. You choose your own perceptions. So consider several possible points of view for a given stressor and decide which would be most advantageous for you. However, be honest with yourself. Convincing yourself a stressor is unimportant to you when it really is important won't save you from that stress.

Stage 3: Your Stress Reactions

Stress reactions, as we discussed in Chapter 12, include both internal thoughts and feelings and outward behavior. You may experience these as mild, medium, or intense. If your reaction is mild, it may be easy to cope with it simply by turning your attention elsewhere. In this case, you don't have to spend time with Stage 2, closely examining your perceptions.

For example, if you feel stressed while trying to complete paperwork that has to be turned in by the end of the day, you might take a ten-minute break in mid afternoon. Even though you aren't working during those five minutes, freeing your mind from the task will enable you to be more focused when you return to it, and will help ensure you turn the papers in on time.

Many of the tips for taking care of yourself in an ongoing manner that I present at the end of this chapter also can be applied in moments of stress. If you practice them regularly, they will become automatic. Then, when minor stress arises, you can deal with it without too much thought. If a stress reaction is more intense, you may need to develop an effective strategy for coping with it. The warning signs in Table 13.2 are indications you need to be more proactive in dealing with your stress. If you ignore these signs, you may find yourself in a state of overwhelm you won't be able to simply will away. You are likely to feel miserable until you do something about it.

Coping with an intense stress reaction calls for you to examine the situation and your feelings. I suggest the following:

1. Stop and notice the warning sign(s). They serve a valuable purpose. If you are, for example, grumpy and irritable, instead of continuing to be that way, recognize this as a warning sign of stress. This is your first step toward freeing yourself of the stress.

2. Go back and review Stage 1. What in your environment is the stressor behind your grumpiness? Did you, for instance, have an unpleasant interaction with a faculty member? Do you recognize one of the known stressors on your Stressors List?

3. Move on to Stage 2 and examine your perceptions. Are they working for you in this situation? Can you change your perceptions in a way that would relieve the stress reaction?

4. It can be helpful to write down how you reformulate your perception. For example, in the case of Dr. Domas, you might say, "I will recognize that it is his style to voice criticism but not compliments. Therefore, if he says nothing about my work, I will know he has no complaints, and I don't need to get upset."

5. Identify actions you can take to minimize your stress reaction. In addition to changing your perception, you might want to speak with the faculty member in question or help him or her with a particular task, or you might need to find ways to distance yourself from the situation. See if you can meet your personal needs in other ways, perhaps by getting appreciation from your friends and family.

Stage 4: Your Consequences

Finally, consider both the short-term and long-term consequences your stress reactions are having on you and on your work with faculty. Are your responses benefiting you, or are you further wounding yourself?

Are you making the situation better or worse for yourself and others?

Sometimes, I've noticed, we tend to react to stress in ways that effectively allow us to shoot ourselves in the proverbial foot. For example, staff who feel overloaded may feel justified in getting stressed out each day as 5 p.m. nears and a huge pile of work stares them in the face. However, the feelings that come with overwhelm don't offer a step toward the solution. What is needed is a step back from the situation. Instead of beating yourself up or blaming someone else about the overload, put your energy into examining how the stress cycle is affecting you, and then come up with creative ways to change the situation. Many of the resilient and effective staff members I know make a prioritized to-do list at the end of the day. They say it helps them leave their work at work, instead of thinking about it at home, and makes it easier for them to start fresh again in the morning.

Stand Up for Yourself

We've been looking at some basic stress management techniques you can apply in your work with faculty. However, not all challenging situations can be handled simply by changing your perceptions and reducing your level of stress. Sometimes you may encounter interactions that call for you to stand up for yourself and protect yourself. I'm not suggesting these kinds of crises are frequent, but they do occur. Consider the case of Kevin.

Kevin is a research assistant for Dr. Carolyn Dawson in the Urban Studies Department. One of his responsibilities is overseeing data analysis for her research projects. Recently it has been crunch time because Dr. Dawson has a major conference presentation coming up. She asked Kevin to do some additional analyses for it. One required that he recode a substantial amount of data. As a result, he's had to stay late at the office several evenings this week.

Kevin likes working for Dr. Dawson—or Carolyn, as he calls her. She is friendly, approximately his age, and often stops by to chat. He wants her presentation to go well, so occasionally working late is not a problem for him.

One evening, after everyone else has left for the day, Dr. Dawson walks by Kevin as he is finishing work. She thanks him for his willingness to go the extra mile. Then she says she'd like to treat him to dinner to show her appreciation. Kevin is taken by surprise, especially when she says the invitation is for that night. But since he sees no reason not to, he agrees to go.

At dinner, Kevin enjoys their discussion about data analysis. However, two days later, Dr. Dawson asks Kevin to go out again. This time it seems almost as if she is asking him on a date. In addition to the fact that he has a girlfriend, Kevin considers dating his boss a conflict of interest. So he makes an excuse not to go.

Dr. Dawson isn't deterred. She starts doing little things, such as bringing him snacks, leaving personal notes, and asking him to go various places with her. All week, he tries to keep up his hard work on the data analysis, while conveying he isn't interested on a personal level. He is afraid he can't get his message across without offending her because she isn't picking up his subtle cues. He's also confused because she's always been friendly, and he wonders if he's just imagining her intentions now are anything other than professional.

Eventually Kevin confides in his girlfriend and asks her to hang out with him at the office while he stays late to complete the last round of data analysis. Dr. Dawson sees them and walks by without even saying hello. Kevin is pleased his strategy seems to be working. However, the next morning he receives an email from Dr. Dawson. In it, she finds fault with his work and insists he redo all the analyses because he didn't follow directions. Yet he knows he did exactly what she asked.

Kevin tries to make an appointment with Dr. Dawson to straighten out any miscommunication, but she schedules it for after the conference. When they finally meet, she is harsh with Kevin, and he backs down from speaking directly about his real concerns. A week later he quits his job. His girlfriend tries to get him to go the Sexual Harassment Office and report Dr. Dawson.

"Are you kidding?" he says. "I'm the guy. If I get blamed for this, I'll never get another job here."

If we review Kevin's actions, we see he made a series of attempts to stand up for himself before he quit. First, he gave an excuse not to go on the "date," when he could have felt obligated to go because Dr. Dawson was his boss. Then he brought his girlfriend in as a way to send the professor a message. Both of these attempts were indirect communications, but although temporarily effective, they didn't solve the harassment problem.

Meeting with Dr. Dawson was a direct attempt to address the issue;

however, Kevin backed down out of fear and perhaps because he didn't have the communication skills for this kind of confrontation. Finally, for similar reasons, he did not attempt to stand up for himself by going to the dean.

What could Kevin have done to stand up for himself that would have been more effective and possibly allowed him to stay in his position?

I think the answer to this question involves several key interrelated elements.

Communication skills. Standing up for yourself requires you to communicate skillfully—both verbally and nonverbally. You have to be firm and congruent. Yet you don't want to upset the faculty member unnecessarily. Using I-messages is helpful, as is maintaining a calm, detached attitude. Be careful how you use terms, such as sexual harassment, that might trigger an investigation. You may want to role-play the conversation with a friend or trusted colleague beforehand so you can anticipate how you would handle your emotions to cope with various possible faculty responses.

Have a third party present. You may find it easier to stand up to a faculty member if a third party is present. This can be someone in an official capacity (e.g., a supervisor or ombudsman) or a colleague.

Understand the power dynamics in your relationships. Obviously this is a vast topic. We touched on it in Chapter 4 in our discussion about systems and power and in Chapter 5 with respect to the value of developing a collegial mindset. Here, at a minimum, it is important to keep in mind that staff who feel the need to stand up for themselves are dealing with the power dynamics of a faculty-staff relationship. These dynamics can lead to feelings of fear, disempowerment, frustration, and intimidation, among others.

Have confidence in yourself and your perceptions. If you are dealing with a manipulator or other difficult faculty member, that person may operate in ways that lead you to doubt the validity of your own perceptions. Kevin was caught between seeing Dr. Dawson as someone he liked and feeling she was wronging him, to the point that he became confused about whether his grievances were real. Giving someone the benefit of the doubt may be the gallant thing to do initially, but that doesn't mean you should excuse repeated wrongful behavior.

Make decisions in your own best interest. Ultimately, the decision about whether to stand up for yourself is yours to make. Despite everything I've just said, there are no guarantees. If a faculty member holds a grudge or is determined to make your life difficult, the complaint may be hard to prove and to stop. I know staff members who have stood up for themselves and ended up either being fired or quitting anyway.

The bottom line is that you need to think about your own best interests in the situation. Is it worth it to you to stay in a job in which you feel poorly treated? The answer may be yes if you feel you can look past the problems or if you plan to be in the position for a short time. On the other hand, you may feel the only way to protect yourself is to stand up for yourself, regardless of the eventual outcome. I encourage you to carefully examine all aspects of a complex situation and then to engage in a thoughtful decision-making process, rather than automatically standing up for yourself or filing a formal grievance.

Know Your Rights

These days, institutions of higher learning have standard policies and procedures in place for reporting grievances and for handing the kinds of situations just discussed. In addition to your supervisor, your Human Resources Department and many other services can assist you with sensitive professional or personal issues. Your institution may offer workshops designed to help you better understand your rights.

The resources available vary widely from campus to campus, and the quality of service can vary as well, depending on the approach and leadership provided by a particular office, department, or program. Table 13.3 lists some of the resources you may find at your institution that can help you understand your difficult situation, sort out your feelings, define your options, and choose your best approach. Keep in mind that the names/titles at various institutions may differ. Even the term *grievance* may have a different meaning, depending on the institution. For example, while some institutions use grievance and complaint interchangeable, one university distinguishes a grievance from a complaint by stating that the former focuses on the effects experienced by the grievant and the latter on the alleged misconduct of another. At another institution, complaints refer to violations of university rules or policies, while grievances refer to conditions of employment not covered by those policies. So inform yourself about the terminology, resources, and procedures at your workplace.

Table 13.3 Institutional Resources for Handling Difficult Situations

Counseling Center and Employee Assistance Programs

- Offers free brief counseling with licensed professionals
- Conducts workshops and peer support groups (work-related and personal issues)

Disability Office

- Assists with disability accommodation, compliance with Americans with Disabilities Act (ADA) and Section 504 of the Rehabilitation Act

Diversity Office

- Resolves issues related to affirmative action, diversity, discrimination

Employee and Labor Relations

- Interprets and applies policies and collective bargaining agreements
- Provides information and assistance for staff concerns

- Mediates employee/supervisor differences, union and non-union grievances and arbitrations

Ombudsman Office or Mediation Services

- Resolves disputes
- Strives to see that faculty, staff, and students are treated fairly and equitably

Sexual Harassment Office

- Establishes sexual harassment policies
- Provides educational programs, problem solving

Union

- Negotiates and enforces union members' rights
- Counsels employees about their rights
- Represents employees with Labor Relations

I have personally benefited from counseling when I found myself in some tough job situations. So I don't hesitate to encourage you to talk with a counselor if you are in a stressful or crisis situation, or otherwise feel the need. You don't have to be falling apart mentally or emotionally to seek out a counselor. Counselors can offer a new perspective, help you think through alternatives, and provide a forum for practicing communication with faculty. They also can inform you about additional resources on campus.

How to Recover from Being Criticized, Beaten Up, or Worn Down

After you have dealt with a difficult situation, you need to allow yourself sufficient time to recover. This is important whether you faced a dramatic crisis requiring you to stand up for yourself or whether it was a protracted situation during which you were gradually worn down. In fact, even if your crisis had a successful outcome, you may still need—and you definitely deserve—recovery time.

Only you can say how much time you need to recover from a given experience. I'm not suggesting you need to leave work during this period. When I say "take time," I'm referring more specifically to an inner process. You may or may not be able to take external time off. However, that doesn't mean you can't look out for yourself in a more personal way.

Perhaps the underlying guideline is simply to be kind to yourself. Here are some tips to help you accomplish that:

- Stop and recognize your overwhelm, shutdown, or depression. If you haven't already, take note of the warning signs discussed at the beginning of this chapter.

- Get professional help to identify and change any self-defeating patterns. Make use of appropriate university resources (Tables 13.3 and 13.4).

- Seek support from friends or colleagues.

- If you can, take some time off to rest, regroup, and reflect.

- Stop and assess the bigger picture before you make any major decisions. Ask yourself, "Is this the right place for me?"

- Distinguish between what you can change and what you can't; accept the givens in your work with faculty.

- Refocus your energy on dealing with the part of a challenge you can control, rather than trying to do it all.

A therapist I know has a sign on her wall that says, "People who are feeling good about themselves will not allow themselves to stay in a situation that is not good for them." I think this is an excellent reminder.

Become More Resilient

Last but not least, let's look at what you can do to cultivate your resilience and take care of yourself in an ongoing manner. Here are some suggestions for taking better care of yourself on a daily basis. I have grouped them loosely by category. Some strategies (e.g., have a solid support system) are important for everyone, while other strategies may appeal more to some than to others. I suggest you review all the tips and find which work best for you.

Rely on a strong network. Build and maintain a support system of friends, coworkers, and colleagues. Every individual may not be available at all times, so have a large enough network.

- Ask for help and support when you need it. Resist the tendency to think asking for help is a sign of weakness or failure.

- Meet regularly with others who work with the same faculty members or have similar job titles to share information and support one another.

- Work closely with a few like-minded colleagues for mutual support with your projects and dilemmas.

- Develop personal signals and slogans you can use with coworkers to show support. For example, my friend Brian, who is a mountain climber, uses the phrase "rope up" to convey a message of support. We use it with one another quite often, like before going into a difficult meeting or when the work is unusually difficult.

- You may find that being active in a civic or other local group provides an additional source of social and emotional support.

Be extra savvy. In Chapter 10 we discussed the importance of being organizationally savvy, being organized, and managing time effectively. I suggest reviewing that chapter and implementing the tips there. All of them will help you take care of yourself. Here are some additional strategies.

- Think about what you want to accomplish in the organization and create a compelling mission for yourself.

- Respond directly and immediately to difficulties and demands by faculty members, rather than avoiding them. Don't let problems fester.

- Avoid seeing problems as insurmountable. Instead of thinking, "I can't do anything about it," ask yourself, "What can I do about it?" Define a first step you can take.

- Take time out when you need to. Don't allow yourself to reach the point of burnout.

- Rethink your approach when things aren't working.

- Give yourself time to reassess. Don't feel pressured to make a snap decision. One staff member who was feeling beleaguered in his job bought a box of 100 Q-tips, and used one each night. He told himself when they were all gone, he would reevaluate his situation and decide whether to look for another job on campus.

• Set limits. Review the discussion in Chapter 8 about how to set healthy boundaries in your work with faculty.

• Arrange to take compensatory time off after you have been working extra-long hours.

Support yourself. Identify ways to nurture yourself. Balance the support you receive from others with the support you give to yourself.

• Avoid workaholism and identifying who you are with your work. Many staff find themselves in a seemingly impossible situation. They have so much work that they can't get everything done, especially not to their high standards.

• Don't base your self-worth on how faculty treat you.

• Make sure you have a meaningful life outside of work. If you let work demands prevent you from getting together with friends, having fun, or pursuing intersts and activities that nurture you, you are more likely to burn out.

• Recognize you have three choices in a stressful situation: you can walk away, you can do something to change it, or you can accept it as it is. Worrying about it and complaining to others are not good choices.

• Understand that stress can be contagious. If faculty or other staff are stressed, try not to catch it.

• Maintain a positive view of yourself, regardless of how you think faculty or others might view you. Review Chapter 8, in which we discussed how to develop and maintain a positive mindset.

• Praise yourself when you do a job well, especially if faculty members don't offer you sufficient appreciation. Give yourself a reward for work well done.

• Develop confidence in your ability to solve problems. Learn to trust your instincts.

• Look for opportunities to expand your horizons, learn new skills, and engage in self-discovery.

• Keep a journal in which you write about and seek to better understand your experiences and challenges. Write a poem. Keep a gratitude journal in which you write five things you are grateful for each day.

Take care of your physical and mental well-being. Our minds and bodies function in tandem, so taking care of your body not only ensures you stay healthy but also helps keep your mind sharp and clear while you do your work. Bennett Tepper and his colleagues (2009) found that employees with abusive supervisors not only experienced reduced job satisfaction and productivity, but also a variety of mental and physical health problems. People who endure stress at work for long periods of time can have difficulty sleeping, feel worthless, be irritable or angry, and suffer from anxiety and depression, among other things. So, consider the following:

• Exercise regularly.

• Maintain a healthful diet.

• Get enough sleep.

• Learn to increase your awareness of how your thoughts and feeling affect your well-being.

• Learn to meditate.

• Read a good book.

• Practice hatha yoga, qigong, tai chi, or other techniques that are simultaneously relaxing and energizing and that foster well-being.

Besides the strategies just described, your institution most likely offers resources that can aid your efforts. Table 13.4 lists resources you may find at your institution that can help you take care of yourself. Again, names and titles may differ.

[See Table 13.4 Institutional Resources for Taking Care of Yourself on the following page.]

Conclusion

In this chapter, we've looked at a range of ways to help you take care of yourself—whether in the midst of a crisis or simply on a routine, day-to-day basis. In fact, if you make the effort to adopt ways to look out for yourself in an ongoing way, you increase the likelihood you will be able to face with equanimity any crises that do arise. I want you to be happy, balanced, and effective. You are important, and your role is important. So, don't burn out, we need your fire!

Table 13.4 Institutional Resources for Taking Care of Yourself

Benefits
* Medical, dental
* Life, disability, retirement
* Time off/leave
* Employee discounts

Campus programs and interest groups
* Entertainment
* Clubs
* Exercise programs

Health and Safety Services
* Health awareness
* Environmental health
* Safety, workers' compensation

Office of Staffing and Employment
* Assists with recruitment (diversity, advertising, screening, job fairs, search strategies)

* Provides lay-off services for employees

Training and Organizational Development
* Consulting to departments
* Staff professional development
* Soft skills training for staff
* Career development for staff
* Staff orientation to the institution

Work Life Office
* Child care
* Parenting education and consultation
* Elder care and care-giving support
* Take Our Daughters and Sons to Work program

Summary

Be Resilient and Recover From Being Criticized, Beaten Up, or Worn Down

- Cultivate the qualities of resilience, including acceptance of change, continuous learning, confidence, self-esteem, recovery from mistakes, and flexibility.

- Learn to identify the warning signs of stress for you; learn to work with the four stages of stress (your stressors, your perception of those stressors, your stress reactions, and their consequences).

- Recognize interactions or situations that call for you to protect yourself, and learn to manage your career wisely. Use the resources available within your institution to get the support you may need.

- Make it a priority to take care of your physical and mental well-being in an ongoing manner.

14

A Career That Works for You

- The Ingredients of Satisfaction
- Job or Career
- Adopt a Career Mindset
- Define a Career Path
- How You Can Further Your Career
- Amplify What Brings Heart and Meaning to Your Work
- Conclusion
- Summary

In the last chapter, I talked about the importance of taking care of yourself day-to-day on the job, of increasing your resilience and taking steps to prevent burnout. In this chapter, we consider what you can do long term to take care of your career. I want you to be satisfied in the work you do, confident your job is a good match and that you're on the right track to succeed.

The Ingredients of Satisfaction

To start, here is a brief assessment I put together, loosely based on research by Frederick Herzberg (1976), David Buckingham and Gale

Coffman (1999), as well as others, that identifies the key factors associated with job satisfaction. I say "loosely" because most of the research in this area doesn't focus specifically on academic staff. Moreover, what people report as satisfactory can vary, depending on their personal preferences and priorities, as well as their age, gender, and even the year in which the research was conducted. Nevertheless, I hope you will find this questionnaire helpful for assessing the extent to which your job is satisfying to you, and if it isn't, why not. Read the statements without giving each one too much thought. Circle the number on the 1–4 scale that you feel best describes your current feelings about your staff position:

Table 14.1—Is Your Job a Good Match?

Key: 1 = Disagree 2 = Somewhat disagree 3 = Somewhat agree 4 = Agree				
Rate how much you agree with each statement	Disagree . . . Agree			
1. My job is interesting and meaningful.	1	2	3	4
2. I make good use of my knowledge and skills in this job.	1	2	3	4
3. I have good prospects for promotion.	1	2	3	4
4. I have a good relationship with faculty I work with.	1	2	3	4
5. I have good relationships with my coworkers.	1	2	3	4
6. My job has satisfactory benefits.	1	2	3	4
7. People pay attention to what I have to say at work.	1	2	3	4
8. I have a reasonable workload.	1	2	3	4
9. My job allows me to balance work and home life.	1	2	3	4
10. My paycheck is satisfactory.	1	2	3	4
11. I receive sufficient recognition for my performance.	1	2	3	4
12. My job is reasonably secure.	1	2	3	4
13. My job allows me to learn and grow.	1	2	3	4
14. I like my job.	1	2	3	4
Calculate the sum of all circled numbers.	Total ____			

If the total of your answers is 42 or greater, chances are your job is a reasonably good match for you. If it is less than 42, notice the specific statements with which you most strongly disagreed. These suggest areas where you might seek improvement in your current position, or areas to pay attention to if you decide it is time to search for a more suitable job.

In his research, Herzberg distinguished between factors associated with satisfaction in the workplace (e.g., recognition for success, responsibility) and factors associated with dissatisfaction (e.g., not being paid enough, work overload). He theorized that it is as important to minimize potential sources of dissatisfaction as it is to maximize sources of positive motivation. Taken together, the following are some of the main ingredients of job satisfaction, in academia as well as elsewhere:

Interest level. A task you find interesting might seem boring or too difficult for another person. Research suggests it is hard to be satisfied with the work you do if you don't take any interest in it. If your work is sufficiently interesting, some of the following probably are true for you.

- I look forward to going to work every day.
- I enjoy the chance to tell others about the work I do.
- I find my work meaningful.
- I don't look at the clock too frequently.

Growth. No one wants to stay stagnant in a job. It is just as important to have work that stimulates our long-term growth as it is to have work we find stimulating and enjoyable on a daily basis. Growth can be measured in any or all of the following ways:

- Gaining new skills and knowledge (e.g., technical, organizational, interpersonal)
- Creating new relationships with colleagues, faculty members, and others beyond your department and the university
- Learning about a faculty member's content area
- Adding job responsibilities or taking on new projects
- Changing jobs (being promoted to a higher level or shifting what you do to another department)

Responsibility. Having sufficient responsibility on the job can add to its general interest level. Few people thrive in situations in which they have little responsibility or are limited to doing exclusively what someone else instructs them to do. Usually, you gain responsibility the longer you stay in a position. Many faculty give staff members training and opportunities to learn and expand their responsibility. In addition, colleges and universities offer opportunities to serve on committees or help with campus events.

Recognition. If we're honest, we can probably admit we all like to be recognized and receive appreciation for the work we do. Just knowing faculty and other staff are satisfied with our work can boost our own level of satisfaction. And it's not just about having to do everything right all the time; that is, we benefit from both praise and constructive criticism. You might assume that positive feedback is what leads to job satisfaction, but some research has shown that it is the process of feedback itself (i.e., what has been called the *feedback environment*) that leads to satisfaction.

Positive relationships. It's hard to be satisfied in a job if your working relationships are not harmonious. Buckingham and Coffman found that having a best friend at work was one of the most important factors associated with productivity and job satisfaction. This doesn't mean that faculty members or your coworkers need to become instant BFFs. However, the kinds of collegial relationships we discussed in Chapter 5, as well as the communication skills described in Chapter 6, are important ingredients.

Working conditions. If you are chronically overloaded at work or are dissatisfied with the working conditions in general, you probably aren't feeling satisfied with your job. Most people are willing to go the extra mile on occasion (e.g., staying late to complete a project), but expectations should be reasonable. If you work with a faculty member who does not want you to take regular breaks or time away for lunch, not only is resentment likely to build, but your health may suffer. Having the right materials and equipment, easy access to important information, and adequate workspace also contribute to your contentment on the job. Attractive, spacious workspaces and private offices typically are in short supply at colleges and universities. Spending hours in an undesirable workspace, such as a basement cubicle without natural lighting, can affect your energy level and productivity, even if you are not consciously aware of it.

244

Money. The size of their paycheck is not the primary motivator or determinant of job satisfaction for many academic staff. They know higher-paying positions probably are available in corporations, but they have reasons for choosing to work at a university. They may choose to stay even if they have reached the top of their pay range, or if the institution is not granting raises at the rate it did in previous years. Nevertheless, this doesn't mean anyone wants to be, or should tolerate being, underpaid. Your skills should be adequately compensated within the academic pay scale.

Job or Career

Some staff look at their work as a job, while others look at it as a career. In general, a career is something you construct based on your training, interests, abilities, and goals. If a job fits into this larger framework, then it is part of your career.

Table 14.2 highlights some of the main distinctions between a job and a career, as these are commonly conceived, both within the academic setting and elsewhere. Perhaps when you can look at this table, you can identify which term best fits your own situation. Or you may not see the two as quite so distinct. For example, you may view your career as consisting of a series of jobs, whereby what you originally thought was a short-term job developed into a long-term position you find satisfying. Again, these generalizations hold much of the time.

Table 14.2 Job and Career Comparison

	Job	Career
Primary purpose	To provide steady income	To fulfill lifelong goals
Requirements	May need minimal training	Special training may be required
Pay	Often has an hourly rate	Salaried
Time frame	Short term	Long term
Characteristics	Stability, safety, freedom from extensive responsibility	Flexibility, allows for risk taking, opportunity to assume greater responsibility

I'd like to suggest that the distinction between jobs and careers can be seen as a matter of mindset, as we discussed in Chapter 5. Moreover, I think you can benefit by adopting a career mindset—regardless of whether you or others view your staff position as a job or as a career. In other words, the technical definitions of job and career are less significant than how you view your work.

Adopt a Career Mindset

Adopting a career mindset allows you to take a big-picture view of your work. In essence, this mindset says, "The work I do is an important aspect of my life. It is my responsibility to take care of it." This perspective encourages you to assess your situation, plan ahead, and assume a more active role in determining your future and your career.

One of the benefits of adopting a career mindset is that it provides you with more options. You see that staff have multiple career paths from which to choose, and that you can set a course for yourself that is most in line with your own strengths and priorities. In the next section, I describe three career paths I have observed among staff:

1. Upward path

2. Level path

3. Alternative path

The key point here is that none of these paths should be regarded as superior to the others. Each can offer its own challenges and each can be satisfying in its own way, depending on the goals of the individuals who follow that path and how they personally define success. Nor do I mean to imply that these are the only satisfying options; they are the ones I see most commonly.

Define a Career Path

Claire, Donna, and Steve are all staff members in academic institutions, but each has carved out a very different path. All three have success stories. As you read about them, see which one you resonate with most.

Upward Path

When Claire graduated from college, she took a part-time position on a research project led by one of her professors in the School of Education. Her main tasks involved scheduling follow-up interviews with several hundred teachers who had participated in the research study. Originally she saw this position as temporary, as a way to make some money over the summer while she decided what jobs to apply for in the local school district. She thought of becoming a teacher's aide to explore whether she might be interested in a career in the classroom. Claire saw herself as ambitious, but she was unsure about what specific direction would be best for her.

That summer, Claire set to work organizing the scheduling process and was able to do it in less than the allotted time. As a result, the project manager asked if she would like to do some of the interviewing herself. This excited Claire, and led to her taking on a full-time position over the next year. She liked the range of responsibilities involved, which included interacting with research participants and staff members, as well as administrative tasks. She was a quick study, always noticing what else needed to be done and tuning into people's needs—both on the project and around the department office in general. She helped her co-workers and others around her to be successful, and worked well with faculty. Everyone appreciated her can-do attitude and the way she partnered with them while maintaining a quiet presence.

Toward the end of her first year, Claire was asked to assist a high-level staff member who was preparing a grant proposal for continued funding in the department. As they worked together, he recognized Claire's potential as an administrator and asked about her career goals and plans. Subsequently, when Claire inquired if he would mentor her, he was happy to do so.

Based on suggestions made by her mentor, Claire volunteered for a committee that gave her a high profile on campus. She attended brown bag lunches and went to staff trainings that helped her improve her skills and her understanding of the university. Throughout this period, she met many people across campus. Her responsibilities expanded and she was promoted three times. Eventually, she decided to go to graduate school to get a master's degree in educational administration. She felt this would allow her to pursue her talents as an administrator, while keeping her within the academic environment she found so stimulating. Claire was able to take all her classes in the evening and continued to work full time, although she had to cut back on some of her cross-campus activities while she was in school.

Within a few years of receiving her advanced degree, and about ten years after taking her initial part-time job, Claire was promoted to associate dean of students. Several years later, the dean of students retired and Claire was promoted to that position. She had successfully made a career in educational administration, rising steadily from a low-level entry job to a position with wide responsibility. Her salary was higher than that of many faculty members. When I met Claire, she had just been named vice chancellor of student affairs. She told me this was a delightful culmination to her career. She found it satisfying to have oversight of so many aspects of the university (e.g., undergraduate admissions, registration, financial aid, housing, fundraising for scholarships, child care services, and career services) and to work in a new capacity with so many people she had known over the years.

Claire is following an upward path in the sense that she climbed the career ladder at her institution, even though it was quite steep at times. Although she didn't initially have clear career goals, she developed them as she went. She matched her ambition with determination and professional growth, and built a strong network within the university that helped her navigate the system.

Level Path

After her three children had reached high school age, Donna took a position as program coordinator at a small local college. She had earned her bachelor's degree at another institution before she got married, but had not held a paying job since. Now her family needed the extra income to save enough to pay for three college educations.

The program coordinator position made Donna a member of the support staff for the School of Arts and Sciences, and she thoroughly enjoyed the work. Her co-workers were friendly, and initially she found herself relying heavily on them to support her as she got up to speed on some of her technical office skills.

Donna, who had frequent contact with faculty members, respected and admired the faculty and their teaching. She saw her job as doing whatever administration and class preparation work would free up the faculty to focus on teaching. She enjoyed working with most of the faculty members, received their appreciation, and liked to help train new program coordinators.

When I spoke with Donna, she had been in this position for eighteen years. She worked closely with three other people who did basically the same type of work. Over the years, they had learned to support one another and had figured out how to work with faculty members who tended to be critical or otherwise difficult to work with. She chuckled when she described some of the creative strategies she had developed to handle faculty who were frequently late getting their class materials ready to be duplicated at the beginning of each term.

Donna had no interest in climbing a career ladder. It was clear she took pride in her work, without the need to seek out anything more. Others might say she was in a "dead-end job," with no prospects for advancement. But Donna didn't see it that way. She had a job she loved and planned to stay until she retired. Donna loved watching the students grow and learn, and enjoyed going to graduation each year. She thrived in the campus environment and culture.

Donna's career follows what you might consider a level path, in the sense that she sought satisfaction and compatibility through a single position, rather than upward mobility. Many of the challenges on which Claire thrived would have been unnecessary hassles to Donna. Like Claire, she relied on a strong social network. However, while Claire used her network to advance herself, Donna used hers for mutual nurturing and to facilitate her daily tasks. Over the past eighteen years, many aspects of her job have evolved, and Donna has grown and expanded as a result.

Alternative Path

When Steve was in first grade, his teacher asked the students to draw a mouse with a piece of cheese. She took one look at Steve's picture and ran to get the principal. Steve thought he'd done something wrong, but the adults were delighted with his work. His artistic talent had been recognized. Steve kept drawing. When he was in junior high, he won a design-a-logo contest and received free ice cream for six weeks.

In high school, a friend's father who had a printing business promised Steve if he got all A's and B's, he would give him a job after graduation. Steve got the grades—and the job. He learned the printing business and received several promotions.

Although Steve's parents wanted him to attend college, they moved to another state just when he was about to apply to schools. As a result, he could not afford college because he would have been charged out-of-state tuition. Instead, he got a job drawing for a T-shirt company, and later worked as an artist for the small-town newspaper. Eventually he was able to start his own business. At age twenty-nine, Steve was on his way to success. He was busy, money oriented, and newly married. Then he was diagnosed with stage-four cancer. He had to stop everything to concentrate on his health. Fortunately, Steve's cancer responded to treatment and he was able to return to work after a few months, with a fresh appreciation for life.

Around that time, a friend who worked in the university's printing department asked Steve to do an illustration job under contract. Steve owed him a favor, so he agreed to a three-month contract. This was followed by a six-month contract, and then a job offer. At first Steve thought accepting the staff position meant his own business had failed. But as he learned more about the university benefits and lifestyle, he began to see the advantage of a steady job after dealing with a life-threatening illness.

When I met him, Steve expressed no regrets for taking the staff position. He had learned a tremendous amount during his five years on staff. Initially, his computer skills were limited, but the university provided training, including face time with several experts. Steve also increased his people skills, which, as an introverted artist doing business on his own, were minimal. He received supervisory training through the university's Learning and Development Program.

Steve earned several promotions. At one point, a few staff members tried to make an issue about his not having a college degree. However, his track record as an artist, his political savvy, and his strong management skills counted more heavily than his lack of a degree, and he was promoted.

Steve works with faculty as what he calls a visual communicator/ visual interpreter. He takes faculty's complex ideas and reinterprets them visually to make the message stronger, using movies, animations, and photos. Three people report to Steve, and he manages an average of 65 projects a week. He also works out of his home on art projects for friends and small companies, which gives him satisfaction as well as extra income. He feels fulfilled by his work and appreciates the flexibility in his work schedule, which allows him to do work that he loves and still have time for family and friends.

An alternative path, such as the one Steve followed, often manifests as a unique mix of career goals and spontaneous opportunities. Staff members who take this relatively unpredictable road tend to be led by what they love to do. They begin with an openness to pursuing their interests, and step in when they find opportunities that provide institutional support. Openness and spontaneity are their trademarks. Many staff members tell me they wind up in jobs that surprise them and bear little relationship to what they originally expected or planned.

How You Can Further Your Career

Regardless of which type of career path you find most fitting for yourself—whether one of the ones I described, or something else—a number of basic elements are likely to contribute to your success. These include setting goals, becoming politically savvy, and developing a support network.

Set goals. Taking care of your career requires that you do some planning. I suggest periodically setting aside time to think about, clarify, and refine what you want for yourself.

- Consider both short-term (1 to 2 year) and long-term (5 and 10 year, or longer) goals.

- Aim high—don't be afraid to go for what you really want or to push your limits. Many people tell me others recognized their potential before they did. A manager or mentor may have inspired them to take on a more complex job or greater responsibility. It was only with hindsight that they realized how much they allowed themselves to be limited by their own assumptions and prior experience. You may want to consider how you limit your horizons. Notice how many of the people you admire started where you are now.

- Consider how your goals relate to the work you currently do, as well as to available opportunities and what will be needed in the future. For example, academic institutions expect accountants to have more analytical skills, and managers to have more business and financial skills, than they used to.

- Back up your goals with specific and realistic action steps when possible.

- Draw upon your institution's professional development and/or counseling resources.

Understand the art and science of office politics. Staff with political savvy get things done efficiently and effectively on a daily basis and are more successful in achieving their career goals than are staff who don't learn about the institution. When you hear the term *office politics*, you may conjure up images of corruption, deception, or manipulation. But politics need not be negative. By office politics, I mean the unwritten, often unspoken rules and etiquette of working with and for others. This includes knowing what is appropriate to say to whom, and when. Avoiding office politics will not serve your career in the long run. Staff who work quietly behind the scenes are less likely to be noticed and may find themselves with fewer career opportunities.

Office politics takes study and finesse to master. Here are some suggestions for developing political savvy:

- View the university or college as a complex human system; make it your business to find out how the different parts operate and how decisions are made.

- See yourself and others (i.e., staff and faculty) as important parts of the greater whole.

- Be willing to be proactive; look for opportunities to demonstrate leadership.

- Anticipate the consequences of your actions and communications.

- Avoid gossip, don't assume what you say will remain a secret.

- Maintain your integrity.

- Pick your battles wisely; consider where and when you are likely to be able to affect change.

- Learn how to work effectively within the existing system, whenever possible.

- Watch other people at work and identify successful behaviors you can use as models.

- In new situations, figure out the group culture before you proceed.

- Listen more than you talk.

Develop relationships across campus. Become a part of multiple networks at your institution. In Chapter 10 we discussed the importance of developing relationships to help support your work with faculty, and in Chapter 13 we talked about the value of relying on a network to build your resilience. Here the purpose of relationships is to support your career. Specifically,

- Establish affiliations of mutual advantage across campus.
- Offer support as often as you receive it, although the balance may not always be equal person to person (i.e., you may give some individuals more support than you receive from them, and vice versa).
- Communicate with members of your network often.
- Seek out and network with staff who are in positions that represent growth and advancement for you; ask them to counsel or mentor you, as appropriate.
- Include faculty members, as appropriate.
- Let others know about your abilities and successes, not just your needs.
- Don't burn your bridges.

Amplify What Brings Heart and Meaning to Your Work

A healthy career grows and evolves. Years ago, when I left academia and joined a small communications training firm in San Francisco, the work suited me perfectly. Later, as director of training for that firm, I enjoyed designing new programs and managing a team of trainers. When I was promoted to vice president, everything changed. I was sitting in an office, and my skill set was less compatible with the corporate VP role than it had been with the trainer and director roles. I felt as though the life had been sucked out of me because I had stopped doing what I loved most: teaching, working with clients, and empowering others.

To get back on track with myself, I left the firm and started my own consulting business. In this capacity, I have found working within academia especially meaningful. Looking back, I see that my process taught me some important lessons. I learned it takes awareness and courage to make difficult decisions to keep our work aligned with what has heart and meaning.

In his book *Authentic Happiness*, Martin Seligman (2002) defines happiness as consisting of pleasure, engagement, and meaning. Meaning refers to using personal strengths to serve a larger end. Similarly,

I think it is important to know in our work with faculty that we are doing what we do well, and that we derive meaning from seeing how our skills contribute to the greater academic community.

I have noticed that staff find heart and meaning in a variety of ways:

- Leading others, building and managing teams
- Working closely with particular faculty and colleagues whom they respect and admire
- Being involved in higher education and research, participating in challenging projects and cutting-edge work
- Serving students, contributing to their learning and success on campus
- Coaching and mentoring others
- Learning new subject matter, practicing new skills, solving complex problems
- Doing whatever they enjoy most: technology, artwork, fund development, event planning, community development, architecture, food service, facilities management, law enforcement, library science

They derive satisfaction from the work itself, their relationships, and their contributions to the mission of the institution.

I suggest you ask yourself what gives heart and meaning to your work. The assessment at the beginning of this chapter may help. Pay more attention to what makes you thrive, and focus less on irritations or what is not working. Define your talents, interests, and skills to assess if you are on track with yourself or if you want to chart a new direction. Find ways to do more of what you like and less of what you don't like. It could mean changing positions, as when I left the VP job to go into consulting. Or it could be as simple as you and a coworker swapping some tasks so you can both do what you like best.

As you take care of yourself and your career, you will clarify your preferences, learn more about human nature and your institution, and refine your abilities. As you become more resilient, you will expand your perspective and flexibility. A broader understanding usually brings patience, empathy for self and others, and courage.

Conclusion

As your guide through the academic world, I have tried to provide you with perspectives and highlight skills that can help you thrive in this world. Academia is not for everyone. I hope by now that you have gained the knowledge, and developed the skills, to have a rewarding experience, perhaps even career, supporting the purpose and mission of the academic institution in which you work.

While I have sprinkled various examples throughout the book to add some reality and flavor, I certainly could not cover all the situations you may encounter. Hopefully I have provided enough principles and examples for you to figure out how to handle any challenges I have not mentioned. If you feel stymied by a situation and wish to discuss it with me, feel free to phone me at 510-222-2992, or email me at Susan@ WorkingWithFaculty.com.

[See Summary—A Career That Works for You on the following page.]

Summary

A Career That Works for You

- Define your talents, interests, and skills to determine if you are on track with yourself or if you want to chart a new direction. Take time periodically to assess whether your current job is a good match for you.

- Adopting a career mindset allows you to take a big-picture view of your work and your life.

- Further your career by setting goals, understanding the art and science of office politics, and developing relationships across campus.

- Ask yourself what gives heart and meaning to your work. Find ways to do more of what you enjoy and do well.

References

Abbott, E. L. (2009). *A brain new way to work: The guide to using your brain style at work for better results with less stress.* Charleston, SC: BookSurge.

Ackerman, D. S., & Gross, B. L. (2007). I can start that JME manuscript next week, can't I? The task characteristics behind why faculty procrastinate. *Journal of Marketing Education,* 29: 97–110.

Altman, H. B. (2003). "Dealing with troubled faculty." In D. R. Leaming (Ed.), *Managing people: A guide for department chairs and deans.* Bolton, MA: Anker Publishing, 139–156.

American Council on Education. (2008, January 17). *Facts about higher education financing.* Retrieved from http://www.usachinacorp.com/ articles/education/facts-about-higher-education-financing.html.

Barron-Tieger, B., & Tieger, P. D. (1995). *Do what you are: Discover the perfect career for you through the secrets of personality type.* Boston, MA: Little, Brown.

Bissell, B. (2003). "Handling conflict with difficult faculty." In D. R. Leaming (Ed.), *Managing people: A guide for department chairs and deans.* Bolton, MA: Anker Publishing, 119–138.

Block, P. (1981). *Flawless consulting: A guide to getting your expertise used.* New York, NY: Pfeiffer.

Buckholdt, D. R., & Miller, G. E. (Eds.). (2008). Special issue: "Faculty stress." *Journal of Human Behavior in the Social Environment*, 17:1 & 2. New York, NY: Routledge.

Buckingham, D., & Coffman, G. (1999). *First, break all the rules: What the world's greatest managers do differently*. New York, NY: Simon & Schuster.

Cavaiola, A., & Lavender, N. (2000). *Toxic coworkers: How to deal with dysfunctional people on the job*. Oakland, CA: New Harbinger.

Connolly, M., & Rianoshek, R. (2002). *Communication catalyst: The fast (but not stupid) track to value for customers, investors, and employees*. New York, NY: Kaplan.

Countries with most universities. (2008). UNESCO data on http://www.aneki.com/universities.html.

Covey, S. R., Merrill, A. R., & Merrill, R. R. (1994). *First things first*. New York, NY: Simon & Schuster.

Dunning, D. (2003). *Introduction to type and communication*. Palo Alto, CA: Consulting Psychologists Press.

Dweck, C. (2006). *Mindset: The new psychology of success*. New York, NY: Random House.

Ellis, A., & Knaus, W. (1977). *Overcoming procrastination*. New York, NY: Institute for Rational Living.

Galanti, G. A. (1991). *Caring for patients from different cultures*. Philadelphia, PA: University of Pennsylvania Press.

Gmelch, W. H. (1993). *Coping with faculty stress (survival skills for scholars)*. Thousand Oaks, CA: Sage Publications.

Goleman, D. (1995). *Emotional intelligence*. New York, NY: Bantam Books.

Goleman, D. (1998). *Working with emotional intelligence*. New York, NY: Bantam Books.

Gottman, J., & Silver, N. (2000). *The seven principles for making marriage work: A practical guide from the country's foremost relationship expert*. New York, NY: Three Rivers Press.

Gunsalus, C. K. (2006). *The college administrator's survival guide*. Cambridge, MA: Harvard University Press.

Hammer, C., & Ferrari, J. R. (1999). *Procrastination prevalence among adults: Midwest vs. Northeast United States.* Unpublished manuscript, DePaul University, Chicago, IL.

Handy, C. (1995). *Gods of management: The changing work of organizations.* New York, NY: Oxford University Press.

Hargie, O. D. W. (Ed.). (1997). *The handbook of communication skills.* New York, NY: Routledge.

Hermanowicz, J. C. (2009). "The faculty of the future: Leaner, meaner, more innovative, less secure." *Chronicle of Higher Education,* 55(41), 26–27.

Herzberg, F. (1976). *The managerial choice: To be efficient and to be human.* Homewood, IL: Dow-Jones Irwin.

Jan, T. (2010, February 16). "Colleges lagging on faculty diversity: Numbers trail makeup of Hub's student bodies." *Boston Globe.*

Kanter, R. M. (1993). *Men and women of the corporation.* New York, NY: Basic Books.

Kemeny, J. (1994). "Accidental adversaries: When friends become foes." *The Systems Thinker,* 5(1), 5.

Kray, L. J., & Haselhuhn, M. P. (2008). "What it takes to succeed: An Examination of the relationship between negotiators' implicit beliefs and performance." In L. H. Crystal, G. R. Goethals, & D. R. Forsyth (Eds.), *Leadership at the crossroads: Leadership and psychology.* New York, NY: Praeger Publishers, 213–229.

Kübler-Ross, E. (1969). *On death and dying.* New York, NY: Macmillan.

Leebov, W., & Scott, G. (2007). *Service quality improvement: The customer satisfaction strategy for health care.* Lincoln, NE: Author's Choice Press.

McDowell, J. E., & Westman, A. S. (2005). "Exploring the use of first name to address faculty members in graduate programs." *College Student Journal,* 39(2), 353.

Mehrabian, A. (1981). *Silent messages* (2nd ed.). Belmont, CA: Wadsworth.

Morgan, R. (2002). *Calming upset customers: Staying effective during unpleasant situations* (3rd ed.). Los Altos, CA: Crisp Publications.

Myatt, M. (2007). "What is the difference between vision and mission?" *Management Matters*. Retrieved from http://cpnmhn.typepad.com/management_matters/2007/09/what-is-the-dif.html.

Oshry, B. (2007). *Seeing systems: Unlocking the mysteries of organizational life*. San Francisco, CA: Berrett-Koehler.

Pulley, M. L., & Wakefield, M. (2002). *Building resiliency: How to thrive in times of change*. San Diego, CA: Pfeiffer.

Richo, D. (1991). *How to be an adult*. Mahwah, NJ: Paulist Press.

Rossett, A., & Gautier-Downes, J. (1991). *A handbook of job aids*. San Diego, CA: Pfeiffer.

Ruch, R. S. (2001). *Higher Ed, Inc.: The rise of the for-profit university*. Baltimore, MD: The Johns Hopkins University Press.

Salter, D. W. (2006). "Testing the attraction-selection-attrition model of organizational functioning: The personality of the professoriate." *The Journal of Psychological Type*, 66(10), 88–97.

Satir, V. (1988). *The new peoplemaking*. Palo Alto, CA: Science and Behavior Books.

Satir, V., Banmen, J., Gerber, J., & Gomori, M. (1991). *Satir model: Family therapy and beyond*. Palo Alto, CA: Science and Behavior Books.

Seligman, M. (2002). *Authentic happiness: Using the new positive psychology to realize your potential for lasting fulfillment*. New York, NY: Simon & Schuster.

Senge, P. (1990). *The fifth discipline: The art and practice of the learning organization*. New York, NY: Doubleday.

Sutton, R. I. (2007). *The no asshole rule: Building a civilized workplace and surviving one that isn't*. New York, NY: Warner.

Tepper, B. J., Carr, J. C., Breaux, D. M., Geider, S., Hu, C., & Hua, W. (2009). "Abusive supervision, intentions to quit, and employees' workplace deviance: A power/dependence analysis." *Organizational Behavior and Human Decision Processes*, 109:156–167.

Twale, D. J., & De Luca, B. M. (2008). *Faculty incivility: The rise of the academic bully culture and what to do about it*. San Francisco, CA: Jossey-Bass.

Seminars and Speeches

Contact Susan at:
Susan@WorkingWithFaculty.com
Toll free 888 408-9059
510 222-2992

Bring Susan Christy to your conference or campus to celebrate and inspire staff and to improve their working relationships with faculty.

Susan welcomes your questions, suggestions, stories, and feedback.

Visit my Website: www.WorkingWithFaculty.com
Information, free resources, blog, and more.

Volume purchases available
Give a copy of *Working Effectively with Faculty* to everyone on your team. Discounts on quantities of books are available to professional associations, colleges and universities, educators, trainers, and others.

A special edition with your institution's logo and/or a letter from your president or dean can be arranged.

Send mail to:
University Resources Press
P.O. Box 237
1748 Shattuck Avenue
Berkeley, CA 94709
or
info@UniversityResourcesPress.com

[See over for a Quick Order Form]

UNIVERSITY
RESOURCES
PRESS

Quick Order Form

Purchaser information (please print)

Name _____

Address _____

_____

City, State, Zip _____

Ship to (if different) _____

_____

Phone _____ Email _____

Please send the following books. I understand that I may return them for a full refund.

Title: *Working Effectively with Faculty: Guidebook for Higher Education Staff and Managers* ISBN: 978-0-9827476-0-5

Quantity: ____ Books x $24.95 = Subtotal: _____

or discount code _____ _____

plus sales tax 9.25% (California only) _____

or resale permit number _____

plus shipping for one copy ($5:00) _____

plus shipping additional copies ($2.00 each) _____

Total enclosed _____

Mail orders: Check payable to **University Resources Press**, to:
PO Box 237, 1748 Shattuck Ave, Berkeley, CA 94709

To pay by PayPal or credit card, go to Website:
www.WorkingWithFaculty.com

Fax orders: 510 222-2770

Email orders: orders@UniversityResourcesPress.com or
www.WorkingWithFaculty.com

For more information and free resources, go to
www.WorkingWithFaculty.com

Breinigsville, PA USA
20 October 2010
247671BV00007B/2/P